THE PASQUOTANK PLATE

coastal
carolina
cuisine

Christ Episcopal Church ECW
Elizabeth City, North Carolina

The Pasquotank Plate contains over 600 favorite recipes of members and friends of Christ Episcopal Church in Elizabeth City, North Carolina. Some are treasured secrets passed down through families while some have evolved from trial and error in individual kitchens. For the most part, no originality is claimed for these recipes. We hope you will find enjoyment in the pages to follow.

The proceeds derived from the sale of these books will be used for the outreach projects and other charitable works of Christ Episcopal Churchwomen. The women of Christ Church sincerely thank all of the persons who contributed recipes and helped to test those that appear.

These recipes were chosen from the many submitted by members and friends. Similarity of content and space limitations prevented us from including all recipes.

Additional copies may be obtained at the cost of $17.95, plus $2.75 postage and handling, each book. North Carolina residents add $1.08 sales tax, each book.

Send to:

Christ Episcopal Church ECW
200 McMorrine Street
Elizabeth City, North Carolina 27909

ISBN: 0-9632518-9-9

First Printing   5,000 copies   October, 1992
Second Printing   5,000 copies   October, 1994

Printed in the USA by

WIMMER
The Wimmer Companies, Inc.
Memphis • Dallas

A Brief Introduction

Four centuries ago, the first Englishmen visited, explored and mapped the area. The DeBry map, dated 1585, appeared in London shortly thereafter.

Pasquotank Precinct was created in 1672 and was named for a band of Indians who inhabited the area.

The fertile soils and temperate climate were an attraction to early settlers. Agriculture was, and is, still a major industry and the 225 frost-free days per year permit multiple crops.

The Pasquotank River invited commerce and ship building and by the late 1600's ship building was a thriving industry. The river, in addition to its commercial value, attracted less desirables headed by Edward Teach "Blackbeard" and his pirates.

In 1660 the first known land deed in North Carolina was executed and is preserved in the Pasquotank Courthouse.

The first public school in North Carolina was established in Pasquotank in 1705.

Pasquotank became a county in 1738, and in 1753, the first town. In 1793, the General Assembly authorized a town at the "Narrows" of the Pasquotank River to be known as Reding. In 1794 the name of the town was changed to Elizabethtown and in 1801 it was changed again to Elizabeth City.

During the first half of the 19th century, Elizabeth City was a major seaport in North Carolina.

The Revolution and the War of 1812 had little impact upon the area. During the Civil War the area was occupied by Union Troops from February 1862 until1865. The effects of the war were severe and recovery was slow. By 1880, however, a new wave of prosperity swept the area. New crops and blooded livestock appeared and the first soybeans in the United States were grown at Bayside Plantation in Pasquotank.

In the 20th century, the economy has continued to grow and today, Elizabeth City is the commercial, medical and educational center of the Albemarle Region. Elizabeth City has a population of 14,292; Pasquotank County – 31,298; and Camden County – 5,904. In addition to our 206-bed modern hospital we have three colleges in our area. College of the Albemarle, a two-year comprehensive Community College; Roanoke Bible College — a four-year institution; and Elizabeth City State University — a four-year Liberal Arts University and a part of the 16 institutions of the University of North Carolina. A municipal airport located in the county operates in conjunction with the U.S. Coast Guard Airfield, however, no commuter service is available.

Within an hour in either of two directions we can be in the Norfolk/Virginia Beach, Virginia area or at the beaches of the Outer Banks of North Carolina. Yet, we still retain the peacefulness and hospitality small towns are noted for. As you may see, we in Pasquotank truly have a lot on our "*Plate*".

Cookbook Committee

Co-Chairmen
Bea Southworth
Tapp Robinson

Assistant Chairman: Gray Little

Proofreaders: Anne Hughes
Joyce Porter
Jane Umphlett
Barbara Waldo
Faye Ellen Weatherly

Typist: Tracy Ewell

Acknowledgements

A special thanks to our artists:

The beautiful cover is taken from a watercolor designed and illustrated by **Becky Wienges** of Orangeburg, South Carolina. Mrs. Wienges, a talented portraitist, is a graduate of art from the University of Georgia. Examples of her work can be seen in homes and corporate offices throughout the South. Appointments are made by contacting the Becky Wienges Studio, 803-533-0450 or 360 South Paul Street, Orangeburg, SC 29115.

The historical landmark illustrations are prints from the beautiful watercolor paintings of **Maxine Sweeney**, a North Carolina native, art teacher and craftsman. Mrs. Sweeney is a graduate from the Maryland Institute of Art in Baltimore, the Strayer Business College in Baltimore and Elizabeth City State University in Elizabeth City, NC, with a B.S. Degree in Art Education.

Christ Episcopal Church Women extend their deep appreciation and gratitude to **Tapp Robinson** and **Bea Southworth** for their dedication and endless hours of hard work in making this cookbook a reality. Proceeds from this project will benefit many who are in need.

Table of Contents

Christ Church – 1856

Elizabeth City, North Carolina

History of Christ Church
Elizabeth City, North Carolina

One of the most familiar landmarks in Elizabeth City is Christ Episcopal Church, a fine example of medieval architecture; but it should be remembered that, though a church has an edifice, a church is people, gathered to worship Almighty God, and scattered to serve him.

The parish had its roots in Jamestown, Virginia, whose colonists began settling the area in about 1630. Under Acting Governor Henderson Walker, the North Carolina Assembly of 1701 designated Pasquotank a parish. The Rev. Mr. Ackers wrote in 1708 to Her Majesty's secretary in London that "The citizens of Pasquotank have agreed to build a Church and two chapels." Though the whereabouts of these are unknown, it is known that two vestries were appointed in 1715 and later consolidated by the General Assembly, meeting in New Bern from December 12, 1754 through September 30, 1756.

The first Christ Church was built during 1825 and 1826; its rector was John Avery, also of St. Paul's Edenton. In 1856 $6,000 was raised for a new church, which was completed in 1857. This was during the ministry of the Rev. E.M. Forbes, best known for his valiant Civil War ministry.

In 1925 the parish house was built and in 1946 Christ Church's rare hammerbeam roof was complemented by her most beautiful memorial gift, a set of eighteen narrative stained glass windows.

In 1986, another beautiful gift was added to the church, thirteen kneelers handmade in needlepoint by nine women of the church. The original designs were created around these Christian symbols: fish, dove, butterfly, lamb, cross and crown, fleur-de-lis, and IHS. The borders of the seven altar rail kneelers match the design of the wrought-iron rails on the front steps of the church.

The present rector of Christ Church, Joshua Tayloe MacKenzie, the 29th rector, dedicated the kneelers on his first Sunday, June 1, 1986.

A mission was accomplished by the members of Christ Church in 1988 when they raised over $400,000 for a major renovation of the Parish House. New heating and air-conditioning systems were installed, along with cement flooring. Outside bricks were cleaned and waterproofed. Inside, the entire Parish House was refurbished and modernized.

Between the church and the Parish House is a small, but beautiful memorial garden landscaped with topiary and evergreen plants. Dedicated on February 4, 1990, the garden features a granite bench, a statue of Jesus, a lamp post, a tall wrought-iron gate, and a granite plaque inscribed with the names of parishioners whose ashes rest in the garden.

With the addition of the gift of a handsome black wrought-iron fence at the rear of the Parish House, and the paving and landscaping of the parking lot in 1991, the task of renovating Christ Church is over. To visitors, local residents, and parishioners alike, it is a landmark to admire.

Christ Church is, indeed, a special place. It was built to seat 450 people when its membership numbered 77. Today there are over 300 communicants in good standing. May we have a faith in the future like that of our forefathers. And may our common purpose continue — "To be a loving family in which Christ is known and proclaimed as Lord and Savior."

Notes

APPETIZERS & BEVERAGES

Becky Wienges '92

Index for Appetizers & Beverages

Aloha Dip

1 (8-ounce) package cream cheese
1 medium can crushed pineapple, drained
1 cup frozen coconut
1½ teaspoons ginger
2 teaspoons lemon juice
½ cup finely chopped nuts
    Assorted crackers

- Beat cream cheese until light and fluffy. Add remaining ingredients.
- Chill and serve with crackers.
- This is attractive when mounded in pineapple halves.

Bell Pepper Dip

(This is wonderful)

2 eggs, beaten
2 tablespoons sugar
2 tablespoons vinegar
2 tablespoons butter
2 (3-ounce) packages cream cheese, room temperature
½ cup chopped onion
½ cup chopped bell pepper

- Cook first 4 ingredients together until mixture is thick; let cool.
- Cream together with cream cheese. Stir in onions and green pepper.
- Serve with crackers or dip-size corn chips.

Yield: 2 cups.

Anchovy Dip

1 (8-ounce) package light cream cheese, softened
¼ cup milk
2 teaspoons lemon juice
    Dash Worcestershire sauce
½ cup chopped fresh parsley
1 teaspoon capers
1 small garlic clove, minced
1 (2-ounce) can anchovy fillets, drained, rinsed and finely chopped

- Mix cream cheese, milk, lemon juice and Worcestershire sauce until smooth. Fold in parsley, capers, garlic and anchovy fillets.
- Let stand covered in refrigerator 1 hour before serving to blend flavors.
- Serve with crackers.

Yield: 1½ cups.

Clam Dip

1 (7-ounce) can minced clams, drained, reserving juice
1 (8-ounce) package cream cheese, softened
2 tablespoons clam juice
1 tablespoon grated onion
1 (4-ounce) can mushroom pieces, drained
    Salt to taste
    Garlic salt to taste
    Hot sauce to taste
    Worcestershire sauce to taste
    Cayenne pepper to taste
    Wheat crackers

- Mix all ingredients together.
- Serve with shredded whole wheat wafers or other crackers of your choice.

Yield: 2 cups.

Cranberry Orange Fruit Dip

1   cup vanilla yogurt
⅔   cup cranberry-orange sauce
½   teaspoon freshly grated lemon peel
¼   teaspoon lemon juice
    Fresh fruits

- Mix together yogurt, cranberry-orange sauce, lemon peel and juice; chill.
- Prepare fruits such as apple wedges, melon balls, pineapple chunks, orange sections, banana slices or grapes for dipping.
- Serve dip with fruit.

Yield: 1⅔ cups.

Easy Mexican Dip

(The easiest, prettiest and best)

1   (16-ounce) can refried beans
1   envelope taco seasoning
1   (8-ounce) container sour cream
    Green Goddess dressing, thin layer
    or frozen avocado dip, thawed
2   medium tomatoes, seeded and
    finely diced
1   medium onion, chopped
6   ounces Monterey Jack cheese,
    shredded
    King size corn chips

- Spread in layers in a 2-quart casserole dish, beginning with the beans and ending with the cheese.
- Serve with king size corn chips.
- If you prefer a warm Mexican dip, you may microwave this for a few minutes.

Yield: 12 to 16 servings.

Dill Dip

8   ounces sour cream
8   ounces mayonnaise
2   tablespoons dill weed
1   tablespoon parsley flakes
1   teaspoon seasoning salt
    Pepper to taste
1   small onion, grated

- Mix all ingredients.
- Refrigerate overnight.
- Serve with fresh veggies as well as corn chips.

Yield: 2 cups.

Mexican Dip

(A real hit at a bowl game)

1   can bean dip
2   ripe avocados, peeled and pitted
2   tablespoons lemon juice
    Salt and pepper to taste
1   package taco seasoning
1   pint sour cream
½   cup mayonnaise
½   cup chopped green onions
1   tomato, seeded and diced
6   ounces Cheddar cheese, shredded
½   cup black olives, chopped

- Spread bean dip in a 2 quart casserole.
- Mash avocados with salt, pepper and lemon juice. Spread over dip.
- Mix taco seasoning with sour cream and mayonnaise. Spread over avocado mixture. Sprinkle onion and tomato over taco seasoning mixture.
- Sprinkle cheese over onion and tomato layer and top with black olives.
- Serve with taco chips.

Yield: 16 to 18 servings.

Layered Nacho

(Very good, colorful and filling)

1   **(16-ounce) can refried beans**
1   **package taco seasoning mix**
1   **(6-ounce) container frozen avocado dip**
1   **(8-ounce) container sour cream**
1   **(4½-ounce) can chopped black olives**
2   **large tomatoes, diced**
1   **small onion, chopped**
1   **(4-ounce) can green chilis, chopped**
6   **ounces Monterey Jack cheese, shredded**
    Taco chips

- Combine beans and seasoning mix. Spread evenly in bottom of 12x8x2-inch Pyrex dish.
- Layer remaining ingredients in order listed, except chips.
- To serve, put dish on table with basket or bowl of large corn chips or taco chips.

Yield: 12 servings.

Braunschweiger Pâté

1   **pound braunschweiger**
½   **pound cream cheese**
    Cognac
    Worcestershire sauce
    Milk
    Parsley
    Mushroom slices

- Mix liverwurst with ¼ pound cream cheese and Cognac to taste. Mold into desired shape and chill.
- Make topping with remaining cheese, softened with milk and Worcestershire sauce. Spread over pâté and decorate with parsley and raw mushroom slices.

Caponata

(This is a perfect appetizer over a leaf or radicchio or regular lettuce, or with pasta as a main course.)

1   **large eggplant, about 1½ pounds**
    Salt, to soak eggplant
2   **large green peppers, diced**
2   **medium-size onions, chopped**
1   **cup chopped celery**
2   **cloves garlic, crushed**
2   **tablespoons green olive oil**
3   **tablespoons capers**
½   **teaspoon Italian herb seasoning**
    Dash of pepper, black or cayenne
½   **cup Sicilian black olives, diced**
1   **tablespoon red wine vinegar**
½   **pound fresh plum tomatoes, peeled and diced**
½   **cup chopped fresh Italian parsley**
    Handful of pignoli nuts (pine nuts)

- Wash eggplant well and cut into small cubes, leaving skin on. Soak the cubes in cold water with 1 tablespoon of salt for each quart of water for ten minutes. Drain, rinse and pat dry.
- In a large sauté pan, cook the peppers, onions, celery, garlic and eggplant in the oil for 6 to 8 minutes. Add the capers, Italian seasoning, pepper, olives, vinegar and nuts and cook for 2 minutes. Add tomatoes and parsley and cook 5 minutes more. Stir and mix well. Serve warm or at room temperature.

Variation: Use mushrooms in place of olives

Yield: 5 cups.

Shrimp Dip

1   (6½-ounce) can shrimp, drained
¼   cup ketchup
1½ tablespoons horseradish
½   cup mayonnaise
1   onion, grated
    Dash hot sauce

- Combine all ingredients.
- Serve with corn chips.

  Yield: 1 cup.

Italian Shrimp Dip

1   (3-ounce) package cream cheese
1   cup sour cream
2   tablespoons lemon juice
1   package dry Italian salad dressing
    mix
½   cup cooked shrimp, finely chopped

- Soften cream cheese and blend with remaining ingredients.
- Chill one hour before serving; serve with crackers.

  Yield: 2 cups.

Caviar Mousse

4   ounces red lump caviar plus 1
    tablespoon
3   tablespoons chopped fresh parsley
    plus 1 tablespoon
2   tablespoons minced Spanish onion
¼   teaspoon pepper
1½ teaspoons unflavored gelatin
2   tablespoons water
½   cup whipping cream, whipped

- Combine caviar, parsley and onion with sour cream and pepper. Blend well.
- Dissolve gelatin in water; add to mixture. Fold in whipped cream. Pour into 2 cup mold and chill until set.
- Unmold and garnish with 1 tablespoon caviar and 1 tablespoon parsley. Serve with sliced cucumbers and melba toast.
- Added treat: Serve with Stoli Vodka. Decorate by placing vodka bottle in an empty milk carton. Fill with water and flowers and freeze. Remove carton from frozen block of ice and serve. Iced Vodka-Delicious!

  Yield: 2 cups.

Vegetables Dip/Spread

(This needs to be made 1 day ahead; fabulous used as little sandwiches when put on bread rounds)

1   (8-ounce) package cream cheese
⅔   cup shredded carrot
¼   cup shredded cucumber
¼   cup shredded onion
¼   cup shredded celery
2   tablespoons lemon juice
2   tablespoons mayonnaise
    Garlic salt to taste
    Seasoned salt to taste
    Salt and pepper to taste

- Mix juice of lemon with cream cheese until fluffy.
- Mix in all vegetables and let stand overnight in refrigerator in covered container.
- Season to taste with garlic salt, seasoned salt and salt and pepper.

  Yield: 2 cups.

Curried Herb Dip

1   cup mayonnaise
½   cup sour cream
1   teaspoon herb seasoning
¼   teaspoon salt
⅛   teaspoon curry powder
1   tablespoon minced parsley
1   tablespoon grated onion
1½ teaspoons lemon juice
½   teaspoon Worcestershire sauce
2   teaspoons capers

• Blend all ingredients together and chill.
• Serve with fresh vegetables.

Yield: 1 pint.

Southern Caviar

2   (15-ounce) cans black-eyed peas, drained
½   cup chopped red onion
½   cup chopped green pepper
1   clove garlic
4   tablespoons cider vinegar
4   tablespoons vegetable oil
4   tablespoons sugar
½   teaspoon salt
    Dash of pepper

• Combine peas, onion, green pepper and garlic in a large bowl.
• Combine vinegar and remaining ingredients in a jar; cover tightly and shake vigorously.
• Pour over pea mixture and toss gently.
• Cover and chill 12 hours.
• Remove garlic clove and drain before serving.
• Serve with crackers.

Yield: 6 to 8 servings.

Curried Chutney Shrimp Dip

(A nice blend of flavors to please all)

2   (8-ounce) packages light cream cheese, softened
1   tablespoon grated onion
1   teaspoon lemon juice
1½ cups cooked shrimp, peeled, deveined and cut in several pieces
4   tablespoons chutney, chopped
2   dashes curry powder
    Assorted crackers

• Mix first 6 ingredients together, blending well.
• Serve on crackers.

Yield: 12 to 15 servings.

Deviled Ham Dip

1   (8-ounce) container whipped cream cheese with chives
1   (4¼-ounce) can deviled ham
½   teaspoon lemon juice
    Mayonnaise (optional)
    Assorted crackers

• Bring cream cheese to room temperature.
• Break up and mash deviled ham.
• Combine ham, cream cheese and lemon juice, blending well until smooth. Thin with mayonnaise to the consistency you like for dips.
• Serve with assorted crackers.

Yield: 1½ cups.

Boursin

(Always a hit with no leftovers)

1   **(8-ounce) package lightly salted whipped butter, room temperature**
2   **(8-ounce) packages cream cheese, room temperature**
1   **teaspoon oregano**
½   **teaspoon garlic powder**
¼   **teaspoon thyme**
¼   **teaspoon marjoram**
¼   **teaspoon dill weed**
¼   **teaspoon coarsely ground pepper**
¼   **teaspoon basil**
¼   **teaspoon chervil**
2   **tablespoons freeze-dried chives**
     Assorted crackers

- Mix all ingredients in an electric mixer; spoon into a bowl and chill.
- Serve with assorted crackers.
- Flavor is best if made a day or two in advance; keeps for 1 to 2 weeks in the refrigerator.
- Allow to come to room temperature before serving.
- May be formed into a ball and refrigerated; when ready to serve, roll in coarse ground pepper.

Yield: 3 cups.

Crab Delight

1   **envelope unflavored gelatin**
3   **tablespoons cold water**
1   **(10¾-ounce) can cream of mushroom soup**
6   **ounces cream cheese, softened**
¾   **cup mayonnaise**
1   **cup chopped celery**
½   **pound fresh lump crabmeat, carefully picked over**
1   **small onion, grated**
     Several large squirts of hot sauce
     Chopped parsley for garnish

- Soften gelatin in cold water.
- Warm soup to simmering. Add softened gelatin and cream cheese. Stir over medium heat until dissolved, about 3 minutes.
- Remove from heat and add mayonnaise, celery, crabmeat, grated onion and hot sauce.
- Rinse a four-cup mold with cold water; pour mixture into mold and refrigerate overnight.
- Unmold on a cold serving platter and garnish with parsley.
- Serve with crackers of your choice.

Yield: 12 servings.

Dill Surprise

3   **to 4 whole dill pickles**
2   **(8-ounce) packages cream cheese, softened**
1   **(2½-ounce) jar thin sliced dried beef**

- Dry pickles with paper towels. Mold cream cheese around pickle, then wrap thin dried beef slices around it. Chill then slice into round pieces and serve.

Yield: 8 to 10 servings.

Crab Mold

1 (10¾-ounce) can tomato soup
2 (3-ounce) packages cream cheese
2 tablespoons unflavored gelatin
  dissolved in ¼ cup cold water
1 cup minced celery
¼ cup minced green pepper
¼ cup minced onion
1 pound fresh crabmeat
1 cup mayonnaise
1 cup cream

- Heat soup and cheese until cheese has melted. Add gelatin; stir in celery, green pepper, onion, crabmeat, mayonnaise and cream.
- Oil one large mold or 2 small molds and pour mixture into molds.
- Refrigerate overnight.
- Serve with crackers.

Yield: 16 servings.

Curried Cheese Spread

1 cup grated sharp Cheddar cheese
½ cup cream cheese, softened
  Small amount of milk to thin
2 tablespoons sherry
1 teaspoon curry powder
  Salt to taste
6 ounces hot chutney
1 bunch scallions, chopped; some green tops also

- Blend cheeses in blender with milk to thin. Add sherry, curry powder and salt.
- Spread in an 8-inch pie plate. Top with chutney and then scallions and green tops.
- Serve with crackers.

Yield: 12 to 15 servings.

Cheese Ball

8 ounces pimento cheese, room temperature
8 ounces sharp Cheddar cheese, shredded, room temperature
8 ounces New York State cheese
3 (3-ounce) packages cream cheese, softened
1 tablespoon garlic
  Juice of 2 lemons
1 onion, grated
  Salt and pepper to taste
  Dash of hot pepper sauce
  Ground ham (optional)
  Chopped pecans (optional)
  Chopped parsley (optional)
  Cayenne pepper (optional)

- Blend all of the cheeses, garlic, lemon juice, onion, salt, pepper, and hot pepper sauce together.
- Roll into 1 large ball or 2 medium balls.
- Garnish with ground ham, parsley leaves, finely chopped pecans, or sprinkle with cayenne pepper.
- Let set at least one day in refrigerator.
- Serve with your favorite crackers.

Yield: 1 large ball or 2 medium balls.

Tuck candles in the refrigerator the day before a party and they'll burn more slowly. Dip the candles into salted water renders the candles dripless.

Crab Spread

1   cup mayonnaise
1   tablespoon salad dressing
4   tablespoons Parmesan cheese
2   teaspoons steak sauce
4   tablespoons ketchup
1   teaspoon curry powder
1   pound fresh backfin crabmeat
    Assorted crackers

- Mix first 6 ingredients together until well blended. Gently fold in crabmeat; chill.
- Serve with crackers.
- Should be prepared several hours before serving.

Yield: 8 to 10 servings.

Easy Cream Cheese Ball

(Freezes well)

1   jar Roka bleu cheese
1   jar Old English cheese
2   (3-ounce) packages cream cheese
½   teaspoon onion salt
½   teaspoon garlic salt
    Dash of Worcestershire sauce
1   cup chopped pecans

- Mix first 6 ingredients with mixer (you can add a few chopped nuts after it is mixed).
- Form into a ball; roll ball in remaining nuts.
- Place on waxed paper in a bowl; chill in refrigerator overnight (it may also be frozen).

Yield: 1 ball.

Frosted Seafood Mold

Mold:

1   (1-pound) can pink salmon, skin and bones removed or 1 pound cooked and cleaned shrimp
¼   cup finely grated sweet onion
1   (8-ounce) package cream cheese, softened
⅛   teaspoon liquid smoke
¼   teaspoon black pepper
    Dash hot pepper sauce

- Blend ingredients in food processor until smooth.
- Line a small bowl with plastic. Mound seafood mixture in the bowl and smooth the top. Cover and chill for several hours or overnight.
- When ready to serve, unmold onto serving dish lined with red-tipped lettuce leaves.
- Garnish with paprika and serve with lightly salted crackers.

Frosting:

½   cup light sour cream
¼   teaspoon cayenne pepper
1   teaspoon dill weed

- Blend sour cream and cayenne pepper together. Frost the mold. Sprinkle the dill weed over the top.

Crabmeat Pizza

12 ounces cream cheese
2 tablespoons mayonnaise
2 teaspoons Worcestershire sauce
½ onion, finely minced
¼ teaspoon paprika
1 tablespoon lemon juice
⅛ teaspoon garlic powder
1 cup seafood cocktail sauce
   Lemon juice to taste
   Horseradish to taste
½ pound fresh crabmeat
   Minced parsley to garnish
   Assorted crackers

- Cream together first seven ingredients; spread on a 12½-inch circular tray, mounding the edges like a pizza crust.
- Combine cocktail sauce, lemon juice and horseradish; spread over the cream cheese "crust."
- Cover with crabmeat and garnish. Refrigerate overnight.
- Serve with crackers.

Dried Beef Cheese Ball

1 (8-ounce) package cream cheese, softened
¼ cup grated Parmesan cheese
1 tablespoon horseradish
⅓ cup stuffed green olives, chopped
1 (2½-ounce) jar dried chipped beef

- Beat first 4 ingredients together with an electric mixer until fluffy and well blended. Mound lightly into a ball and chill.
- Shred ½ of the jar of chipped beef; reserve remainder for another use. Sprinkle the shredded beef over cheese mound and serve with crackers.

Yield: 1 ball.

Frosted Artichokes with Caviar

1 (8-ounce) package cream cheese, softened
2 tablespoons sour cream
2 teaspoons mayonnaise
1 teaspoon lemon juice
2 teaspoons grated onion
1 teaspoon garlic salt
1 (8½-ounce) can artichoke hearts, drained and chopped
1 (2-ounce) jar caviar
   Assorted crackers

- Cream together the first 6 ingredients. Mound the chopped artichoke hearts on a serving tray. Ice with the cream cheese mixture. Sprinkle with the caviar.
- Garnish and serve with crackers.

Yield: 10 to 12 servings.

Garlic Herb Cheese Spread

3 cloves garlic
2 tablespoons minced chives
1 tablespoon crumbled dry parsley
1½ teaspoons dill weed
3 (8-ounce) packages cream cheese, softened
¾ cup butter, softened

- Chop first four ingredients in blender. Mix well with cream cheese and butter; chill.
- Bring to room temperature before serving.
- Serve with toast rounds and assorted crackers

Yield: 12 servings.

Bacon and Almond Topped Cheese Ball

1 (8-ounce) package cream cheese, softened
½ cup sour cream
2 cups shredded sharp Cheddar cheese
2 cups shredded Swiss cheese
3 tablespoons grated onion
3 tablespoons sweet pickle relish
1 tablespoon prepared horseradish
¼ teaspoon salt
¼ teaspoon lemon-pepper seasoning
⅛ teaspoon garlic powder
6 slices bacon, cooked and finely crumbled
¼ cup minced fresh parsley
¼ cup finely chopped almonds, toasted

- Combine cream cheese and sour cream in a large mixing bowl; beat at medium speed of electric mixer until smooth. Add Swiss and Cheddar cheeses, onion, relish, horseradish and seasonings. Beat with mixer until well blended. Cover and chill thoroughly.

- Combine bacon, parsley and almonds; stir well.

- Shape chilled cheese mixture into one large ball or two medium-size balls; roll in bacon mixture. Press bacon mixture into cheese ball with hands.

- Wrap cheese ball in wax paper and chill until ready to serve.

Note: Can make ahead of time and freeze.

Yield: 1 large cheese ball or 2 medium cheese balls.

Frosted Chicken Salad

1 tablespoon lemon juice
2 cups diced apples
4 cups finely chopped, cooked chicken
1½ cups finely chopped celery
1 cup green grapes, cut in half
¾ cup salad dressing
½ teaspoon salt
¼ teaspoon pepper
1 (8-ounce) package cream cheese, softened
¼ cup salad dressing

- Sprinkle lemon juice over apples; add chicken, celery, grapes, salad dressing and seasonings, mixing lightly.

- Press mixture into 1½-quart bowl; chill several hours.

- Unmold on serving platter; combine cream cheese and salad dressing, mixing until well blended.

- Frost chicken salad; garnish as desired. Serve with crackers.

Yield: 8 to 12 servings.

Shrimply Divine Mold

2 envelopes plain gelatin
2 cups cold water, divided
1 cup tomato soup
3 (3-ounce) packages cream cheese
1 cup mayonnaise
½ cup chopped celery
½ cup chopped green pepper
¼ cup grated onion
1½ cups finely chopped shrimp
   Lemon juice and hot pepper sauce
   to taste
   Assorted crackers

- Dissolve gelatin in ½ cup cold water.
- Heat soup and 1½ cups cold water; melt cream cheese in soup mixture. Add gelatin and beat well until dissolved; cool.
- Add mayonnaise and blend well; add the remaining ingredients and pour into well-oiled fish mold or any other mold and chill for 24 hours.
- Serve with assorted crackers.
- Individual molds may be used and serve on lettuce.

Jezebel Sauce

(Serve over cream cheese)

1 (18-ounce) jar pineapple preserves
1 (18-ounce) jar apple jelly
1 (5-ounce) jar prepared horseradish
   or to taste
1 to 2 tablespoons dry mustard

- Combine all ingredients, blending well; store in refrigerator.
- Serve over cream cheese as an hors d'oeuvre or on roast beef and chicken sandwiches.
- Keeps indefinitely in refrigerator in a covered container.

Yield: 1 quart.

Pineapple Cheese Ball

2 (8-ounce) packages cream cheese, softened
1 (8½-ounce) can crushed pineapple, drained
¼ cup finely chopped green pepper
2 tablespoons chopped onion
1 tablespoon seasoned salt
2 cups chopped pecans, divided
   Crackers

- Combine first 5 ingredients; add 1 cup pecans and mix well.
- Refrigerate until firm and shape into a ball; roll in remaining pecans, then serve.
- Garnish as desired.
- Serve with an assortment of crackers.

Yield: 3 cups.

Green Pepper Jelly

(Serve with cream cheese over crackers)

 6   large green peppers, seeded and coarsely chopped
 1½ cups vinegar, divided
 1   teaspoon crushed red pepper
 6   cups sugar
 ½   teaspoon salt
 2   (3-ounce) packages liquid pectin

- Place half of green peppers and ¾ cup vinegar in food processor. Process on high until smooth; repeat with rest of peppers and vinegar.

- Combine puréed peppers, red pepper, sugar and salt in large Dutch oven. Bring to a boil and add pectin. Cook, stirring often for 30 minutes or until mixture sheets from a metal spoon.

- Quickly pour into sterilized jars with ½-inch head space. Seal jars and cover with metal lids.

  Yield: 6 half pints.

New Orleans Shrimp Spread

 1   (3-ounce) package cream cheese, room temperature
 ⅔   cup shrimp, cooked and chopped
 2   teaspoons minced onion
 1   teaspoon lemon juice
 2   tablespoons mayonnaise
 3   tablespoons butter, melted
 1   teaspoon anchovy paste

- Mix all the ingredients except onion and shrimp until creamy smooth. Add onion and shrimp.

- Serve on crackers.

  Yield: 6 to 8 servings.

Smoked Salmon Ball

 1   pound smoked salmon, crumbled
 1   (8-ounce) package cream cheese, softened
 1   tablespoon lemon juice
 2   teaspoons grated onion
 1   teaspoon Worcestershire sauce
 ¼   teaspoon salt (optional)
     Chopped parsley (optional)
     Chopped nuts (optional)

- Blend first 6 ingredients together; shape into a ball.

- Cover with parsley or nuts.

  Note: If you can't find smoked salmon, you can use regular salmon and add liquid smoke.

  Yield: 12 to 15 servings.

Special Cheese Ring

1 **pound sharp Cheddar cheese,
   grated**
1 **cup finely chopped nuts**
1 **cup mayonnaise**
1 **small onion, finely grated**
   Black pepper to taste
   Strawberry preserves (optional)
   Assorted crackers

- Mix all ingredients except preserves; place in a 5 or 6 cup lightly greased mold. Refrigerate until firm.
- To serve, unmold; make an indention in the center and fill with strawberry preserves.
- Serve with assorted crackers.

Yield: 12 to 16 servings.

Sun Dried Tomato and Cheese Spread

1 **(8-ounce) package cream cheese,
   softened**
½ **cup margarine, softened**
½ **cup grated Parmesan cheese**
½ **cup oil-packed dried tomatoes,
   drained, reserving oil**
2 **tablespoons oil from tomatoes**
1 **tablespoon chopped fresh basil
   or 1 teaspoon dried**
   Pita toast triangles

- Combine first 6 ingredients in food processor; pulse several times until smoothly blended.
- Spoon mixture into a cheese crock or bowl; cover and chill until ready to serve.
- Bring to room temperature before serving.
- Serve with pita toast triangles.

Yield: 2 cups.

Sweet Cheese Ball

1 **(8-ounce) package cream cheese,
   softened**
½ **cup salted peanuts or pecans,
   chopped**
½ **cup chopped crystallized ginger**
4 **tablespoons chutney**
   Worcestershire sauce to taste
   Green hot pepper jelly
   Coconut (optional)

- Combine first 5 ingredients together; shape into a ball.
- Cover the cheese ball with the jelly; sprinkle coconut over the jelly if you prefer.

Brie in Pastry with Fruit Glaze

1½ **cups sweet butter, melted**
11 **sheets phyllo pastry**
1 **whole Brie, approximately 5
   pounds**
1 **(12-ounce) jar fruit preserves,
   apricot is wonderful**

- Butter large shallow pan; place 5 sheets of phyllo on buttered pan, staggering layers to make a circle and brushing butter between each layer.
- Place Brie on top of phyllo and spread top and sides with preserves; fold phyllo over and up around the cheese.
- Cover top of cheese with 6 sheets of phyllo, brushing butter on each. Tuck ends of pastry under cheese; brush top and sides with butter.
- Bake at 350° for 20 to 25 minutes; let stand at least 30 minutes before serving.

Yield: 20 to 25 servings.

Chutney and Bacon Brie

(Can be heated in microwave or conventional oven)

1 (15-ounce) mini Brie round
½ cup chutney
¼ cup bacon bits
    Water wafers
    Apple and pear wedges

- Remove rind from top of Brie round, cutting to within ½ inch of outside edges
- Place cheese on a microwave-safe dish; spread chutney over top and sprinkle with bacon.
- Microwave, uncovered, at HIGH 1½ to 2 minutes or until the cheese softened. Turn dish a half-turn after 1 minute.
- Serve with unsalted crackers, such as water wafers, or pear and apple wedges.

Yield: 12 to 15 servings.

Crabmeat Dip

1   (8-ounce) package cream cheese
1   tablespoon milk
2½   teaspoons Worcestershire sauce
1   (7½-ounce) can crabmeat, drained and flaked
2   tablespoons minced onion
2   tablespoons slivered almonds

- Combine with mixer, cream cheese, milk and Worcestershire sauce. Add crabmeat and onion to cream cheese mixture. Place in a small greased baking dish and top with almonds.
- Bake at 350° for 15 minutes
- Serve with assorted crackers.

Yield: 4 servings.

Crab Mornay

½   cup butter
1   small bunch green onions, chopped
½   cup finely chopped parsley
2   tablespoons flour
1   pint half-and-half
½   pound Swiss cheese, shredded
1   tablespoon sherry
    Salt to taste
    Red pepper to taste
1   pound crabmeat
    Assorted crackers

- Sauté onions and parsley in butter over low heat; cook just until soft, not brown.
- Blend in flour, half-and-half and cheese cooking gently until the cheese has melted. Add sherry, salt and red pepper. Gently fold in crabmeat.
- Serve warm from a chafing dish with crackers.

Yield: 24 servings.

Cranberry-Topped Brie

(This baked cheese recipe will be a favorite all year)

⅓ cup cranberry-orange sauce
2 tablespoons firmly packed brown sugar
¼ cup chopped pecans
1 tablespoon brandy
1 round (2 pounds) Brie cheese
Water wafer crackers

- Preheat over to 500°.
- In a small bowl, combine cranberry-orange sauce, brown sugar, pecans and brandy; mixing well. Set aside.
- Cutting to within ¼-inch of the outside edge, remove the rind from the top of the cheese. Place the cheese on an oven-proof platter or glass pie plate.
- Spread the cranberry mixture over top of the cheese.
- Bake 5 to 8 minutes or until cheese is heated through, but not melted.
- Serve with neutral-flavored crackers.

  Note: Can use the cranberry mixture on smaller rounds of cheese. Any leftover will keep in the refrigerator for several weeks.

Yield: 12 to 15 servings.

Hot Artichoke Spread

(Always a pleaser!)

1 (14-ounce) can artichoke hearts, drained and finely chopped
1 cup mayonnaise
6 ounces Monterey Jack cheese, finely cubed
8 ounces freshly grated Parmesan cheese
  Dash of cayenne
  Dash of Tabasco
  Sesame seeds

- Combine all ingredients except sesame seeds. Place in a 9-inch pie plate and sprinkle with sesame seeds.
- Bake at 350° for 30 minutes. Serve with crackers.
- Can be made in the morning and refrigerated until 1 hour before serving. Let stand at room temperature for 15 minutes before cooking.

Hot Chicken in Chafing Dish

1   (10¾-ounce) can cream of mushroom soup, undiluted
1   (8-ounce) package cream cheese
2   ounces sautéed sliced mushrooms
1   teaspoon Worcestershire sauce
⅛   teaspoon garlic
⅛   teaspoon pepper
1   tablespoon steak sauce
1   (2¼-ounce) package slivered almonds
2   cups minced, cooked chicken
    Crackers

- Combine all ingredients except chicken in a saucepan, stirring often until blended and heated through.
- Add chicken.
- Serve hot in chafing dish with bland crackers.

Yield: 12 servings.

Cheese Straws

1   cup all-purpose flour, sifted
½   teaspoon baking powder
½   cup butter
1   cup shredded sharp Cheddar cheese
3   tablespoons cold water

- Sift flour and baking powder into bowl. Cut in butter and cheese as for pie crust, using pastry blender or two knives; add water and mix well.
- Fill cookie press; form straws on ungreased cookie sheets using star form. Cut into desired lengths.
- Bake at 375° for 8 to 10 minutes.

Yield: 3 to 4 dozen.

Shrimp-Crabmeat Spread

½   pound fresh crabmeat
½   pound shrimp, cooked and dressed
2   (3-ounce) packages cream cheese, softened
½   cup chopped almonds
2   teaspoons lemon juice
1   teaspoon minced onion
1   teaspoon horseradish
2   tablespoons dry white wine
1   teaspoon dry mustard
½   teaspoon salt
¼   teaspoon white pepper
    Dash red pepper
    Freshly grated Swiss cheese
    Cherry tomato slices
    Olive slices

- Combine first 3 ingredients. (This will be a thick consistency; if too thick, thin with a little cream).
- Stir together the almonds, lemon juice, horseradish, wine, mustard, salt and peppers. Fold into the crab-shrimp mixture.
- Spread in a Pyrex dish and top with the grated Swiss cheese.
- Bake at 325° until mixture is hot and bubbly.
- Garnish with either tomato or olive slices; serve immediately with crackers.

Barbecued Shrimp

½ cup oil
1 teaspoon salt
1 teaspoon black pepper
3 tablespoons chili sauce
1 tablespoon Worcestershire sauce
3 tablespoons vinegar
¼ cup parsley
   Dash of hot pepper sauce
1 clove garlic crushed (optional)
3 pounds fresh shrimp, shelled and deveined
   Hot cooked rice (optional)

- Place all ingredients except shrimp in blender and blend well. Add to cleaned shrimp, cover and refrigerate at least 4 hours or overnight.

- Thread on skewers, head to tail, and grill over hot coals, basting occasionally, about 10 minutes.

- Shrimp can be skewered first, sauce poured over, covered and then refrigerated to marinate as above. Can also be served as a main entrée over rice.

Yield: 6 servings.

Broiled Crab Meltaways

½ cup butter or margarine, softened
1 (5-ounce) jar Old English sharp Cheddar cheese
8 ounces fresh crabmeat or substitute with canned
2 tablespoons mayonnaise
½ teaspoon garlic salt
½ teaspoon seasoning salt
6 English muffins, cut in half

- Mix first 6 ingredients together and spread on English muffin halves.

- Freeze; must be frozen before broiling to serve.

- Broil until bubbly and golden brown, from 5 to 15 minutes.

- Cut each muffin into halves or quarters to serve.

Yield: 48 servings.

Cheese Wafers

1 **cup butter or margarine, softened**
2 **cups grated extra sharp Cheddar cheese**
2 **cups flour**
¼ **teaspoon salt**
¼-½ **teaspoon red pepper**
2 **cups rice cereal**
½ **cup chopped pecans**

- Blend first 5 ingredients together; add cereal and pecans. Roll in balls the size of marbles and flatten in hand; place on ungreased cookie sheet.
- Bake at 350° for 10 minutes or until lightly brown.

Yield: 14 dozen.

Dilly Ranch Crackers

(Easy to make, really a hit)

1 **(11-ounce) package bite size oyster crackers**
1 **bag goldfish crackers**
1 **package dry Ranch dressing**
2 **tablespoons dill weed**
¾-1 **cup vegetable oil**

- Mix crackers with dill weed and Ranch dressing in a plastic bowl; mix well.
- Pour oil over crackers; mix well. Stir often for several hours.
- Keep in plastic container in refrigerator.
  Note: Do not use a wooden bowl, it will absorb the oil.

Yield: 12 servings.

Clam Shells

(A great luncheon dish or appetizer)

1 **cup chopped onion**
1 **cup chopped celery**
½ **cup chopped green pepper**
½ **cup butter**
4 **tablespoons flour**
2 **teaspoons Parmesan cheese, grated**
   Dash of Worcestershire sauce
   Dash of hot pepper sauce
½ **teaspoon salt**
½ **teaspoon pepper**
2 **(8-ounce) cans minced clams and juice**
30 **buttered crackers, crushed**

- Sauté onion, celery and green pepper in butter. Add flour, Parmesan cheese, Worcestershire sauce, hot pepper sauce, salt and pepper. Mix in a medium bowl and add clams and juice.
- Crush crackers and mix half the amount to the clam mixture.
- Fill 6 buttered cooking shells.
- Add a little butter to remaining cracker crumbs and sprinkle over the clam mixture in the shells.
- Bake at 350° for 15 minutes.

Yield: 8 servings.

Crab Stuffed Mushrooms

36 large whole fresh mushrooms, with stems removed
½ pound fresh crabmeat
1 tablespoon minced parsley
1 tablespoon chopped pimento
  Capers
½ teaspoon dry mustard
½ cup mayonnaise

- Wash and dry the mushrooms.
- Combine crabmeat, parsley, pimento and capers. Mix dry mustard and mayonnaise then fold gently into crab mixture. Fill each cap with crabmeat filling.
- Bake at 375° for 10 to 15 minutes.

Yield: 3 dozen.

Marinated Broccoli

(Can be served as an appetizer or a vegetable on a cold plate)

3 large bunches of broccoli flowerets
1 cup cider vinegar
1 tablespoon sugar
1 tablespoon dill weed
1 tablespoon Accent
1 teaspoon salt
1 teaspoon coarsely ground pepper
1 teaspoon garlic salt (optional)
1½ cups vegetable oil

- Mix all ingredients except broccoli.
- Put broccoli in large leak-proof container.
- Pour mixture over the broccoli. Refrigerate for 24 hours. Turn every 4 hours to insure a thorough mixing.

Yield: 20 servings.

Marinated Broccoli with Lime Dip

2 cups sour cream
2 cups mayonnaise
½ cup fresh lime juice
1 scant tablespoon horseradish
1 tablespoon zest of lime
2 teaspoons Dijon mustard
1 teaspoon salt
6 bunches broccoli, cut into florets
¾ cup Italian dressing
  Lime slices for garnish

- Combine first 7 ingredients to make lime dip; chill overnight.
- Stream broccoli florets until color is bright green, about 2 minutes.
- Remove from heat and immediately immerse in cold water to halt cooking; drain well and chill.
- To serve, lightly dress flowerets with Italian dressing, arrange on a platter accompanied by lime dip.

Yield: 25 servings.

Divine Cocktail Shrimp

6	slices bacon, cut in thirds
	Hot mustard
18	large shrimp, shelled and deveined
	Thousand Island Dressing
	Seafood cocktail sauce

- Brush each strip of bacon with mustard.
- Wrap 1 piece of bacon around each shrimp and secure with a toothpick.
- Broil on grill until crisp, turning once.
- Be careful not to overcook shrimp.
- Serve with sauces if desired.

Yield: 18 shrimp.

Oysters à la Mochie

24	oysters
24	saltine crackers
	Worcestershire sauce
	Hot pepper sauce
	Lemon juice
	Margarine

- Open oysters and leave in scallop side of shell with juice.
- Crumble one saltine on each oyster.
- Add dash of Worcestershire sauce, hot pepper sauce, lemon juice and a pat of margarine.
- Broil until oysters curl and cracker becomes toasted.
- Remove from oven and serve hot.

Yield: 24 servings.

Meatballs with Pineapple Sauce

Meatballs:

1	pound lean ground beef
¾	cup finely chopped celery
¾	cup finely chopped almonds
¼	cup finely chopped onion
1	teaspoon salt
¼	teaspoon black pepper
½	cup bread crumbs
1	tablespoon soy sauce
2	eggs, beaten
	Cornstarch
2	tablespoons cooking oil

- Combine first 6 ingredients, mixing well. Add bread crumbs, soy sauce and eggs.
- Shape into small meatballs and roll into cornstarch.
- Heat oil in skillet and brown meatballs.
- Serve in chafing dish covered with pineapple sauce.

Yield: 35 to 40 meatballs.

Pineapple Sauce:

⅓	cup sugar
3	tablespoons cornstarch
1	cup chicken broth
½	cup white wine vinegar
2	tablespoons soy sauce
½	cup pineapple juice
1	green pepper, cut in thin strips
1	cup pineapple chunks

- Combine sugar and cornstarch in a saucepan. Stir in broth, vinegar and soy sauce. Stir in pineapple juice and stir until thick.
- Add remaining ingredients and cook over low heat for 2 to 3 minutes.

Muffin Appetizers

½ cup salad dressing
½ cup mayonnaise
5-6 green olives, chopped
3-4 green onions or scallions, chopped
1 cup shredded sharp cheese
6 English muffins

- Separate English muffins into halves and toast lightly.
- Mix together salad dressing, mayonnaise, olives, scallions and cheese. Spread muffins with cheese mixture.
- Broil until cheese melts; cut in quarters and serve.

Yield: 48 servings.

Herbed Pita Triangles

(Easy and a crowd pleaser)

½ cup unsalted butter, melted
1 tablespoon fresh rosemary or
  1 teaspoon dried
1 tablespoon fresh oregano or
  1 teaspoon dried
1 tablespoon fresh thyme or
  1 teaspoon dried
1 package pita breads

- Combine butter with herbs and let stand 1 hour or more to blend flavors.
- Preheat oven to 300°.
- Slice open pita to make 8 pieces; brush with herb butter. Cut each round into 6 wedges.
- Place on cookie sheet and bake 18 to 20 minutes until crisp.
- Serve on antipasta platter with sundried tomatoes; sweet roasted peppers and Asiago (Italian hard cheese).

Yield: 48 servings.

Mushroom Turnovers

9 ounces cream cheese, softened
½ cup butter, softened
1½ cups all-purpose flour

- Mix cream cheese and butter; add flour and blend well. Chill for 30 minutes.
- Roll dough ⅛ inch thick on lightly floured board and cut into 3 inch rounds. Place 1 teaspoon of filling on each and fold dough over; press edges with a fork and prick the top.
- Bake at 450° on ungreased cookie sheet for 15 minutes or until lightly browned.

Note: Can be frozen before baking; bake frozen.

Yield: 50 turnovers.

Filling:
3 tablespoons butter
1 large onion, minced
½ pound mushrooms, chopped
¼ teaspoon thyme
½ teaspoon salt
  Pepper to taste
2 tablespoons flour
¼ cup sour cream

- Combine onions with butter in a saucepan; brown lightly. Add mushrooms and cook for 3 minutes. Add thyme, salt, pepper and flour. Stir in sour cream and cook slowly until thickened.

Note: Can substitute sweet cream for sour cream.

Seafood Nibbles

½ pound fresh crabmeat
1 (5-ounce) can shrimp, drained
2 (3-ounce) packages cream cheese, softened
    Cream to thin, if necessary
½ cup chopped almonds
2 teaspoons lemon juice
1 teaspoon minced onion
1 teaspoon horseradish
2 tablespoons dry white wine
1 teaspoon prepared mustard
½ teaspoon salt
¼ teaspoon white pepper
    Hot pepper sauce to taste
6 English muffins or sandwich rolls, split
    Grated Swiss cheese
    Tomatoes
    Ripe olives

- Combine crabmeat, shrimp and cream cheese; thin with cream if necessary.
- Stir together almonds, wine, lemon juice, onion, horseradish, mustard, salt, pepper and hot pepper sauce. Fold into crabmeat mixture; mixture will be stiff.
- Spread on muffins or rolls; sprinkle with grated Swiss cheese.
- Bake at 325° until cheese is melted and mixture is hot; cut into quarters.
- Garnish with tomato slices and ripe olives.

Yield: 48 servings.

Spinach Balls

2 (10-ounce) packages frozen, chopped spinach
2½ cups herb-flavored stuffing
¾ cup margarine, melted
6 eggs, beaten
½ cup grated Parmesan cheese
2 small onions, minced
    Seasoned salt to taste
    Pepper to taste
    Garlic powder to taste

- Cook spinach, uncovered, until thawed and drain well.
- Combine all ingredients and roll into small balls.
- Bake 20 minutes on a greased cookie sheet.
- Freezes well.

Yield: 75 balls.

Sausage Stuffed Mushrooms

1 pound fresh mushrooms
1 pound bulk pork sausage
1 teaspoon garlic
2 tablespoons chopped parsley
1½ cups grated extra sharp Cheddar cheese

- Rinse mushrooms and pat dry; remove stems.
- Chop stems and combine with sausage, garlic and parsley; cook until sausage is browned, stirring to crumble.
- Drain well; stir in cheese and mix well.
- Spoon mixture into mushroom caps; place in a 9x13-inch dish and bake for 20 minutes at 350°.

Sausage Pinwheels

2   cups all-purpose flour
½   teaspoon salt
3   teaspoons baking powder
5   tablespoons shortening
⅔   cup milk
1   pound mild sausage, uncooked

- Preheat oven to 400°.
- Sift together the first 3 ingredients; cut in shortening. Add milk and mix.
- Divide dough into 2 rectangles; roll ¼ inch thick. Spread dough with sausage and roll "jelly-roll" style; chill until firm. Slice ¼ inch thick and bake 10 minutes.
- The rolls may be wrapped and frozen before slicing.

Yield: 30 pinwheels.

Lemonade Concentrate

(Refreshing in the summer)

1¼   cups sugar
1   tablespoon grated lemon peel
1½   cups boiling water
1½   cups lemon juice

- Put sugar and lemon peel in a jar with a tight-fitting lid.
- Stir in boiling water until sugar dissolves; stir in lemon juice then cover and refrigerate.
- For each serving, pour ¼ cup concentrate over ice in tall glass and fill glass with water.
- Can freeze individual ¼ cup portions so they will always be handy.

Banana Ale

(Everyone will rave over this)

6   cups water
4   cups sugar
5   oranges, juiced
4   lemons, juiced
7   ripe bananas, mashed
2   (46-ounce) cans pineapple juice
4-5   quarts ginger ale, chilled

- Boil water and sugar for 3 minutes or until it comes clear.
- Add the next 4 ingredients in order.
- Pour in a container and freeze for 3 hours. Can be done up to this stage several days ahead of time.
- When ready to serve, remove from the freezer and let it sit for about 45 minutes.
- Add mixture and ginger ale together.
- Add vodka to it if you need a "spiked" punch.
- Food coloring, a few drops, can be added to make a specific color.

Yield: 1 gallon.

Jazzy Tea

11   cups water
6   ounces frozen lemonade, undiluted
½   cup low calorie instant tea with lemon and sugar
1   liter Sprite

- Mix the water, lemonade and instant tea.
- When ready to serve, add Sprite.

Yield: 15 to 20 servings.

Limeade Tea

5   regular size tea bags
5   cups boiling water
1   cup sugar
1   (6-ounce) can limeade, undiluted
5   cups cold water
    Mint sprigs

- Steep tea bags in the boiling water for 8 minutes. Remove tea bags and discard.
- Add sugar to tea and stir to dissolve sugar. Stir in limeade and cold water.
- Serve over ice. Garnish with mint sprigs.

Yield: 2 quarts.

Apple Cider

1   gallon apple cider
1   (1-pound) box brown sugar less ¼ cup
2   teaspoons whole allspice
6   inches of cinnamon sticks
    Dash of nutmeg
½   teaspoon salt
2   sliced oranges

- Heat all ingredients to boiling. Reduce heat and simmer for 20 minutes
- Remove cinnamon sticks and orange slices
- Serve.

Yield: 1 gallon.

Christmas Punch

2   cups water
1   (3-ounce) package cherry gelatin
1   small package cherry flavored drink mix, unsweetened
1   cup sugar
1   can pineapple juice
1   quart ginger ale, chilled

- Bring 2 cups of water to a boil; add gelatin, drink mix and sugar; stir until dissolved. Pour into gallon jug; add pineapple juice and fill the jug with water. Shake well. Can make ahead and refrigerate until ready to use.
- Pour into punch bowl and add ginger ale.
- Strawberry gelatin may be used with strawberry drink mix.
- 12 gallons will serve 300 people.

Yield: 25 servings.

Russian Tea

1   cup sugar
2   cups water
2   sticks cinnamon
12-18 whole cloves
1   quart sweetened tea
1   quart orange juice
1   (46-ounce) can pineapple juice
       Juice of 1 lemon

- Boil sugar, water and spices for 5 minutes. Remove spices.
- Add juices and tea to mixture and heat to boiling.

Yield: 1 gallon.

Russian Tea Mix

(Makes a great gift)

1¼ cups orange powdered breakfast drink
⅓ cup instant tea mix
½ cup sugar
½ teaspoon cinnamon
¼ teaspoon ground cloves

- Mix all ingredients together and store in an airtight container.
- Use 2 or 3 generous teaspoonfuls of mix to 1 cup hot water.

Yield: 1 pint.

Bloody Mary Mix

(Spicy, excellent for a brunch)

9 tablespoons Worcestershire sauce
7 tablespoons lemon juice
1 tablespoon horseradish
1 tablespoon Tabasco
3 tablespoons seasoning salt
1 tablespoon celery salt
¼ teaspoon pepper

- Mix all ingredients in a tightly covered jar; shake well.
- Store in refrigerator for unlimited time.
- Use ½ to 1 teaspoon of the mix in any brand of tomato juice per drink.

Mint Iced Tea

3 cups boiling water
4 small tea bags
12 sprigs mint
1 cup orange juice
¼ cup lemon juice
1 cup sugar
6 cups cold water

- Combine boiling water, tea bags and mint; allow to cool. Remove mint and tea bags and discard.
- Combine orange juice, lemon juice, sugar and cold water. Stir until sugar is dissolved. Strain and combine both mixtures.
- Pour over ice and garnish with orange slices or mint sprigs.

Yield: 6 to 8 servings.

Bloody Marys

1 (46-ounce) can V-8 juice
1 (10½-ounce) can beef bouillon soup
4 ounces lemon juice concentrate
10 ounces vodka
1 teaspoon salt
½ teaspoon pepper
1 teaspoon Worcestershire sauce
½ teaspoon hot pepper sauce
   Celery sticks

- Mix all ingredients except celery together and serve individual drinks with a celery stick.
- For individual serving, mix all ingredients except vodka; let each person add his own amount of vodka.

Yield: 8 to 10 servings.

Cranberry Daiquiris

1 (8-ounce) can cranberry jelly
1 tablespoon sweetened lime juice
3 tablespoons liquid daiquiri mix
½ cup plus 2 tablespoons light rum

- Combine ingredients in blender.
- Add crushed ice to fill the blender; blend well.

Yield: 3½ cups.

Frozen Peach Daiquiri

3 fresh peaches, pitted but not peeled
1 tablespoon confectioners sugar
1 (6-ounce) can frozen lemonade, undiluted
1 lemonade can of rum
 Ice

- Mix ingredients in blender and add ice to top, blend and serve.
- May also be poured into plastic cups and frozen until ready to serve.

Yield: 6 servings.

Fuzzy Navel

(Not only pretty but good)

1 ounce Peach Schnapps
2 ounces orange juice
1 ounce vodka
2 ounces cran-raspberry juice
 Squirt of lime

- Mix all ingredients and serve over ice.

Yield: 1 serving.

Spicy Holiday Cheer

(Can be fixed ahead of time if needed)

1 quart apple juice
1 quart cranberry juice cocktail
2 tablespoons brown sugar
2 cinnamon sticks (2-inch)
¾ teaspoon whole cloves, it helps to put these in a tea ball
½ lemon, thinly sliced

- Combine all ingredients, cover and simmer for 20 minutes.
- May be served over an orange wedge.
- To microwave: bring to a boil and remove and steep for 20 minutes.

Kir Royale

2 (10-ounce) packages frozen raspberries, thawed
1 (32-ounce) bottle club soda, chilled
1 cup crème de cassis, chilled
3 bottles champagne, chilled

- Place one package of raspberries in a blender; process until smooth.
- Strain; pour raspberry purée into punch bowl with club soda and cassis. Stir gently.
- Break up remaining package of raspberries and add to punch bowl.
- Slowly pour champagne around bowl stirring gently; serve at once.

Yield: 3½ cups.

Kahlúa

3 cups sugar
¼ cup instant freeze dried coffee
3 cups water
1 fifth vodka
6 teaspoons vanilla flavoring

- Mix together sugar and coffee in a large saucepan; add water and stir. Boil slowly for 15 minutes; cool overnight.
- The next day add the vodka and vanilla to the mixture. Pour into bottles and let it set for 2 weeks before drinking.
- Keeps for months.

Fruit Spritzers

2 (12-ounce) cans frozen cranberry juice concentrate, thawed and undiluted
4 lemon slices
4 orange slices
4 lime slices
2 (750-milliliter) bottles champagne, chilled

- Combine first 4 ingredients in a large pitcher; cover and refrigerate 8 hours or overnight.
- Remove fruit; add champagne to cranberry juice, stirring gently.
- Garnish with lemon, orange and lime slices.
  Note: Two (23-ounce) bottles chilled sparkling mineral water may be substituted for champagne.
  Yield: 24 servings.

Margarita Daiquiris

(Great on a hot summer day)

1 (6-ounce) can limeade, undiluted
½ limeade can tequila
½ limeade can Triple Sec
½ limeade can Sweet and Sour mix or bottled Whiskey Sour mix
  Dash of lime juice
¼ lime, unpeeled

- Mix all ingredients in blender; add crushed ice to top of blender and blend well.
- Serve in salt-rimmed glasses or plain, unsalted glasses.
- Store any leftover in freezer.
  Yield: 6 servings.

Old Southern Eggnog

6 eggs, separated
½ pint whipping cream
1½ cups sugar
¾ cup whiskey
1 cup milk
  Nutmeg to taste

- Whip egg whites until stiff.
- Whip cream.
- Whip egg yolks and gradually add the sugar and whiskey.
- Fold together the egg whites, whipped cream and egg mixture; add milk.
- Freeze the mixture overnight in a covered container.
- Pour individual servings and thin with up to 2 tablespoons milk; garnish with nutmeg.

Sangría

1 (25.4-ounce) bottle dry red wine
¼ cup brandy
2 tablespoons orange flavored liqueur
3 cups red Hawaiian punch
3 oranges, thinly sliced
2 lemons, thinly sliced
2 bananas, sliced (optional)

- Combine wine, brandy, orange flavored liqueur and punch in a 4-quart container. Mix well; add fruit, stirring gently.
- Refrigerate at least 4 hours.
- Serve over ice.

Make Ahead Whiskey Sours

½ cup water
½ cup sugar
1 cup lemon juice
¾ cup fresh orange juice
1 fifth whiskey

- Boil water and add to sugar in a pitcher. Stir well to dissolve. Add lemon and orange juices and chill until serving time.
- Add whiskey to pitcher with plenty of ice and stir vigorously.

Yield: 18 servings.

Ruby Slipper

1 (12-ounce) can frozen orange juice, undiluted
2 cups pineapple juice
4 cups cranberry juice
1½ cups vodka

- Mix orange juice with pineapple juice and cranberry juice; add vodka.
- For a bright red color, tint with red food coloring; pour into plastic pitchers and freeze to a slushy consistency.
- Allow 2 to 3 hours in freezer.
- Stir and pour into Jefferson cups or sour glasses.

Yield: 8½ cups.

Passion Potion

1 (32-ounce) bottle cranberry juice
1 bottle champagne
   Lemon or lime twist

- Combine first 2 ingredients to taste and serve with fruit twist.

Pimm's Cup

9 ounces Pimm's
18 ounces ginger ale or lemon flavored soda
6 lemon slices
6 cucumber sticks (3x½-inch)

- Pour 1½ tablespoons of Pimm's into each of 6 tall glasses or balloon wine glasses.
- Fill with ice; add 3 ounces soda to each.
- Garnish with lemon and cucumber slices.

Yield: 6 servings.

Rum Punch

2 cups rum
28 ounces ginger ale
48 ounces cranberry juice
12 ounces frozen orange juice,
    undiluted
1 cup sugar

- Mix all ingredients together.
- Serve over ice.

Yield: 10 to 12 servings.

Sangre Y Arena

*(Best enjoyed in winter by the
fireplace)*

Fresh-squeezed orange juice
Red vermouth
Scotch
Cherry brandy

- Mix and pout together in "rocks" glass and
  add a few ice cubes.

Yield: 1 serving.

The Recipe

2 (6-ounce) cans frozen lemonade,
    undiluted
1 (6-ounce) can frozen orange juice,
    undiluted
6 ounces fresh lemon juice
72 ounces ginger ale
1 fifth bottle whiskey

- Mix lemonade, orange and lemon juice; add
  whiskey.
- Add ginger ale and chill for 4 hours.
- Serve in whiskey sour glasses

Yield: 12 to 16 servings.

Southern Iced Tea

(A definite "Stay at home" drink)

1 cup cola-flavored beverage
½ cup sweet and sour mix
2 tablespoons gin
2 tablespoons vodka
2 tablespoons light rum
2 tablespoons tequila
2 tablespoons Triple Sec
2 tablespoons lemon juice
2 tablespoons lime juice
3 cups crushed ice

- Combine all ingredients in a pitcher.
- Serve over additional crushed ice.

Yield: 4 servings.

Easy Wassail

1 gallon apple cider
2 quarts apricot nectar
3 cups dark rum
1½ cups firmly packed brown sugar
6 tablespoons lemon juice
6 (3-inch) cinnamon sticks
3 small oranges
1½ teaspoons whole cloves

- Bring the first 6 ingredients to a boil in a
  large Dutch oven, reduce heat and simmer
  uncovered for 1 hour.
- Stick cloves into oranges in a random
  pattern and add to hot cider.
- Serve hot.

Yield: 1½ gallons.

Wine Cooler

6 ounces lemonade
2 ounces Claret
Sprig of mint
Maraschino cherry

- Pour lemonade over crushed ice, then add claret.
- Garnish with mint and cherry.
- Refreshing on a hot summer day.

Yield: 1 serving.

Whiskey Sour Punch

(Looks festive with cherries frozen in block of ice or round mold for Christmas)

3 (32-ounce) bottles lemon-lime carbonated drink
1 (6-ounce) can frozen orange juice, undiluted
1 (6-ounce) can frozen lemonade, undiluted
1 (6-ounce) can plain lemon juice, undiluted
1 fifth of bourbon

- Mix all ingredients and pour over large block of ice in punch bowl.

Yield: 30 servings.

Hot Buttered Rum

(Wonderful on a cold night by the fire)

2 cups butter, softened
1 (16-ounce) box light brown sugar
1 (16-ounce) box confectioners sugar
2 teaspoons cinnamon
2 teaspoons nutmeg
1 quart vanilla ice cream, softened
Light rum
Boiling water

- Combine first 5 ingredients, beating until fluffy; add ice cream and blend well then place in a 2-quart container and freeze.
- To serve, place 3 heaping tablespoons of mixture and 1 jigger of rum in a large mug; fill with boiling water and stir well.

Yield: 16 to 18 servings.

Hot Buttered Coffee

(Takes the chill off a cold winter's night)

2 teaspoons brown sugar
½ teaspoon butter
Pinch each nutmeg and cinnamon
Strip of orange rind
1½ ounces bourbon, or to taste
Hot coffee
Cream (optional)

- Combine sugar, butter and spices in mug; stir until smooth.
- Add orange rind and bourbon; fill with hot coffee and stir well.
- Add cream if desired.

Yield: 1 serving.

BREADS

Index for Breads

Albemarle Hospital – 1914

This was the first established hospital building in the Albemarle Area. Founded by the Pasquotank Association in 1914 and later taken over by Dr. John Saliba. The hospital was designed by Wilson, NC architects Benton and Moore. It was built on original point in 1914 and enlarged in the 1950's.

Breakfast Pumpkin Bread

1   teaspoon nutmeg
1   teaspoon cinnamon
1½ teaspoons salt
3   cups white sugar
4   eggs
1   cup vegetable oil
1   cup pumpkin
3   cups all-purpose flour
2   teaspoons baking soda

- Combine first 6 ingredients and mix well.
- Add pumpkin, flour and soda. Mix until flour is dampened.
- Grease 3 (1-pound) coffee cans. Divide batter equally in the 3 cans.
- Bake at 350° for 1 hour.
- Remove from cans.
- Eat one, freeze one and take one to a friend.

Yield: 3 loaves.

Light-Hearted Hotcakes

1   package dry yeast
¼   cup warm water
1   tablespoon oil
1   cup milk
1   egg
1   cup pancake mix

- Sprinkle yeast into warm water; stir until dissolved. Add remaining ingredients and beat with rotary beater until smooth.
- Use a lightly greased griddle to cook.

Yield: 8 to 10 pancakes.

Cinnamon Leaf Ring

2   cups milk, scalded
2   packages active dry yeast
¾   cup shortening
¼   cup butter or margarine
½   cup sugar
2   teaspoons salt
4   egg yolks or 2 eggs, beaten
6   cups flour, sifted
1   cup butter or margarine, melted
2   tablespoons ground cinnamon
2   cups sugar

- Cool milk to lukewarm and sprinkle yeast over top; let stand to soften.
- Cream shortening and butter; add sugar and salt then cream together until light and fluffy. Add egg yolks, yeast mixture and enough flour to make soft dough.
- Knead until smooth and elastic on lightly floured cloth or board.
- Place in greased bowl; cover and let rise until doubled, about 1 hour.
- Mix together the cinnamon and sugar; set aside.
- Divide dough in half; roll out dough to ¼-inch thickness.
- Cut into rounds with 2-inch biscuit cutter; dip each round in melted butter and then in cinnamon and sugar mixture.
- Place rounds on end in two well buttered 8½-inch ring molds; bake at 350° for 25 minutes or until done, then cool in pans on racks a few minutes. Turn out onto racks.

Yield: 2 coffee cakes.

Oatmeal Pancakes

(Everyone will enjoy these)

¾ **cup regular rolled oats**
1½ **cups milk**
2 **eggs, beaten**
¼ **cup shortening, melted**
1¼ **cups flour**
2 **tablespoons sugar**
1 **tablespoon baking powder**
1 **teaspoon salt**
¾ **teaspoon cinnamon**
½ **cup raisins**

- Combine oats and milk; let stand 5 minutes. Add eggs and shortening; mix well. Combine dry ingredients; add to oatmeal mixture. Stir until just blended; add raisins.
- Drop by tablespoonfuls on greased griddle.
- Freezes well.

Yield: 4 to 5 servings.

Marmalade Muffins

1 **egg, beaten**
¼ **cup orange juice**
2 **tablespoons sugar**
1 **tablespoon salad oil**
1 **cup buttermilk baking mix**
¼ **cup orange marmalade**

- Preheat oven to 400°.
- Combine egg, juice, sugar and oil. Add baking mix and beat for 30 seconds; stir in marmalade.
- Fill greased muffin tins ⅔ full and bake 15 to 20 minutes.
- Freezes well.

  Note: These are very good reheated in microwave after being frozen, 35 seconds per muffin.

  Yield: 8 muffins.

Blueberry Muffins with Streusel Topping

1¾ **cups all-purpose flour**
½ **cup sugar**
2¾ **teaspoons baking powder**
2 **teaspoons grated lemon rind**
¾ **teaspoon salt**
1 **egg, beaten**
¾ **cup milk**
⅓ **cup vegetable oil**
1 **cup fresh blueberries**
1 **tablespoon all-purpose flour**
1 **tablespoon sugar**
¼ **cup sugar**
2½ **tablespoons all-purpose flour**
½ **teaspoon ground cinnamon**
1½ **tablespoons butter**

- In a large bowl combine the first 5 ingredients. Combine egg, milk and vegetable oil; stirring well; add to dry ingredients, stirring until moistened.
- Combine blueberries, 1 tablespoon flour and 1 tablespoon sugar, tossing gently to coat; fold this mixture into batter.
- Grease regular size muffin pans; spoon batter into pans, filling ⅔ full.
- Combine ¼ cup sugar, 2½ tablespoons flour and cinnamon; cut in 1½ tablespoons butter with a pastry blender until mixture resembles coarse meal. Sprinkle over batter.
- Bake at 400° for 20 minutes or until golden.

  Yield: 16 muffins.

Cranberry Coffee Cake

½ cup margarine
1 cup sugar
2 eggs
1 teaspoon baking powder
1 teaspoon soda
2 cups all-purpose flour
½ teaspoon salt
1 (8-ounce) carton sour cream
1 teaspoon almond flavoring
1 (7-ounce) can whole cranberry
   sauce
½ cup chopped nuts
¾ cup confectioners sugar
2 tablespoons warm water
½ teaspoon almond flavoring

- Cream margarine and sugar. Add eggs, one at a time.

- Sift together baking powder, soda, flour and salt.

- Add dry ingredients to creamed mixture, alternating with the sour cream. Stir in almond flavoring.

- Grease and flour tube pan or 2 loaf pans. Pour ½ batter into tube pan or ¼ batter into 2 loaf pans. Spread cranberry sauce over batter. Pour remaining batter over cranberry sauce; sprinkle nuts on top.

- Bake at 350° for 55 minutes; smaller pans might take less time.

- Remove from oven and cool.

- While bread is baking, mix together confectioners sugar, water and almond flavoring; set aside.

- Remove bread from pan and ice with sugar topping.

Yield: 1 tube cake or 2 loaves.

Bran Muffins

(Serve with a hearty breakfast)

5 cups all-purpose flour
2 cups sugar
1 cup vegetable oil
3 teaspoons baking soda
1 teaspoon salt
4 eggs
1 quart buttermilk
1 (20-ounce) box raisin bran or bran
   flakes
   Nuts, raisins, dates or fresh fruit
   (optional)

- Combine all ingredients and mix well; refrigerate. Batter will keep in refrigerator for 6 weeks.

- Do not thin out further; when ready to bake, add fresh fruit bits, nuts, raisins or dates.

- Fill greased muffin thins ⅔ full and bake 15 to 20 minutes at 400°; check after 15 minutes.

- Freezes well.

Carrot Muffins

(Will disappear quickly)

4   cups all-purpose flour
2½ cups sugar
4   teaspoons baking soda
4   teaspoons cinnamon
1   teaspoon salt
4   cups peeled and grated apples
1   cup raisins
1   cup chopped nuts
1   cup shredded coconut
1   cup grated carrot
6   eggs
2   cups vegetable oil
4   teaspoons vanilla

- Preheat oven to 350°.
- Grease 36 large muffin cups or several small tins.
- In a large bowl, sift flour, sugar, soda, cinnamon and salt; stir in the next 5 ingredients, mixing well.
- Combine eggs, oil and vanilla, blending well; add to flour mixture and stir just until blended.
- Spoon batter into prepared tins, filling ⅔ full.
- Bake for 35 minutes for large muffins and no more than 20 minutes for miniature muffins.
- Cool in pans on wire rack for 5 minutes then remove from pans to rack; cool completely.
- Freezes well.

Yield: 36 large muffins or 100 mini muffins.

Carrot, Zucchini and Apple Muffins

(Great snack)

2   cups all-purpose flour
2   cups shredded carrots
1¼ cups sugar
1   cup shredded zucchini
1   yellow apple, cored and finely chopped
¾   cup golden raisins
¾   cup unsweetened shredded coconut
½   cup almonds, coarsely chopped
1   tablespoon cinnamon
2   teaspoons baking soda
1½ teaspoons grated orange peel
1   teaspoon vanilla extract
½   teaspoon salt
3   large eggs
1   cup vegetable oil

- Preheat oven to 375°.
- Grease large size muffin cups.
- Mix all ingredients except eggs and oil in large bowl.
- Beat eggs and oil in large bowl to blend.
- Stir flour mixture into the eggs; spoon ¼ cup batter into each cup.
- Bake until tester inserted in centers comes out clean.

Yield: 24 muffins.

To freshen stale raisins, etc., place them in a strainer and steam them for a few minutes.

Cheddar Cheese Muffins

(Wonderful with chili or soup)

3 ounces sharp Cheddar cheese, grated
1 large green onion, including top, chopped
1 cup all-purpose flour
⅓ cup yellow cornmeal
2 teaspoons baking powder
1 teaspoon red pepper flakes (optional)
½ teaspoon baking soda
½ teaspoon salt
1 tablespoon sugar
¾ cup sour cream
⅓ cup vegetable oil
2 eggs

- Preheat oven to 375°; grease muffin cups.
- Combine all ingredients in a food processor and process until well blended.
- Fill muffin cups ⅔ full.
- Bake for 15 minutes; serve warm.

  Note: May be frozen for 2 months.

  Yield: 10 to 16 muffins.

Miniature Cranberry Muffins

1 cup fresh cranberries, chopped
1 cup all-purpose flour, divided
½ cup whole wheat flour
1 teaspoon baking powder
½ teaspoon baking soda
⅓ cup sugar
1 cup orange juice
½ cup morsels of wheat bran cereal
2 tablespoons vegetable oil
1 egg, slightly beaten
1 teaspoon vanilla extract
Vegetable cooking spray

- Toss cranberries with ¼ cup all-purpose flour; set aside.
- Combine remaining all-purpose flour and whole wheat flour and next three ingredients in a large mixing bowl. Make a well in center of mixture.
- Combine orange juice and the next 4 ingredients and add to dry ingredients, stirring just enough to moisten. Stir in chopped cranberries. Spoon into miniature muffins pans that have been coated with vegetable spray; fill ¾ full.
- Bake at 350° for 10 to 12 minutes.

  Yield: 3 dozen.

*Chill cheese to grate
it more easily.*

Oatmeal Muffins

¾ cup oats
¼ cup bran
1 cup buttermilk
1 cup firmly packed brown sugar
1 egg, slightly beaten
1 cup all-purpose flour
¾ cup whole wheat flour
1 teaspoon baking powder
1 teaspoon baking soda
1 teaspoon salt
½ teaspoon ground cinnamon
½ teaspoon ground cloves
½ teaspoon allspice
½ cup vegetable oil
1 lemon rind, grated
   Juice of 1 lemon
½ cup raisins

- Combine oats, bran and buttermilk; let stand 30 minutes. Add brown sugar and egg; mix well.
- Combine next 8 ingredients; stir into oat mixture.
- Stir in oil, grated lemon rind, lemon juice and raisins.
- Spoon into greased muffin pans, filling ½ full; use the small tins or regular size muffin tins.
- Bake at 375° for 12 to 15 minutes for small tins; longer for larger tins.
- Wrap any leftovers in foil and freeze.

Sweet Potato Muffins

½ cup butter, softened
1¼ cups sugar
2 eggs
1¼ cups mashed sweet potatoes
1½ cups all-purpose flour
2 teaspoons baking powder
¼ teaspoon salt
1 teaspoon cinnamon
¼ teaspoon nutmeg
1 cup milk
½ cup finely chopped pecans
½ cup chopped raisins (optional)

- Preheat oven to 400°.
- Cream margarine and sugar; add eggs, mixing well. Blend in sweet potatoes. Mix in dry ingredients, which have been sifted together, alternately with milk. Be careful not to overmix. Fold in nuts and raisins.
- Grease muffin tins and fill ⅔ full. Bake for 25 minutes.

  Note: These may be frozen and reheated.

  Yield: 24 large muffins or 72 small ones.

Biscuits

2 cups self-rising flour
⅓ cup oil
⅓ cup canned milk
⅓ cup water
   Dash of salt

- Put flour in a bowl.
- Mix remaining ingredients together and pour into bowl with flour; stir until well blended. Knead lightly on a floured board; cut into desired size.
- Bake 12 to 16 minutes at 400°.

  Yield: 18 to 36 biscuits.

Beer Bread

3 cups self-rising flour
4 tablespoons sugar
1 (12-ounce) can of beer

- Mix together in a bowl with spoon. Pour into a greased loaf or round pan.
- Bake in oven at 400° for 30 minutes.
  Yield: 1 loaf.

Broccoli Bread

1 (10-ounce) package frozen chopped broccoli, thawed and drained
3 spring onions plus part of tops, chopped
1 (16-ounce) carton small curd cottage cheese
½ cup butter, melted
4 eggs, beaten
1 (8½-ounce) box corn muffin mix

- Mix the first 5 ingredients together; add the muffin mix.
- Pour into a 9x13-inch greased pan. Bake at 400° for 20 to 25 minutes.
  Yield: 12 servings.

Buttermilk Biscuits

5 cups self-rising flour
1⅓ cups butter-flavored shortening
½ teaspoon baking powder
2½ cups buttermilk

- Mix ingredients, knead, and form into desired size.
- Place in non-stick pan and bake at 400° for about 20 minutes.
- Check biscuits about half way through baking to see if they are browning on both top and bottom evenly.

Cheese Biscuits

½ cup margarine, softened
¼ pound sharp Cheddar cheese, shredded and room temperature
   Dash cayenne pepper or hot pepper sauce
1½ cups self-rising flour

- Cream margarine, cheese and pepper well. Add flour and work in well, first with fork, then with hands; it should be a smooth ball.
- Pinch off dough and roll into balls according to desired size. Flatten with fork or hand.
- Bake in 350° oven on ungreased cookie sheet for 10 to 15 minutes.
- Do not brown.

Hot Crab Bread

½ pound fresh crabmeat, flaked
⅓ cup mayonnaise
⅓ cup sour cream
2 tablespoons chopped parsley
2 teaspoons lemon juice
¼ teaspoon garlic salt
1 loaf French bread
1-2 tablespoons butter, softened
¼ pound sliced Swiss cheese

- Combine crabmeat, mayonnaise, sour cream, parsley, lemon juice and garlic salt.
- Slice bread in half lengthwise; arrange on baking sheet. Spread cut side with butter; top with cheese slices, trimmed to fit bread. Pile crab mixture on top of cheese.
- Bake in 350° oven until lightly browned, about 20 minutes.
- Cut across into serving pieces.

Corny Cornbread

1 (8½-ounce) box corn muffin mix
2 eggs, lightly beaten
1 (8¾-ounce) can creamed corn
1 (8¾-ounce) can regular corn, drained
1 (8-ounce) carton sour cream
½ cup butter, softened

- Mix all ingredients together, blending well; pour into a greased 7x11-inch Pyrex dish.
- Bake at 350° for 25 to 30 minutes.
- Freezes well; doubles easily.

Yield: 10 servings.

Dog Biscuits

(A treat for man's best friend!)

2½ cups whole wheat flour
½ cup powdered dry milk
½ teaspoon salt
½ teaspoon garlic powder
1 tablespoon brown sugar
6 tablespoons margarine, shortening or meat drippings
1 egg, beaten
½ cup ice water

- Combine flour, dry milk, salt, garlic powder and sugar. Cut in shortening until mixture resembles cornmeal. Mix in egg. Add enough water so that mixture form a ball.
- Pat dough ½-inch thick with your fingers on a lightly oiled cookie sheet. Cut out with dog bone shaped cookie cutters or shape of your choice. Remove scraps. Pat over the scraps and continue cutting biscuits.
- Bake at 350° for 25 to 30 minutes. Remove from oven and cool on cake rack.

Gilroy Garlic Bread

¾ cup butter, room temperature
¾ cup freshly grated Parmesan cheese
6 tablespoons mayonnaise
3 large garlic cloves, minced
2 tablespoons chopped fresh parsley
¼ teaspoon dried oregano, crumbled
1 (1-pound) loaf French bread, halved lengthwise

- Combine first 6 ingredients in medium bowl. Can be prepared 2 days ahead. Refrigerate.
- Bring to room temperature before continuing. Preheat oven to 375°.
- Spread garlic spread on cut sides of bread; wrap each bread half in foil.
- Place bread on baking sheet cut side up, bake 20 minutes.
- Remove foil from bread.
- Broil about 2 minutes until golden brown.

Yield: 8 to 12 servings.

Spoon Bread

2 cups boiling water
1 cup white cornmeal
1 teaspoon salt
1 teaspoon sugar
1 cup milk
2 eggs, separated
1 tablespoon shortening

- Mix water and dry ingredients; cool. Add milk and beaten egg yolks. Fold in beaten egg whites.
- Melt shortening in 9x12-inch baking dish.
- Pour batter into greased baking dish and bake at 400° for 30 to 40 minutes.

Yield: 6 to 8 servings.

Herbed Cheddar Cheese Bread

4 cups unbleached white flour
¼ cup sugar
2 tablespoons baking powder
2 teaspoons salt
1½ teaspoons dried thyme
½ teaspoon celery seeds
⅛ teaspoon freshly ground pepper
   Dash allspice
3 cups grated sharp Cheddar cheese
1 bunch green onions, chopped
   including green tops
1 egg
1¾ cups skim milk

- Combine first 8 ingredients together in large bowl. Add cheese and onions and stir to coat. Beat egg with milk in a separate bowl and pour into dry ingredients. Mix until blended. Batter will be stiff.
- Spoon into 2 greased 9x5-inch loaf pans and let rise 10 minutes.
- Bake at 375° for 45 minutes or until wooden pick inserted in center of loaves comes out clean.

Yield: 2 loaves.

Mile High Biscuits

3 cups all-purpose flour
2 tablespoons sugar
1 tablespoon plus 1½ teaspoons
   baking powder
¾ teaspoon cream of tartar
¾ teaspoon salt
¾ cup shortening
1 egg, beaten
¾ cup milk

- Preheat oven to 450°.
- Combine first 5 ingredients, mixing well.
- Cut in shortening with a pastry blender until mixture resembles coarse meal.
- Combine egg and milk, add to flour mixture, stirring until dry ingredients are moistened.
- Turn dough out onto a lightly floured surface; knead 8 to 10 times.
- Roll dough out to 1-inch thickness. Cut with a 2½-inch biscuit cutter.
- Place biscuits on an ungreased pan.
- Bake for 15 minutes or until golden brown.

Yield: 12 to 15 biscuits.

Parmesan French Bread

1 cup Parmesan cheese
1 cup mayonnaise
1 loaf French bread, sliced

- Mix cheese and mayonnaise together.
- Spread cheese and mayonnaise on each slice of bread.
- Bake in 400° oven until toasted, about 10 minutes.

Yield: 12 servings.

Spice Zucchini Bread

- 3 cups all-purpose flour
- 2 teaspoons soda
- 1 teaspoon salt
- ½ teaspoon baking powder
- 1½ teaspoons cinnamon
- 1 teaspoon nutmeg
- ⅛ teaspoon ground cloves
- ¾ cup chopped pecans
- 3 eggs
- 1⅔ cups white sugar
- ⅓ cup brown sugar
- 1 cup salad oil
- 2 teaspoons vanilla
- 2 cups zucchini, unpeeled and shredded
- 1 (8-ounce) can crushed pineapple, well drained

- Combine flour, soda, salt, baking powder, cinnamon, nutmeg, cloves and nuts; set aside.

- Beat eggs lightly in a large mixing bowl; add sugars, oil and vanilla; beat until creamy.

- Stir in zucchini and pineapple; add dry ingredients, stirring only until dry ingredients are moistened.

- Spoon batter into 2 well-greased and floured 8½x4½x2⅝-inch loaf pans; bake at 325° for 45 to 60 minutes then cool 10 minutes before removing from pans.

  Yield: 2 loaves.

Spinach Squares

(Great side dish with chili and other casual dishes)

- 1 (10-ounce) package frozen chopped spinach, thawed and drained well
- ½ cup chopped onion
- ¼ cup margarine, melted
- 1 (8½-ounce) box corn muffin mix
- 2 eggs, beaten
- ½ cup chunky bleu cheese salad dressing
- 1 cup grated sharp Cheddar cheese
- ¼ teaspoon garlic powder

- Sauté chopped onions in margarine; add spinach, corn muffin mix, eggs, dressing, cheese and garlic powder.

- Mix well then bake for 25 to 30 minutes at 350° in a greased 9x9-inch pan or baking dish.

- This dish freezes well after cooking; it can be cut into smaller portions and served as appetizers.

Sweet Potato Biscuits

- 6 cups buttermilk biscuit mix
- 5 medium sweet potatoes, steamed, peeled and puréed
- ½-¾ cup light brown sugar
- ⅓-½ cup water

- Combine all ingredients in a large bowl, starting with ⅓ cup water and adding more until mixture is moist.

- Knead gently; roll out dough to ½-inch thick. Cut into 2½-inch circles.

- Place on lightly greased pan.

- Bake at 325° for 10 to 15 minutes.

  Yield: 24 biscuits.

Strawberry Bread

3	cups all-purpose flour
1	teaspoon salt
1	teaspoon soda
1	tablespoon ground cinnamon
2	cups sugar
3	eggs, well beaten
1¼	cups salad oil
20	ounces fresh strawberries, capped and chopped
1¼	cups chopped pecans

- Combine flour, salt, soda, cinnamon and sugar; add eggs and oil, stirring mixture until dry ingredients are moistened.
- Stir in strawberries and pecans.
- Spoon mixture into 2 lightly greased loaf pans.
- Bake at 350° for 1 hour or until done. Allow to stand overnight before slicing.

Yield: 2 loaves.

Tar Heel State Hush Puppies

1	pound cornmeal
1	egg
1	tablespoon salt
2	tablespoons sugar
	Pinch soda
1	cup buttermilk
¼	cup chopped onion (optional)
	Water

- Mix all ingredients, except water, together. Add water until you get a thick consistency.
- Drop in deep fat fryer which has been heated to 375°.
- When hush puppies become golden brown, remove and drain on paper towels.

Angel Biscuits

1	package yeast
¼	cup warm water
2½	cups all-purpose flour
½	teaspoon baking soda
1	teaspoon baking powder
1	teaspoon salt
⅛	cup sugar
½	cup shortening
1	cup buttermilk

- Dissolve yeast in warm water and set aside.
- Mix all dry ingredients together in the order listed. Cut shortening into the dry mixture. Stir in buttermilk and the yeast mixture.
- Knead lightly or store in refrigerator until ready to use.
- After removing dough from the refrigerator, it should be allowed to set at room temperature to rise.
- Roll dough on floured board. Cut with biscuit cutter.
- Place on greased pan and let rise a little before baking.
- Bake at 400° for 12 to 15 minutes.

Dip the spoon in hot water to measure shortening, butter, etc., the fat will slip out more easily.

Sour Dough Bread

(Everybody will want to know how to make it)

- To make 1 cup of sour dough starter mix, combine the following ingredients:

  4 tablespoons sugar
  3 tablespoons instant potatoes
  1 cup warm water
  ½ package dry yeast

- Put this initial starter mixture in the refrigerator for 3 to 5 days. Take out of the refrigerator and add:

  4 tablespoons sugar
  3 tablespoons instant potatoes
  1 cup warm water

- Mix well and leave out on the counter for 8 to 12 hours. This does not rise but bubbles.

- After 8 to 12 hours, stir mixture well and take out 1 cup to use to make the bread. Put the rest of the starter back into the refrigerator.

- The starter has to be fed every 3 to 5 days. Keep mixture in a quart jar covered with foil that has holes punched into it.

- To the 1 cup of starter mix, add the following ingredients:

  ½ cup corn oil
  1½ teaspoons salt
  1½ cups warm water
  ¼ cup sugar
  6 cups bread flour, unsifted

- Mix well; transfer to a large greased bowl, and cover with a clean dishcloth. Let mixture rise overnight.

- Next morning, punch down dough with fist; divide into 2 equal balls.

- Knead on lightly floured board; place into 2 large greased loaf pans; cover with a cloth.

Let rise 4 to 5 hours or all day.

- Bake at 350° for 35 to 40 minutes or until golden brown; brushed with melted butter.

Whole Wheat Bread:

4 cups bread flour
1 cup whole wheat flour
½ cup oatmeal
½ cup Wheetena
¼ cup sugar
1½ teaspoons salt
½ cup oil
1 cup starter
1½ cups warm water

- Prepare the same way as for the Sour Dough Bread.

  Note: You must feed the starter every 3 to 5 days. If you do not have time to make bread, still feed the starter and throw 1 cup of starter away or give it to a friend.

Surprise Banana Bread

½ cup unsalted butter, softened
½ cup sugar
2 eggs
3 very ripe bananas, mashed
2 cups all-purpose flour
1 teaspoon baking soda
½ cup chopped honey-roasted peanuts or other nuts
⅓ cup semi-sweet chocolate chips

- Cream together butter and sugar; add eggs, scraping bowl well. Add bananas, flour and baking soda; mix in nuts and chocolate chips, blending well. Pour into a greased 5x9-inch loaf pan.

- Bake at 350° for 1 hour.

Yield: 1 loaf.

Dilly Bread

(Leftovers are delicious sliced and toasted with butter)

1   **package dry yeast**
¼   **cup warm water**
1   **cup cottage cheese, room temperature**
1   **tablespoon minced onion**
2   **tablespoons sugar**
1   **tablespoon butter**
2   **teaspoons dill seed**
1   **teaspoon salt**
¼   **teaspoon baking soda**
1   **egg, unbeaten**
2¼-2½   **cups plain flour, sift before measuring**
    Melted butter

- Soften yeast in warm water.
- Combine in mixing bowl, cottage cheese, sugar, onion, butter, dill seed, salt, soda, egg and softened yeast.
- Add flour, a little at a time, mixing well after each addition.
- Cover and let rise in a warm place for an hour or until doubled in bulk.
- Punch down and turn into greased bread pan.
- Let dough rise again until doubled; bake at 350° for 30 to 35 minutes.
- Turn out immediately and brush with melted butter.

Yield: 1 loaf.

Light Yogurt Crescent Rolls

(Crescent rolls with half the fat and less calories)

⅓   **cup vegetable oil**
1   **(8-ounce) carton plain low-fat yogurt**
½   **cup sugar**
2   **packages dry yeast**
½   **cup warm water**
1   **egg**
1   **egg white**
4   **cups all-purpose flour, divided**
1   **teaspoon salt**
    Vegetable cooking spray

- Combine first 3 ingredients; set aside.
- Dissolve yeast in warm water in a large mixing bowl; let stand for 5 minutes then stir in yogurt mixture, egg and egg white.
- Combine flour and salt; stir 2 cups flour into yogurt mixture and beat at medium speed until smooth.
- Gradually stir in remaining flour mixture; cover and refrigerate for 8 hours.
- Punch dough down and divide into 4 equal portions; roll each portion to a 10-inch circle on a floured surface then coat with cooking spray.
- Cut each circle into 12 wedges; roll up each wedge, beginning at wide end.
- Spray baking sheet with cooking spray; place crescents on sheet with point side down.
- Cover and let rise in a warm place for at least 45 minutes or until doubled in bulk.
- Bake at 375° for 10 to 12 minutes or until golden brown.

Yield: 4 dozen.

English Muffin Loaf

(A great gift with a jar of homemade preserves)

6   cups flour, divided
2   packages yeast
1   tablespoon sugar
2   teaspoons salt
½   teaspoon baking soda
2   cups milk
½   cup water
    Cornmeal

- Put 3 cups flour into bowl with yeast and other dry ingredients.

- Heat milk and water to 130°; pour over dry ingredients until well blended. Add rest of flour and mix well.

- Grease 2 loaf pans and sprinkle with cornmeal. Divide dough into 2 pans. Cover and let rise for 45 minutes or until just below rim of pans.

- Preheat oven to 400°; bake for 25 minutes.

- Cover with foil after 15 minutes if the bread begins to brown too quickly.

- Slice and toast as you would English muffins. Freezes well.

Yield: 2 loaves.

Pimento Cheese Biscuits

2   cups flour
3   teaspoons baking powder
1   tablespoon sugar
1   teaspoon salt
¼   teaspoon cayenne pepper
1½   cups shredded sharp Cheddar cheese
8   tablespoons butter
¼   cup chopped pimento, drained
¼   cup finely chopped green bell pepper
¾-1 cup milk

- Preheat oven to 450°. Combine flour, baking powder, sugar, salt and cayenne pepper. Add cheese and mix well.

- Cut butter into flour until consistency of coarse cornmeal. Add pimento and green pepper.

- Make a well in the dry ingredients and add ¾ cup milk. Using a fork, stir to combine until mixture forms a ball. Add additional milk as needed.

- Turn dough onto floured surface and knead 8 to 10 times. Roll out ½-inch thick and cut into 1-inch rounds. Biscuits may be placed on a cookie sheet and frozen at this point. When frozen, store in freezer in zip lock bags until ready to bake. Bake biscuits on ungreased cookie sheet 12 to 15 minutes. Do not thaw frozen biscuits before baking.

Yield: 50 small or 15 2-inch biscuits.

SOUPS & SANDWICHES

Becky Wienges '92

Index for Soup and Sandwich

Apple Soup

(A refreshing summertime soup for the ladies)

1 pound green apples, peeled, cored and quartered
3 cups water
1 teaspoon grated lemon rind
2 teaspoons lemon juice
½ cup sugar
½ teaspoon cinnamon
¼ teaspoon nutmeg
   Sour cream (optional)

- Place all ingredients except sour cream in a saucepan; simmer for 20 minutes.
- Purée in blender until smooth.
- Serve hot or cold.

   Note: A dollop of sour cream can be served on top of each serving.

Gazpacho

3 (6-ounce) cans spiced vegetable juice
½ medium tomato, finely chopped
¾ cup finely chopped cucumber
¾ cup finely chopped celery
⅓ cup finely chopped green pepper
¼ cup finely chopped onion
¼ cup finely chopped parsley
1 clove garlic, pressed or powdered
2 tablespoons lemon juice
   Hot pepper sauce to taste

- Add vegetables and seasonings to vegetable juice.
- Chill at least 4 hours prior to serving.

   Yield: 2 servings.

Cantaloupe Soup

(Summertime favorite)

1 ripe peach
1 ripe cantaloupe
¾ cup unfiltered apple juice
2 teaspoons lemon juice
¼ teaspoon vanilla extract
2 tablespoons fresh mint leaves, chopped
½ pint blueberries for garnish

- Peel and chop the peach; cut the cantaloupe into small chunks. Place the fruit in a medium saucepan and add the apple juice.
- Cook over medium heat until the fruit is soft, 7 to 8 minutes; stir in the lemon juice and vanilla.
- Purée the soup in a blender or food processor. Transfer to bowl and fold in the chopped mint leaves.
- Chill for 2 hours; garnish with fresh blueberries and serve.
- Great as a low calorie snack or for breakfast.

Dilly Tomato Soup

2 (10¾-ounce) cans tomato soup
2 soup cans of buttermilk
2 tablespoons lemon juice
½ teaspoon onion powder
¼ teaspoon garlic powder
   Salt to taste
1 tablespoon crushed dill seed

- Whisk all ingredients together; refrigerate overnight.
- Serve cold.

   Yield: 5½ cups.

Cold Potato Soup

4 cups peeled, cubed potatoes
1 cup sliced celery
1 cup chopped onion
2 cups water
1 teaspoon salt
1 cup milk
1 cup whipping cream
3 tablespoons butter
1 tablespoon parsley
⅛ teaspoon pepper
½ teaspoon ginger
  Sherry (optional)

- Combine first 5 ingredients in large Dutch oven and simmer, covered about 20 minutes.
- Add milk and remaining ingredients to cooked potato mixture and heat slowly.
- This can be put in blender and a little sherry makes it even better!
- Can be served at room temperature or chilled for 4 hours.

Beef Goulash

(Quick meal with salad and French bread)

1 cup uncooked macaroni
1 pound ground beef
1 (8-ounce) can sliced mushrooms, drained
1 cup chopped onion
1 garlic clove, minced
1 (6-ounce) can tomato paste
¼ cup water
1 cup tomato ketchup
1 small bay leaf
1 teaspoon sugar

½ teaspoon pepper
¼ teaspoon oregano
¼ teaspoon basil

- Cook macaroni; drain and set aside.
- Brown ground beef with mushrooms, onion and garlic; drain and add remaining ingredients then simmer gently for 15 minutes.
- Add cooked, drained macaroni and simmer 5 minutes. Remove bay leaf before serving.

Yield: 4 servings.

Borscht

(Something different on a cold night)

¼ cup butter
1 large onion, chopped
2 cans beef consommé
1½ quarts water
2 cans whole beets, julienned
1 (14½-ounce) can tomatoes, puréed in blender
  Juice of 1 lemon
2 tablespoons sugar
½ teaspoon salt
½ teaspoon pepper
  Sour cream

- Sauté onion in melted butter in Dutch oven until transparent. Add consommé, water and beets; simmer for 30 minutes. Blend in tomatoes and simmer for 30 more minutes. Add lemon juice, sugar, salt and pepper to desired sweet and sour taste.
- Serve with spoon of sour cream in each bowl.
- As soup simmers, skim off foam caused by blending tomatoes. Can simmer for hours.

Iced Lemon Soup

4 cups chicken stock
2 tablespoons cornstarch
2 cups half-and-half
6 egg yolks, lightly beaten
1 cup fresh lemon juice
 Dash ground red pepper
1 lemon, sliced thin
1 tablespoon chopped fresh parsley

- In medium saucepan, blend small amount of stock into cornstarch, and whisk until smooth. Gradually add in remaining stock and half and half. Place over low heat and stir constantly until soup begins to thicken.
- Do not boil.
- Gradually whisk a little soup into egg yolks and blend yolk mixture back into soup. Stir in lemon juice and red pepper. Let soup cool and refrigerate at least 8 hours.
- Serve very cold, garnished with lemon slices and parsley.

Yield: 12 servings.

Broccoli and Chicken Soup

1 bunch broccoli, cleaned and coarsely chopped
1½ cups water
2 (10¾-ounce) cans cream of chicken soup, undiluted
1 cup light cream
 Salt to taste
 White pepper to taste
 Cayenne pepper to taste
 Croutons
 Parmesan cheese

- Bring water to a boil in large saucepan. Add broccoli and cook until tender. Purée broccoli with all liquid in a food processor.
- Return to saucepan, add soup and cream. Blend with wire whisk. Season to taste.
- Heat to simmering. Top with croutons and grated Parmesan cheese.

Yield: 1 quart.

Brunswick Stew

1 pound ham hock
4 pounds beef
4 pounds chicken, skinned
3 large onions, chopped
1-2 pods red pepper
1 gallon butter beans
1½ gallons tomatoes, undrained
3 (16-ounce) cans white corn, drained
5 pounds potatoes, cooked and mashed, reserving water
½ bottle Worcestershire sauce
2 cups butter
1 cup sugar
 Salt and pepper to taste

- Combine all meats in a Dutch oven and cover with water. Cook until tender and bone meats; add onions, pepper, salt and butter beans. When almost tender, add tomatoes and cook for an additional 15 minutes. Add corn and continue cooking until all are tender. Add mashed potatoes and remaining seasonings; simmer for a while before serving. Even better if served after reheating the next day.

Yield: 35 to 40 servings.

Broccoli Bisque

3   tablespoons butter
1   large clove garlic, minced
3   medium onions, coarsely chopped
1   carrot, sliced
3-4 stalks of broccoli (1 bunch) cleaned
     and coarsely chopped
4   cups chicken stock
1   tablespoon chicken bouillon
     granules (optional)
2   cups light cream (or lowfat milk)
2   tablespoons dry sherry
     Pepper to taste

- Sauté garlic, onion and carrot, in butter, in large soup pot. Add cut broccoli and sauté briefly. Add chicken stock, cover and simmer until tender.

- Purée in blender until smooth. Add cream and sherry. Add pepper to taste.

- Reheat to serving temperature.

  Yield: 8 servings.

Carrot Bisque with Ginger

¼   cup plus 2 tablespoons unsalted
     butter
2   pounds carrots, peeled, thinly
     sliced
2   large onions, chopped
1   tablespoon minced, peeled fresh
     ginger
2   teaspoons grated orange peel
½   teaspoon ground coriander
5   cups chicken broth, divided
1   cup half-and-half
     Salt and pepper to taste
½   cup minced fresh parsley

- Melt butter in heavy saucepan over medium heat; add carrots and onions. Cover saucepan and cook until vegetables begin to soften; stirring occasionally, about 15 minutes.

- Mix in ginger, orange peel and coriander; add 2 cups stock. Reduce heat to medium-low; cover pan and simmer soup until carrots are tender, about 30 minutes.

- Purée soup in batches in processor or blender; add remaining 3 cups stock and half-and-half to soup. Season with salt and pepper (this can be prepared to this point a day ahead, covered and refrigerated).

- Cook over medium heat until warm; ladle into bowls and sprinkle with parsley.

  Yield: 8 servings.

Cheese Soup

2½   pints chicken stock
½   cup chopped celery
½   cup chopped carrots
½   cup chopped onion
¼   teaspoon Accent
½   teaspoon dry mustard
2   tablespoons Parmesan cheese
1   (7-ounce) bottle beer
½   cup butter
½   cup flour
6   ounces Cheddar cheese

- Boil vegetables in chicken stock; add Accent, dry mustard, Parmesan cheese and beer. Melt butter in saucepan and blend in flour; add Cheddar cheese. Stir until melted, keeping heat low. Add cheese mixture to stock mixture and simmer.

- Do not boil.

- Serve with croutons.

Chicken and Sausage Gumbo

Roux:
- 1 cup flour
- ¾ cup oil

- In a heavy skillet, make the roux.

- 1 young chicken, cut into serving pieces
  Roux
- 1 large onion, chopped
- 1 bell pepper, chopped
- 1½ pounds sausage (fresh pork, smoked, andouille or kielbasa)
  Salt to taste
  Black and red pepper to taste
- 1 bunch green onions or shallots, chopped
- 1 bunch parsley, chopped

- Place chicken in a large gumbo pot.
- Add enough cold water to cover completely.
- Bring to a boil then simmer for ½ hour.
- Remove chicken and discard bones and skin; reserve stock in gumbo pot.
- When roux is dark brown, immediately add onion and bell pepper and sauté until wilted.
- Add sausage and brown well in same pot.
- Add one quart cold water to roux-sausage mixture.
- Stir and transfer to gumbo pot with chicken and chicken broth.
- Cook slowly for 1 to 1½ hours.
- Add more water if necessary; add salt and pepper to taste.
- In the final 15 minutes add parsley and green onions.

Yield: 10 to 12 servings.

Favorite Oyster Stew

- 1 quart oysters, reserve liquid
- 1 quart milk
- 2 tablespoons butter
- 1 tablespoon finely chopped parsley
- 4 teaspoons onion juice
- ½ teaspoon salt
  Dash pepper

- Pick over oysters to remove only shell particles; set aside.
- Heat reserved liquid in saucepan. Scald milk in top of double boiler, stir in oyster liquid and remaining ingredients. Place over simmering heat, add oysters and heat about 5 minutes or until oysters curl.

Yield: 6 servings.

Clam Chowder

- 8 strips bacon, chopped
- 2¾ cups chopped onion
  Water
  Clam juice from clams and bottled if needed
- 1 bay leaf
- 4½ cups diced potatoes
- 4 carrots, diced
- 1½ quarts fresh clams, about 80 medium to large, chopped
  Salt and pepper to taste
  Hot pepper sauce to taste
  Parsley

- In large Dutch oven, brown bacon; add onions and sauté. Pour in enough water and clam juice to cover vegetables; add bay leaf, potatoes and carrots. Simmer until tender; remove bay leaf and stir in clams. Add seasonings to taste and a sprinkle of parsley; heat thoroughly.
- Not adding the clams until the end keeps them from becoming tough.

Chicken Soup

1 **large fryer, disjointed**
2 **(14½-ounce) cans stewed tomatoes**
2 **medium onions, coarsely chopped**
2 **stalks celery, coarsely chopped**
1 **small green pepper, chopped**
3 **carrots, diced**
¾ **cup uncooked rice, more if desired**
Salt and pepper to taste
Celery salt to taste
Seasoning salt, if desired
Worcestershire sauce to taste

- Cook fryer pieces with water in large soup pot until tender. Remove chicken from pot and cool.
- Take chicken off bones; discard skin and bones. Cut cooked chicken into bite size pieces.
- Add vegetables and rice to chicken broth and cook until vegetables are tender and rice is done.
- Return chicken to pot; season to taste.

Yield: 6 to 8 servings.

Corny Cheese Soup

(A good Sunday supper served with spinach cornbread)

1 **medium onion, chopped**
2 **stalks celery, chopped**
2 **medium carrots, chopped**
¼ **cup butter or margarine**
3½ **tablespoons flour**
3 **cups chicken broth**
½ **pound sharp Cheddar cheese, shredded**
1½ **cups milk**
1 **(5½-ounce) can corn niblets, drained**
Chopped parsley

- Sauté onion, celery and carrots in butter. Add flour and cook until bubbly. Add chicken broth, stirring constantly, until boiling.
- Add cheese a little at a time until all is melted. Add milk, do not boil. Add corn and heat.
- Serve hot with chopped parsley.

Yield: 6 servings.

Chili Con Carne

(For those in a hurry)

3 **pounds lean ground beef**
⅓ **cup olive oil**
1 **bay leaf**
½ **cup water**
2 **tablespoons chili powder (2 more for those who like it hot)**
1 **teaspoon salt**
1 **large onion, chopped**
1 **green pepper, diced, include seeds**
1 **teaspoon oregano**
1½ **teaspoons cumin seeds**
3 **(16-ounce) cans red kidney beans, undrained**
3 **tablespoons yellow cornmeal**
Longhorn cheese for garnish

- In large Dutch oven, over moderate heat, brown meat in olive oil. Add bay leaf, water and next 6 ingredients. Let simmer 5 to 7 minutes, covered.
- Add beans and cornmeal; allow to cook another 5 to 7 minutes.
- Serve, garnished with strips (¾-inch pieces) of cheese.

Yield: 6 to 8 servings.

Lentil Soup

(Good with broccoli cornbread or cheese bread)

2 tablespoons oil
2 carrots, pared and sliced
1 large onion, chopped
½ teaspoon thyme
½ teaspoon marjoram
3 cups stock or seasoned water
1 cup dry lentils
   Salt to taste
1 (16-ounce) can tomatoes, undrained
¼ cup fresh chopped parsley
¼ cup white wine or sherry
⅔ cup grated Cheddar cheese

- Sauté carrots and onion 3 to 5 minutes in oil. Add thyme and marjoram and sauté 1 minute more. Add stock, lentils, salt, tomatoes and parsley.
- Simmer, covered for 45 minutes; add wine. Top with cheese; serve.

Yield: 6 servings.

Hamburger-Vegetable Soup

1½ pounds ground chuck
2   onions, chopped
1   (16-ounce) can okra
1   (16-ounce) can butter beans
1   (16-ounce) can tomatoes
2   (10¾-ounce) cans tomato soup
1½ soup cans of water
1   tablespoon chili powder
1   tablespoon oregano
    Garlic salt, salt and pepper to taste

- Brown and drain meat and add onion to meat. Add all remaining ingredients and season.
- Simmer 20 minutes
- Let cool so flavors can transfer. Reheat to serve.
- Freezes well.

Yield: 6 to 8 servings.

Hatteras Shrimp Combo

1   pound shrimp, cleaned and deveined
2   cups fresh sliced okra or 1 (10-ounce) package frozen sliced okra
⅓   cup vegetable oil
½   teaspoon pepper
1   clove garlic, chopped
⅔   cup chopped green onion
1½ teaspoons salt
2   cups hot water
1   cup canned tomatoes
2   whole bay leaves
6   drops hot pepper sauce
1⅓ cups cooked rice

- Sauté okra in oil about 10 minutes or until okra appears dry. Add garlic, onion, salt, pepper and shrimp, stirring constantly. Cook about 5 minutes and add water, tomatoes and bay leaves.
- Cover and simmer for 20 minutes. Remove bay leaves and add hot pepper sauce. Place ⅓ cup rice in bottom of bowls. Fill with gumbo.

Yield: 4 servings.

Duck Soup

6   **cups basic duck or chicken stock**
1   **tablespoon Shaohsing wine or you may substitute vermouth**
4   **slices thin fresh ginger**
6   **scallions, green tops only, chopped and divided**
12 **medium dried shiitake (Chinese black) mushrooms, cut in strips and soaked in water, reserving 1 cup liquid**
1   **tablespoon cornstarch**
¼ **cup cold water**
8   **ounces bok choy, cut into ¾-inch strips**
    Salt to taste

- Simmer stock, wine, ginger, 4 scallions and mushroom liquid for 20 minutes. Add mushroom strips and simmer for 10 minutes.
- Combine cornstarch and water together to make a paste. Mix in cornstarch paste to thicken soup. Add bok choy, cover, and let stand, off heat, for one minute.
- Add salt to taste and serve immediately.

Yield: 8 servings.

Outer Banks Crab Soup

1   **cup margarine**
2   **tablespoons flour**
2   **cups milk**
¼ **teaspoon cayenne pepper**
¼ **teaspoon mace**
¼ **teaspoon nutmeg**
1   **teaspoon salt**
1   **pound fresh backfin crabmeat**
3   **cups thin coffee cream**
    Sherry

- Melt margarine in double boiler; add flour and blend.
- Stir in milk and cook until thick; add all seasonings and gently fold in crabmeat.
- When ready to serve, add the cream; heat but Do Not Boil.
- Pour one bouillon spoon of sherry in each bowl; add soup.

Yield: 6 to 8 servings.

French Onion Soup

(Perfect on a chilly night)

2   **tablespoons unsalted butter**
¼ **cup vegetable oil**
3½ **pounds onions, thinly sliced**
2   **cups dry white wine**
6   **cups chicken stock or canned broth**
    Salt and pepper to taste
12 **slices French bread, toasted**
1½ **cups grated Gruyère cheese**

- Melt butter with oil in large pot over medium heat. Add onions, cover and cook until lightly colored, approximately 45 minutes, stirring often; add wine and bring to a boil. Cook for 5 minutes; add chicken stock and simmer for 1½ hours then season to taste.
- Preheat broiler; ladle soup into 6 oven-proof soup bowls. Place 2 bread slices on top of soup; sprinkle equal portions of cheese on top of bread.
- Broil until cheese melts; serve immediately.

Yield: 6 servings.

Hot and Sour Soup

2	teaspoons cornstarch
2	teaspoons vegetable oil
1	teaspoon soy sauce
1	teaspoon dry sherry
¼	pound boneless pork
2	tablespoons vegetable oil
2	medium onions, chopped
5	cups chicken broth
1	(16-ounce) can bean sprouts, drained
1	(8-ounce) can water chestnuts, drained and chopped
1	(8-ounce) package cubed tofu (soy bean curd), firm
4	fresh mushrooms, sliced
2	tablespoons red wine vinegar
1½-2	tablespoons soy sauce
1	tablespoon lemon juice
½-1	teaspoon pepper
½	teaspoon hot sauce
1	egg, beaten
1	teaspoon sesame seed oil
3	tablespoons water
2	tablespoons cornstarch
1	green onion, minced

- Combine first 4 ingredients; stir well. Partially freeze pork; slice across grain into 3x¼-inch strips. Stack strips, and slice as finely as possible. Stir pork into soy mixture, and set aside.

- Heat 2 tablespoons oil in a Dutch oven; add onion, and sauté until tender. Stir in pork and next 10 ingredients; bring soup to a boil. Cover; reduce heat, and simmer 1 hour.

- Combine egg and sesame seed oil; stir well, and set aside. Combine water and 2 tablespoons cornstarch, stirring well. Add cornstarch mixture to soup; boil 1 minute, stirring constantly. Remove from heat.

Slowly pour beaten egg mixture into soup, stirring constantly. (The egg forms lacy strands as it cooks).

- Sprinkle with onion, and serve immediately.

Yield: 9 cups.

Hot and Spicy Chili

2	pounds ground turkey
½	cup margarine
1	tablespoon garlic powder
1½	teaspoons coarse ground pepper
1	large onion, diced
1	large green pepper, diced
1	carrot, diced (optional)
½	cup fresh parsley, chopped
1	(26-ounce) can kidney beans, drained
1	(15-ounce) can pinto beans, drained
⅓	cup chili powder
2	quarts tomatoes with juice
1½	teaspoons cumin
	Salt to taste
8	slices American cheese

- Spray Dutch oven with non-stick vegetable spray. Brown ground turkey and add margarine. Add garlic, pepper, onion, green pepper, carrot, parsley and continue to cook until onions are softened.

- Add beans, chili powder, tomatoes, cumin and salt. If tomatoes are not home canned, a little more water to tomato juice may need to be added as chili cooks. Simmer covered for at least 1 hour.

- When serving, place a slice of cheese in bottom of bowl and ladle chili on top.

- Serve with salad and crusty French bread and lots of water!

Yield: 6 to 8 servings.

Nine Bean Soup

2 cups nine bean soup mix (make your own combination, if you wish)
2 quarts water
1 pound country ham, cut up
1 onion, chopped
1 clove garlic, minced
1 (16-ounce) can tomatoes, undrained
1 (10-ounce) can tomatoes and green chilies, undrained

- Cover beans with water and soak overnight; drain.
- Put beans, 2 quarts water, ham, onion and garlic in large pot and cook until beans are tender, about 2 hours.
- Add tomatoes and tomatoes with chilies. Cook 1 hour. Serve hot.

Yield: 8 servings.

Okra Gumbo

1 large onion, chopped
1 large green pepper, chopped
2 tablespoons vegetable oil
4 cups sliced fresh okra
3 ripe tomatoes, peeled and chopped
1 cup corn
1 tablespoon white vinegar
½ teaspoon salt
¼ teaspoon black pepper
⅛ teaspoon red pepper

- Sauté onion and green pepper in oil in a large skillet until tender; add okra and remaining ingredients, and cook over medium heat 15 minutes, stirring frequently.
- Serve immediately.

Yield: 8 servings.

Portuguese Kale Soup

4 quarts beef or chicken broth
3 cups diced potatoes
3 cups cabbage, coarsely chopped
8-10 cups torn kale
8 ounces kielbasa, cut in bite size pieces
1 (26-ounce) can red kidney beans, drained
1 (16-ounce) package frozen green peas

- Cook potatoes, cabbage, kale and kielbasa until tender.
- Add kidney beans; simmer 2 to 3 hours. One hour before serving add peas.

Yield: 12 to 15 servings.

Tomato Broth

(A nice sipping soup, served in mugs)

1 (10¾-ounce) can condensed tomato soup
2 soup cans water
2 beef bouillon cubes
1 tablespoon lemon juice
⅛ teaspoon dried cloves
⅛ teaspoon oregano
   Dash of white pepper
   Salt to taste

- Mix all ingredients together and stir until smooth.
- Heat just to boiling, but do not boil.
- Serve immediately with clove studded lemon slice as a garnish.

Yield: 4 servings.

Pork and Turnip Stew (Fricassé)

2½   pounds pork backbone
      Salt and pepper to taste
2½   tablespoons oil
1   large onion, chopped
½   bell pepper, chopped
2   cloves garlic or ½ teaspoon garlic
      powder
½   teaspoon ground cumin
1½   quarts water
      Roux
6-8 peeled turnips
      Onion tops
      Parsley

- Season pork well with salt, black pepper and some red pepper if desired.
- Heat oil in heavy pot and brown meat well. Add onion, bell pepper, garlic, and cumin and sauté with meat. Add 1½ quarts water and enough roux to make a rich brown gravy. Add turnips, cut in halves or fourths and some onion tops and parsley.
- Let simmer partially covered for 1½ hours, stirring occasionally. Add additional onion tops and parsley about 15 minutes before serving.

Roux:
1   cup flour
¾   cup oil

- Roux is a cooked mixture of flour and oil that lends taste and texture to many dishes Louisiana Cajuns make (especially to stews and gumbos).

- To make a roux use a heavy skillet. Combine one cup flour and ¾ cup oil. Mix into a paste, cook over medium heat, stirring very often.
- When color begins to darken, stir continuously. Cook until rich dark chocolate-brown.
- Remove from heat immediately.

Vegetable Beef and Barley Soup

3½-4 quarts water
1   pound lean, stew beef
1   pound beef bones
1   large potato, diced
3   large onions, coarsely chopped
5-6 celery stalks, coarsely chopped
2   large carrots, diced
2   (16-ounce) cans tomatoes
2   small (8-ounce) cans or 1 large (15-ounce) can tomato sauce
1   tablespoon chopped parsley
1   tablespoon beef bouillon granules
4   whole bay leaves
½   cup barley
1   (8½-ounce) can green peas
1   (10-ounce) box frozen okra
1-3 tablespoons Worcestershire sauce
      Salt and pepper to taste

- Place beef, bones, potatoes, onions, celery, carrots, tomatoes, tomato sauce, parsley, bouillon granules and bay leaves in large soup pot with the water.
- Bring to a boil and simmer for 1 hour or until beef is tender.
- Add barley, green peas, okra and Worcestershire sauce, salt and pepper. Simmer for 1 more hour.
- Serve hot.

Senate Bean Soup

1½ pounds dried navy beans
 2 tablespoons butter
 4 large yellow onions, chopped
 1 large clove garlic, chopped
 6 sprigs parsley
 ¾ teaspoon thyme
1½ large bay leaves
 1 carrot, chopped
 ½ lemon, sliced
 1 pound smoked ham hock
    Freshly ground pepper
 1 tablespoon salt

- Soak beans in water, covered by 4 to 5 inches, overnight.
- Next day, drain beans, rinse well under hot water. Put in heavy kettle; add 3 quarts of water.
- Melt butter in saucepan; sauté onions and garlic about 5 minutes; add to beans.
- Tie parsley, thyme, bay leaves, carrot and lemon in cheesecloth; add to kettle. Add ham.
- Bring to boil; cover; cook over low heat for 3 hours or until liquid is reduced by half and beans are done.
- Discard cheesecloth bag; remove ham and cool.
- Remove 2 cups beans with a little liquid; purée through sieve or in a food processor; return to soup.
- Cut ham into small pieces; add to soup. Salt and pepper carefully. Reheat over low heat, stirring occasionally.

Yield: 12 to 16 servings.

Quick Crab Soup

 1 (8-ounce) package cream cheese with chives
 1 quart half-and-half
 1 (10¾-ounce) can cream of tomato soup
 2 (10¾-ounce) cans cream of celery soup
 1 pound crabmeat
 ½ cup sherry
    Sour cream

- Over very low heat, warm the cream cheese, half and half and cream soups.
- Stir in crab and sherry.
- Heat until steaming.
- Ladle into bowls and top with a dab of sour cream.

Vegetable Cream Soup

 2 (14½-ounce) cans chicken broth
 1 carrot, chopped or sliced
 1 onion, coarsely chopped
 1 stalk celery with leaves, coarsely chopped
 1 potato, cubed
 1 (10-ounce) package frozen green peas
 1 tablespoon curry powder
    Salt, pepper and hot pepper sauce to taste
 ½ pint half-and-half

- Cook all vegetables together in broth until done.
- Purée in food processor or blender until smooth; season to taste and add half-and-half.
- Heat and serve.

Yield: 4 servings.

Sherried Wild Rice Soup

2 tablespoons butter
1 tablespoon minced onion
¼ cup flour
4 cups chicken stock
½ teaspoon salt
1 cup light cream
¼ cup dry sherry
½ cup wild rice, cooked according to package directions
Minced parsley

- Melt butter in saucepan; add onion and cook to a light golden brown. Blend in flour, broth and salt, stirring constantly until thickened. Simmer 5 minutes.

- Blend in cream and sherry; simmer until heated through.

- Place equal amounts of wild rice in bottom of 6 soups bowls; ladle soup over rice and garnish with parsley.

Yield: 6 servings.

Oyster Soup

½ tablespoon butter
2 tablespoons chopped green onion
½ pint oysters and liquid

- Melt butter in heavy 1½-quart saucepan; add onion and sauté but do not brown. Add oysters and liquid; cook on medium heat until oysters are plump and edges are curly. Remove oysters to soup bowls with slotted spoon.

- Continue cooking liquid to reduce to ¼ cup. While liquid reduces, make white sauce in microwave oven.

White Sauce:
1½ tablespoons butter
2 tablespoons flour
1 cup lowfat milk
1 cup half-and-half
Fresh ground pepper to taste
Green onion to garnish

- Pour white sauce into saucepan with reduced liquid; blend with wire whip. Add half-and-half; continue to blend. Add to oysters and reheat in microwave to eating temperature. If small oysters are available, cooking time is reduced.

- Grind fresh pepper over soup and garnish with green onion.

Sailing Stew

(Easy to fix on board)

1 stick butter
2 pounds shrimp or 1 pound shrimp and 1 pound cut up fish (any kind)
2 (8-ounce) cans minced clams and juice
1 (10½-ounce) can cream of mushroom soup or cream of shrimp if using all fish and no shrimp
2 (19-ounce) cans tomato base chunky clam chowder
¼ teaspoon garlic powder
Pepper to taste
1 cup dry white wine
Parsley

- Combine ingredients in a saucepan and simmer for 30 minutes.

- Can be done in crockpot or on stove.

Yield: 4 servings.

Variety Mushroom Bisque

½ **ounce dried porcini mushrooms**
1 **cup warm water**
4 **tablespoons unsalted butter**
¼ **cup olive oil**
5 **shallots, peeled and sliced**
3 **garlic cloves, minced**
1 **medium white onion, diced**
4 **leeks, washed, trimmed and sliced**
½ **pound button mushrooms, sliced**
½ **pound shiitake mushrooms, stemmed and sliced**
½ **pound cremini or oyster mushrooms, sliced or torn into medium pieces**
Salt and fresh ground pepper to taste
2 **sprigs thyme**
2 **small turnips, peeled and sliced**
1 **small apple, peeled and sliced**
1 **bay leaf**
1½ **quarts chicken stock**
½ **cup Madeira wine**
1 **cup heavy cream**
Chopped fresh chives, for garnish

- Any combination of mushrooms can be used depending upon availability; be sure to use more than one kind, though, for maximum flavor.

- Soak porcini in warm water for about 20 minutes, until soft; drain, squeeze gently, chop and set aside.

- In large saucepan, over low heat, melt butter; add oil, shallots, garlic, onion and leeks then cook until soft, about 20 minutes.

- Add all mushrooms except porcini and cook for 5 to 10 minutes until slightly soft; season lightly and add leaves of 1 thyme sprig.

- Add turnips, apple and bay leaf and cover with stock (you may not need to use all of stock); simmer for 30 minutes, adding porcini the last 10 minutes then remove from heat.

- Remove bay leaf and purée soup in food processor in small batches; place in clean pot and gently reheat.

- Add Madeira, cream and remaining thyme leaves; add more stock if soup is too thick then add salt and pepper to taste.

- Serve in warmed bowls with a sprinkle of chives.

Yield: 2 quarts.

Zucchini Soup

3 **chicken bouillon cubes**
1 **teaspoon curry powder**
2½ **cups boiling water**
1 **pound zucchini, peeled and sliced**
1 **large onion, chopped**
½ **cup milk**

- Mix all ingredients except milk in a Dutch oven and simmer for 30 minutes; cool then purée in blender.

- Stir in milk and reheat.

- Can be frozen but do not add the milk until it is thawed.

Yield: 1¼ quarts.

Wild Rice Soup

¼ cup mushroom slices
¾ cup each: finely chopped celery, carrots and green pepper
¼ cup margarine
½ cup flour
2 (13¾-ounce) cans chicken broth
½ cup ½% milk
2 cups cooked long grain and wild rice or only wild rice
8 ounces soft cream cheese with chives and onion or lite sour cream
3 tablespoons sherry

- Cook and stir vegetables in margarine in a large saucepan until tender.
- Mix flour and broth together until well blended. Gradually add flour mixture to vegetables; cook, stirring constantly, until mixture thickens. Remove from heat.
- Stir in milk, rice and cheese or sour cream. Stir until well blended. Add sherry; cook on low heat stirring constantly, until thoroughly heated. Do not boil.

Yield: 8 one cup servings.

Williamsburg's Cream of Peanut Soup

(A tradition too good to pass up)

1 medium onion, chopped
2 ribs celery, chopped
¼ cup butter
1 tablespoon all-purpose flour
2 quarts chicken broth
1 cup smooth peanut butter
2 cups light cream
Peanuts, chopped for garnish

- Sauté onion and celery in butter until soft. Stir in flour and blend well. Add chicken broth, stirring constantly and bring to a boil.
- Remove from heat and rub through a sieve. Add peanut butter and cream and stir to blend. Return to low heat; do not boil.
- Serve garnished with nuts.

Yield: 10 to 12 servings.

Venison Stew

(Can be made with beef)

2 slices bacon
1 pound venison, cut in ¾-inch cubes
1 medium onion, chopped
1½ cups beef broth
¾ cup apple cider or apple juice
¼ teaspoon crushed dried thyme
1 cup peeled winter squash, cut in ½-inch cubes
1 cup sliced parsnip
1 apple, peeled, cored and sliced
¼ cup raisins
2 tablespoons cold water
4 tablespoons flour

- In Dutch oven, cook bacon until crisp. Remove, drain, and crumble.
- Brown meat and onions in drippings; drain fat. Add broth, juice/cider, thyme and dash of pepper. Cover and simmer 1 hours, until meat is almost tender.
- Add squash, parsnip, apple, raisins and bacon. Cover and simmer 10 minutes, or until vegetables are tender.
- Blend cold water into flour; add to stew. Cook and stir until bubbly.
- Can also be made with beef, but this is really perfect with venison.

Vegetable Soup with Ground Beef

(Great for dinner with crusty bread and salad)

1	pound lean ground beef
1	cup chopped onion
1	clove garlic, minced
1	(15-ounce) can kidney beans
1	cup sliced carrots
1	cup sliced celery
¼	cup uncooked rice
2	(16-ounce) cans stewed tomatoes
1	(16-ounce) package frozen mixed vegetables
3½	cups water
5	beef bouillon cubes
1	tablespoon chopped parsley
1	teaspoon salt
¼	teaspoon basil
⅛	teaspoon pepper
1	cup fresh or frozen green beans

- Cook beef in skillet with onion and garlic until browned. Drain off fat.
- Combine all ingredients and place in a soup pot. Cover and cook on low 2 to 3 hours.
- V-8 juice can be used for part of water. Any leftover meat, veggies, rice or potatoes can be tossed in.

Yield: 6 to 8 servings.

Asparagus and Crab Topped Muffins

(Delicious for brunch or a light supper)

1	cup whipping cream
2	cups grated Monterey Jack cheese
2	tablespoons butter
1	pound fresh crabmeat
	Butter, room temperature
4	English muffins, split and toasted
40	asparagus spears, trimmed to 4-inch, blanched

- Cook cream in saucepan over medium heat until just heated through; add cheese and cook until cheese melts, stirring occasionally; keep warm.
- Melt 1 tablespoon butter in heavy skillet over medium heat; add crab and stir until heated through.
- Butter muffins and toast until light brown. Place 5 asparagus spears on top of each muffin half. Divide crabmeat among muffins; spoon cheese sauce over muffins.

Yield: 8 servings.

Crab-Avocado Sandwich

4 English muffins, split
1 (8-ounce) package cream cheese, softened
1 tablespoon Worcestershire sauce
3 drops hot pepper sauce
1 tomato, sliced
1-2 hard-boiled eggs, sliced
1 avocado, pitted and sliced
1 pound fresh crabmeat or cooked shrimp, cleaned
   Chili sauce
   Mayonnaise
   Chopped olives

- On English muffin halves spread cream cheese softened with Worcestershire sauce and hot pepper sauce.
- Layer each muffin half with tomato slice, egg slice, and avocado slice. Salt and pepper.
- Top each muffin half with equal portions of crabmeat or shrimp.
- Make your own sauce with chili sauce, mayonnaise and olives. Spoon over the sandwich.

Yield: 4 to 8 servings.

Boulevard Sandwich

1 slice rye bread
   Leaf lettuce (Boston, if possible)
1 slice Swiss cheese
1 slice tomato
1 slice chicken breast
1 slice bacon
2 hard-boiled egg slices

- Place ingredients on bread according to the way they are listed.

Dressing:

1 pint mayonnaise
¼ cup chili sauce
½ cup ketchup
1 tablespoon Worcestershire sauce
1 tablespoon paprika
¼ cup sweet pickle relish
½ cup chopped green pepper
1 tablespoon minced onion

- Make dressing; pour over sandwich and serve. Garnish with parsley.

Yield: 1 serving.

Crab Soufflé Sandwich

12 slices bread, trimmed and buttered
8 ounces crabmeat
½ cup finely chopped celery
2 hard-cooked eggs, sliced
¼ cup finely chopped bell pepper
¼ cup finely chopped onion
½ cup light mayonnaise
½ teaspoon salt
¼ teaspoon white pepper
1 cup grated sharp Cheddar cheese
3 cups milk
5 eggs
½ teaspoon dry mustard

- Butter a 9x13-inch baking dish; place 6 slices bread in dish.
- Mix celery, eggs, bell pepper, onion, mayonnaise, salt, pepper and cheese together; gently fold in crab and cover bread slices with this mixture. Place remaining bread slices on top.
- Combine milk, eggs and mustard and pour over all; chill for several hours or overnight.
- Bake for 1 hour at 350°.

Yield: 6 servings.

Cheese Puff Sandwiches

(Serve with a spinach salad for a luncheon)

½ **pound sharp Cheddar cheese, grated**
¼ **pound butter, softened**
¼ **pound margarine, softened**
1 **egg**
1½ **loaves sandwich bread**

- In a processor, cream cheese, butter and margarine until smooth and well blended. Add egg and mix well.

- Spread cheese mixture on each slice of bread. Stack 3 pieces of bread on top of each other to make a sandwich. Place on a cookie sheet and freeze for 30 minutes.

- Remove from freezer; slice off crusts. Spread the remaining cheese mixture on sides and top (not bottom) of sandwiches.

- Place on cookie sheet and freeze. After frozen, wrap individually and store in freezer in storage bags.

- To serve, unwrap sandwich, cut in half diagonally, place on cookie sheet and bake at 350° for 15 minutes.

Yield: 10 to 12 sandwiches.

Crab Muffins

½ **pound fresh lump crabmeat**
1 **(8-ounce) package cream cheese**
2 **tablespoons mayonnaise**
2 **teaspoons Worcestershire sauce**
½ **teaspoon seasoning salt**
4 **English muffins, split**
8 **slices tomato**
8 **slices Old English cheese**

- Mix crabmeat, cream cheese, mayonnaise, Worcestershire sauce and salt together; place on muffin halves. Place on each muffin a slice of tomato and a slice of cheese.

- Bake at 225° for 1 hour.

- May be frozen for about 1 month without the tomato and cheese. Thaw in refrigerator and cook as above.

Yield: 8 servings.

Crabmeat Burgers

1 **large package Velveeta cheese**
1 **pound fresh crabmeat**
1 **egg yolk, slightly beaten**
1 **teaspoon Worcestershire sauce**
Salt and pepper to taste
Dash hot pepper sauce
4-5 **hamburger buns, split**

- Melt cheese in double boiler and add seasonings; add egg yolk and then fold in crabmeat. Mix well but be careful not to break up crabmeat. Divide crabmeat mixture among hamburger buns; sprinkle with paprika.

- Place on ungreased baking sheet and place under broiler until golden.

- Can be prepared ahead of time and refrigerated until ready to broil.

Yield: 8 to 10 servings.

Curried Chicken Salad in Pita Pockets

(A nice luncheon dish)

4   chicken breast halves, skinned
4   cups water
1   bay leaf
½   teaspoon dried minced onion
    Dash of garlic powder
4   medium sweet pickles, chopped
2   celery hearts, chopped
1   large carrot, grated
1   medium onion, chopped
1   medium apple, chopped
½   cup raisins
1   cup mayonnaise
1   tablespoon curry powder
½   teaspoon salt
¼   teaspoon white pepper
3   (6-inch) pita bread rounds, cut in half
2   cups alfalfa sprouts

- Combine first 5 ingredients together in a large saucepan. Bring to a boil; cover, reduce heat, and simmer 30 minutes or until tender.

- Drain chicken and cool; remove chicken from bones and cut into ½-inch pieces.

- Combine chicken, pickles and next 5 ingredients.

- Combine mayonnaise, curry powder, salt and pepper, stirring well; add to chicken mixture and toss gently, then cover and chill.

- To serve, fill each pita bread half with chicken salad and top with alfalfa sprouts.

Yield: 6 servings.

Gyro Sandwiches

(A spicy Greek sandwich served in pita rounds)

Patties:

1¼   pounds ground beef
1¼   pounds ground lamb
2   tablespoons dried oregano
1½   tablespoons onion powder
1   tablespoon garlic powder
¾-1½   tablespoons black pepper
1   teaspoon dried thyme
¾   teaspoon salt

- Combine all ingredients for the patties in a bowl; shape into hamburger patties. Cook over medium heat or grill to desired degree of doneness.

Sauce:

½   cup plain yogurt
½   cup sour cream
¼   cup finely chopped cucumber
¼   cup finely chopped onion
2   teaspoons olive oil
    Garlic powder
    Salt and freshly ground pepper
4-6   large pita bread rounds, cut in half
    Thinly sliced onion rings

- Combine first 5 sauce ingredients in a small bowl; add garlic powder, salt and pepper to taste.

- To assemble the sandwiches; slice the hamburger patties into desired thickness. Place chopped lettuce in the bottom of each pita round; top with sliced hamburger patties. Top with yogurt sauce and onion rings.

Note: May use all hamburger meat and add diced tomatoes to the sandwich.

Yield: 8 to 12 servings.

Ham and Swiss Kaiser

1 **package Kaiser rolls**
1 **package boiled ham**
1 **package Swiss cheese**
  Margarine
  Mustard

- Slice the rolls in half. On one half spread margarine and on the other half spread mustard.

- Place one slice ham and one slice Swiss cheese on one half of the roll. Close the rolls and wrap each in aluminum foil.

- Heat at 400° for 10 minutes.

  Note: These can be refrigerated 24 hours ahead or frozen.

Hot Grinder Sandwich

1 **green pepper, cut into rings**
3 **tablespoons oil**
½ **teaspoon onion salt**
½ **pound ham, thinly sliced**
2 **tomatoes, thinly sliced**
1 **loaf French bread, split lengthwise**
½ **teaspoon dried whole oregano**
2 **cups shredded Mozzarella cheese**

- Sauté green pepper with onion salt in oil; reserve oil.

- Layer ham, tomatoes and green pepper on bottom half of French bread. Drizzle oil mixture over green pepper.

- Sprinkle with oregano; top with shredded Mozzarella cheese. Cover with top of bread.

- Wrap loaf in aluminum foil; bake at 350° for 30 minutes.

- Slice before serving.

  Yield: 6 servings.

Hot Chicken Sandwiches

4 **cooked chicken breasts**
  Cooked mushroom caps for each sandwich
4 **strips of cooked bacon**
4 **slices of toast**

- Put 4 slices of toast in a flat oven-proof dish. Place a chicken breast on top of each piece of toast; pour a generous amount of sauce over the breasts. Top with bacon and mushroom caps; place in hot oven under broiler until brown and bubbly.

Sauce #1:

⅔ **cup butter**
1 **medium sized onion, minced**
⅔ **cup flour**
6 **cups hot milk**
2 **teaspoons salt**
  Dash red pepper

- Melt butter in saucepan; add onion and cook slowly until light brown. Add flour and blend until smooth; add milk, salt and red pepper.

- Cook 25 to 30 minutes, stirring constantly, until sauce is thick and smooth.

Sauce #2:

4 **cups Sauce #1**
4 **eggs yolks**
1 **cup grated Parmesan cheese**
2 **tablespoons butter**

- In separate saucepan, add egg yolks to 4 cups of Sauce #1; stir and remove from heat when sauce begins to boil. Add cheese and butter.

  Yield: 4 servings.

Hot Ham and Cheese Rolls

½ pound boiled ham, cut in ¼-inch cubes
½ pound sharp Cheddar cheese, cut in ¼-inch cubes
⅓ cup sliced green onion
½ cup thinly sliced olives
3 tablespoons mayonnaise
½ cup chili sauce
12 split hot dog rolls

• Combine first 4 ingredients.
• Mix mayonnaise and chili sauce together.
• Add to ham, cheese, onions and olives. Mix and spread in rolls.
• Wrap each roll in aluminum foil, twisting ends securely.
• Bake at 400° or until rolls are hot.

Yield: 12 servings.

Marvelous Spread

(Good sandwich spread)

1 pint mayonnaise
1 bunch spring onions, finely chopped, including some tops
Salt and pepper to taste
Dash of red pepper

• Mix all ingredients together in a bowl. Adjust seasonings to taste.
• Put in jar and store in refrigerator for at least 12 hours before using.
• Can be used on crackers as hors d'oeuvres.

Yield: 2 cups.

Layered Chicken-Cheese Melt

White or wheat pita pocket bread
Cream cheese, soft
¼ avocado, sliced
1 tomato, sliced
1 onion, diced
Alfalfa sprouts
Fresh mushrooms, sliced
1 lettuce leaf
Provolone cheese
Chicken, boiled and chunked

• Spread inside of pita pocket with cream cheese and layer remaining ingredients.
• Salt and pepper to taste.
• Heat until cheese just begins to melt.

Yield: 1 serving.

Open Face Sandwich

1 tablespoon mustard with horseradish
2 tablespoons mayonnaise
1 teaspoon sesame seed
1 (10-ounce) package frozen broccoli spears
4 slices Jewish rye bread, toasted
4 slices lean, cooked ham
4 sliced processed American cheese

• Combine first 3 ingredients and set aside.
• Cook broccoli according to package directions omitting salt; drain and set aside.
• Spread mayonnaise mixture evenly over bread slices. Place 1 slice ham on each slice of bread. Arrange broccoli spears over ham and top with cheese slices. Broil until cheese melts.

Yield: 4 servings.

Sloppy Joe Hamburgers

(An old stand-by)

1½ pounds extra lean hamburger meat
¼ cup chopped onion
½ cup chopped celery
½ teaspoon salt
   Dash of pepper
1 tablespoon brown sugar
1 teaspoon prepared mustard
1 cup ketchup
½ cup water
2 tablespoons vinegar
2 tablespoons Worcestershire sauce
6 hamburger buns

- Brown together ground beef and onion; drain and add remaining ingredients. Simmer for 30 minutes, stirring constantly. Serve on heated hamburger buns.
- Can use ½ pound ground turkey and ½ pound ground beef.

Yield: 6 servings.

Soft Crab Sandwiches

4 large soft crabs
   Salt and pepper to taste
6 tablespoons butter or oil
1 egg, lightly beaten
½ cup all-purpose flour
4 round rolls
   Sliced tomato
   Lettuce
   Sliced onion
   Mayonnaise
   Old Bay Seasoning

- Clean the crabs and sprinkle them with salt and pepper.
- Heat the butter or oil over medium heat in a pan large enough to hold the crabs in one layer.
- Dip the crabs in the egg, then dredge lightly in the flour. Put them in the pan, belly side down. Fry until they are golden red-brown and the back feeler legs are crisp, 5 to 6 minutes on each side. Drain.
- Season the mayonnaise with Old Bay Seasoning. Spread each roll half with the mayonnaise. Top one half of each roll with a tomato slice, lettuce, onion and one crab. Top with the other roll half.

Yield: 4 servings.

Spicy Chicken Avocado Sandwich

¼ cup mayonnaise
½ teaspoon chili powder
¼ teaspoon cumin
2 boneless chicken breasts, cooked and cut in bite-size pieces or may substitute 1 (5-ounce) can chunk white chicken
2 slices rye bread
1 medium avocado, peeled and sliced
¼ cup Monterey Jack cheese, shredded

- Mix first 4 ingredients together; spread on bread slices. Top with avocado slices and cheese.
- Broil until cheese melts.

Yield: 2 servings.

Pimento Cheese

1 (5-ounce) can evaporated milk
1 pound sharp Cheddar cheese, grated
1 egg, beaten
2 (4-ounce) jars chopped pimento, drained
½ teaspoon salt
½ teaspoon dry mustard
½ teaspoon cayenne
½ teaspoon Worcestershire sauce
½ teaspoon garlic salt
½ teaspoon onion salt
½ cup finely chopped, sweet relish (or more, to taste)

- Heat milk; add cheese and stir until melted. Remove from heat and add remaining ingredients. Cool, cover, and refrigerate.
- It will thicken as it cools.
- Thin, if necessary, with milk, not mayonnaise.

Tuna Puff Sandwiches

(Children love this)

1 (7-ounce) can tuna, drained and flaked
1½ teaspoons mustard
¼ teaspoon Worcestershire sauce
¼ cup mayonnaise
1½ teaspoons grated onion
2 tablespoons chopped green pepper
3 hamburger buns, split
6 tomato slices
½ cup mayonnaise
¼ cup grated cheese

- Blend first 6 ingredients; pile onto bun halves.
- Top each with tomato slice. Blend mayonnaise with cheese. Spread on tomato slices.
- Broil 4 inches from heat until topping puffs and browns.

Yield: 6 servings.

Unbelievable Pimiento Cheese

1 pound Velveeta cheese
1 pound medium Cheddar cheese
1 pound sharp Cheddar cheese
1 pint of your favorite mayonnaise or salad dressing
8 ounces pimento, drained and chopped
3 tablespoons sugar
Salt to taste
Pepper to taste

- Grate cheeses or cut into small pieces. Allow to soften at room temperature. Combine all ingredients and blend using a mixer or food processor. Unless you have an unusually large mixing container it may be necessary to divide this into two batches.
- This may be frozen so don't worry about the large quantity it makes.

Yield: 2 quarts.

Marinated Chicken Breast Sandwiches

8　chicken breast halves, skinned and boned
1　cup soy sauce
½　cup pineapple juice
¼　cup sherry
¼　cup firmly packed brown sugar
1　teaspoon minced fresh garlic
8　slices Monterey Jack cheese
8　Kaiser rolls, split in half
　　Mustard sauce
　　Leaf lettuce

- Place chicken in a large, shallow dish. Combine soy sauce, pineapple juice, sherry, sugar and garlic, mixing well. Pour over chicken and let marinate for 1 hour or longer. Remove from marinade.

- Grill chicken breasts over hot coals about 25 minutes or until done. Turn and baste every 5 minutes with the marinade. Place slice of cheese on each chicken breast and grill an additional 3 minutes or until cheese melts. Remove chicken from grill.

- Spread each side of rolls with the mustard sauce; place chicken breast on bottom half of each roll, top with lettuce. Cover with roll top and serve.

Mustard Sauce:

½　cup dry mustard
⅔　cup white vinegar
⅔　cup sugar
1　egg

- Combine all ingredients in container of blender or food processor and process. Pour mixture into top of a double boiler.

- Bring water to a boil, reduce to low. Cook, stirring constantly, about 7 minutes or until smooth and thickened.

Yield: 8 servings.

Béarnaise Sauce

(Can be used for sandwich spread or topping for vegetables)

½　cup dry white wine
4　tablespoons tarragon vinegar
2　teaspoons dried tarragon
½　teaspoon freshly ground pepper
8　egg yolks, room temperature
4　tablespoons lemon juice
½　teaspoon hot sauce
2　cups butter, melted and hot

- In a small saucepan, combine wine, vinegar, tarragon and pepper. Bring to a boil and reduce to ¼ cup.

- Meanwhile, in the food processor with steel blade in place, combine egg yolks, lemon juice and hot sauce. Process for 15 seconds. With machine running, in a steady stream add hot butter and then the reduced mixture.

- Cover and refrigerate if desired. Bring to room temperature before serving.

Yield: 3 cups.

SALADS

Becky Wienges '92

Index for Salads

Artichoke and Rice Salad

1 (8-ounce) package chicken-flavored vermicelli-rice mix
1 (6-ounce) jar marinated artichokes, drained, reserving the marinade
4 green onions, chopped
12-18 green olives, sliced
1 can sliced water chestnuts, drained
⅓ cup mayonnaise
¼ teaspoon curry

- Prepare rice according to package directions.
- In a separate bowl combine rice, artichokes, green onions, olives and water chestnuts.
- In a separate container combine mayonnaise, marinade from artichokes and curry, stirring well. Mix into salad ingredients.
- Serve immediately — warm or cover and refrigerate until desired time, allowing time to adjust to room temperature.

Yield: 6 to 8 servings.

Colonial Crabmeat Salad

1 pound backfin crabmeat
1 cup diced celery
⅓ cup mayonnaise
1 tablespoon lemon juice
½ teaspoon salt
Dash white pepper
Hot pepper sauce to taste
¼ teaspoon Worcestershire sauce
2 tablespoons French dressing

- Combine all ingredients together except crabmeat. Gently fold in crabmeat.

Yield: 4 servings.

Chicken-Pecan Salad with Cranberry Ring

1½ cups sliced, peeled peaches
3 cups cubed, cooked chicken
1 cup diced celery
¼ cup coarsely broken pecans
½ cup mayonnaise
2 tablespoons salad oil
1 tablespoon vinegar
½ teaspoon salt

- Combine peaches, chicken and celery; set aside.
- In a small bowl combine mayonnaise, oil, vinegar and salt; pour over chicken mixture and toss well. Chill.
- Just before serving stir in pecans; toss again.
- Serve in the center of the cranberry ring.

Cranberry Ring Mold:

2 cups orange juice, divided
1 cup boiling water
2 (3-ounce) packages lemon gelatin
¼ teaspoon salt
1 (16-ounce) can whole cranberry sauce

- Heat 1 cup orange juice and water to boiling; add gelatin and salt and stir until dissolved. Stir in one cup of additional orange juice; chill until partially set. Fold in cranberry sauce.
- Pour into ring mold and chill for at least 6 to 8 hours.

Yield: 8 servings.

Brown Rice Salad with Sweet and Sour Creamy Dressing

3 cups brown rice, uncooked
3 cups water
2 large carrots, peeled and finely chopped
8 water chestnuts, finely chopped
2 scallions, finely chopped, green tops included
1 stalk celery, finely chopped
1 cup Sweet and Sour Creamy Dressing
　Salt and freshly ground pepper to taste
　Sesame seed

- Bring water to a boil and add rice, reduce heat and simmer slowly for 40 minutes or until liquid is absorbed and the grains are tender.

- In a large bowl combine the rice with the remaining ingredients and stir until well mixed.

- Stir the dressing into the rice mixture. Cover and chill for 4 hours or overnight.

- Season with salt and pepper, top with sesame seed. Serve chilled.

Sweet and Sour Creamy Dressing:

¾ cup plain low fat yogurt
¼ cup buttermilk
2 tablespoons mayonnaise
1 tablespoon cider vinegar
1 tablespoon sugar
1 teaspoon Dijon mustard
½ teaspoon celery seed
　Pinch cayenne pepper
　Salt and pepper to taste

- Combine all dressing ingredients together and whisk until smooth.

Fresh Tuna Salad

(Easy to prepare and very tasty)

2 cups water
½ cup white wine vinegar or dry white wine
1 teaspoon freshly ground pepper
1 sprig rosemary, crushed
1 pound fresh tuna
½ cup mayonnaise or ¼ cup mayonnaise and ¼ cup ranch dressing
2 tablespoons fresh lemon juice
1 celery rib, minced
2 tablespoons minced fresh parsley
　Salt and freshly ground pepper to taste
　Chopped onions (optional)
　Sweet pickles (optional)
1 hard-boiled egg, chopped (optional)

- In a large saucepan, combine the first 4 ingredients; bring to a simmer. Add tuna and continue to simmer, covered, until tuna turns opaque in color and flakes with a fork, about 3 to 5 minutes.

- Cut tuna into small pieces; set aside.

- In a small bowl, combine mayonnaise, lemon juice, celery and parsley; mixing well. Season with salt and pepper to taste.

- In a bowl combine tuna and dressing. Can add chopped onions, egg and sweet pickles if you prefer those in your salad.

Yield: 4 servings.

Chutney Chicken Salad

4 cups cubed chicken
1½ cups chopped celery
1 cup mayonnaise
2 tablespoons lemon juice
2½ tablespoons soy sauce
1 tablespoon onion juice
½ cup chutney
½ cup toasted almonds
½ cup sliced water chestnuts
1 cup seedless green grapes, halved

- Combine first 7 ingredients a day ahead.
- Just before serving add last 3 ingredients.
  Yield: 6 servings.

Chicken Salad Delight

4-6 chicken breasts, cooked and shredded
¼ cup sugar
¼ cup white vinegar
1 teaspoon salt
½ teaspoon pepper
½ cup salad oil
½ cup toasted almonds
½ cup chow mein noodles
¼ cup toasted sesame seeds
1 head iceberg lettuce, shredded
3-6 green onions, thinly sliced

- Combine sugar, vinegar and seasonings; heat until sugar dissolves. Cool, then blend in oil.
- Just before serving, toss together chicken, almonds, noodles, sesame seeds, lettuce and onions.
- Pour dressing over and toss again.
  Yield: 8 servings.

Hot Turkey or Chicken Salad

2 cups cooked and diced chicken or turkey
1 cup chopped celery
1 cup chopped green pepper
½ cup chopped onion
1 cup mayonnaise
3 hard-boiled eggs, chopped
2 teaspoons Worcestershire sauce
1 teaspoon seasoning salt
½ cup or more slivered almonds
Buttered bread crumbs

- Blend all ingredients except bread crumbs.
- Pour into 2-quart greased casserole. Top with bread crumbs.
- Bake in 350° oven for 35 minutes.
  Yield: 6 servings.

Spicy Shrimp Mold

6 ounces small shrimp, cooked and deveined
½ cup chili sauce
¼ cup ketchup
½ teaspoon sugar
1 tablespoon grated onion
1 envelope unflavored gelatin
½ teaspoon Worcestershire sauce
½ teaspoon horseradish
1½ tablespoons lemon juice
Dash hot pepper sauce

- Combine all ingredients except shrimp and heat until gelatin is dissolved; add shrimp and stir.
- Pour into a mold, individual molds or a Pyrex dish; chill until congealed.
- Unmold and serve on lettuce.

Linguine Salad

(Make ahead)

1   pound linguine, cooked, rinsed and
    drained
1   (8-ounce) bottle Italian dressing,
    not creamy style
½   bottle Salad Supreme seasoning
1   Bermuda onion, thinly sliced
    Parmesan cheese, freshly grated
    (optional)
    Sliced cucumbers, broccoli
    flowerets, chopped tomatoes
    (optional)

• Mix all ingredients and refrigerate overnight.

• Serve on your favorite lettuce.

Yield: 12 servings.

Macaroni Salad

1   cup mayonnaise
2   tablespoons vinegar
1   tablespoon prepared mustard
1   teaspoon sugar
1   teaspoon salt
¼   teaspoon pepper
1   (8-ounce) package elbow macaroni,
    cooked and drained
1   cup sliced celery
1   cup chopped green or sweet red
    pepper
¼   cup chopped onion

• Combine first 6 ingredients in a bowl and
  stir until smooth; add remaining ingredients,
  tossing to coat well.

• Cover and chill for several hours.

Yield: 10 servings.

Old-Fashioned Chicken Salad

3   cups cooked, diced chicken
1½ cups diced celery
3   eggs, hard-boiled and mashed
3   sweet pickles, diced
1   teaspoon salt
    Mayonnaise
    Paprika

• Mix first 5 ingredients together in a bowl.
  Add enough mayonnaise to hold together.

• Serve on a bed of lettuce.

Yield: 8 to 10 servings.

Apricot Nectar Salad

1   (12-ounce) can apricot nectar
1   (3-ounce) package lemon gelatin
⅓   cup water
1   tablespoon lemon juice
1   (11-ounce) can mandarin oranges,
    drained
½   cup halved, seedless green grapes
¼   cup chopped, unpeeled red apples

• Bring apricot nectar to a boil; add gelatin,
  stirring until dissolved. Stir in water and
  lemon juice. Chill until consistency of
  unbeaten egg whites.

• Stir in last three ingredients and pour into
  4-cup mold; chill until firm. Unmold and
  serve.

  Note: This can also be made in individual
  molds.

Yield: 6 to 8 servings.

Shrimp and Crabmeat Salad

(Serve with marinated asparagus and ham biscuits)

¼ cup Italian dressing
⅓ cup salad dressing
⅓ cup sour cream
1½ cups cooked shrimp
1 cup fresh crabmeat
2 cups cooked white rice
1 cup chopped celery
1 cup frozen peas, cooked until they boil, drain well
½ cup diced green pepper
¼-½ cup chopped onion
⅓ cup chopped fresh parsley
Salt and pepper to taste
Paprika
Mandarin oranges

- Combine the first 3 ingredients together, mixing well. Set aside.
- Combine the next 8 ingredients and gently fold into the salad dressing mixture.
- Line plates with red-tipped lettuce. Divide salad equally and place on lettuce.
- Garnish with mandarin orange sections.

Apricot Salad Delight

(A refreshing salad)

1 (13-ounce) can evaporated milk
1 #2 can crushed pineapple, undrained
½ cup sugar
1 (6-ounce) package apricot gelatin
1 (8-ounce) package cream cheese, softened
1 cup chopped celery
1 cup chopped nuts

- Chill milk in freezer until icy, about ½ hour, and it will whip better.
- Heat pineapple with juice and sugar in a saucepan until sugar is dissolved; remove from heat and add dry gelatin; stir well. Add cream cheese and allow to cool for a few minutes. Add chopped celery and nuts.
- Whip milk and fold into above mixture.
- Rub mold or 13x9x2-inch dish with mayonnaise. Pour mixture into dish and cover; refrigerate.
- Keeps well for 2 to 3 days.

Yield: 8 to 10 servings.

Asparagus Salad

¼ cup sugar
1 cup water
½ cup white wine vinegar
1 envelope unflavored gelatin
½ cup cold water
1 cup chopped celery
1 (4-ounce) can diced pimento, drained
2 tablespoons grated onion
1 (10½-ounce) can asparagus tips, drained and cut in 1-inch pieces
½ cup finely chopped pecans
Juice of ½ lemon
Dash of salt

• Combine first 3 ingredients in a saucepan, bring to a boil and cook 5 minutes.

• Soften gelatin in cold water; let stand 5 minutes; add vinegar mixture. Stir in next 7 ingredients.

• Pour mixture into a 4-cup mold, Pyrex dish or individual molds and chill until firm.

• Unmold and serve on lettuce leaves with mayonnaise.

Yield: 8 servings.

Banana Salad

(Well worth the effort)

3 medium ripe bananas, sliced
1 (8-ounce) can crushed pineapple, drained, reserving juice
1 (6-ounce) package lemon gelatin
1 cup hot water
3 cups sugar
1 tablespoon margarine
1 egg, beaten
1 tablespoon all-purpose flour
⅓ cup water
Juice of one lemon
1 cup miniature marshmallows
1 (1.4-ounce) package whipped topping
⅓ cup mayonnaise

• Dissolve lemon gelatin in hot water; add bananas and pineapple, set aside. To the reserved pineapple juice add sugar, margarine, egg, flour, ⅓ cup water and lemon juice. Cook over medium heat until it thickens, stirring constantly; add marshmallows and stir until melted.

• Fold in gelatin mixture and pour into individual molds or a Pyrex dish. Refrigerate overnight, covered.

• Prepare whipped topping according to directions; add mayonnaise and mix well. Spread on top of salad when ready to serve.

Yield: 8 to 10 servings.

To peel oranges more easily, place them in boiling water for three or four minutes. They will also be more juicy.

Berry Layered Salad

1   (3-ounce) package vanilla pudding
1   (3-ounce) package lemon gelatin
2   cups water
2   tablespoons lemon juice
1   (3-ounce) package raspberry
    gelatin
1   cup boiling water
1   (16-ounce) can whole cranberry
    sauce
½   cup chopped celery
¼   cup chopped pecans
1   (1.4-ounce) package whipped
    topping mix
½   teaspoon ground nutmeg

• Combine first 3 ingredients in a saucepan; cook, stirring constantly until gelatin dissolves. Stir in lemon juice. Chill until consistency of unbeaten egg white.

• Dissolve raspberry gelatin in 1 cup boiling water. Stir in cranberry sauce; blend well. Stir in celery and pecans. Chill until partially set.

• Prepare whipped topping mix according to package directions, adding nutmeg. Fold into lemon gelatin mixture. Spoon 1½ cups mixture into a lightly oiled 7-cup mold. Chill until set.

• Spoon raspberry gelatin mixture over lemon mixture; chill until set. Spoon remaining lemon mixture over raspberry layer. Chill until firm. Unmold on lettuce leaves.

Yield: 12 to 14 servings.

Cherry Cola Salad

1   (16-ounce) can tart cherries,
    undrained
1   (16-ounce) can crushed pineapple,
    undrained
¾   cup water
1   (6-ounce) package cherry gelatin
½   packet plain gelatin, dissolved in
    part of water listed above
⅓   cup chopped celery
12 ounces cola-flavored beverage

• Boil cherries and juice, pineapple and juice and remaining water. Pour over gelatin and dissolved gelatin; stir.

• Cool slightly; add celery and cola.

• Place in square or angel food cake pan and place in refrigerator to congeal.

Yield: 16 servings.

Frozen Fruit Salad

½   cup chopped pecans
1   (15¼-ounce) can pineapple chunks,
    drained
1   (16½-ounce) can pitted dark sweet
    cherries, drained
1   (12-ounce) container frozen
    whipped topping, thawed
1   (8-ounce) carton lemon-flavored
    yogurt
½   cup mayonnaise

• Combine first 3 ingredients, mixing well.

• Combine remaining ingredients and fold into fruit mixture.

• Spoon into a 12x8x2-inch baking dish; freeze until firm. Cut into squares to serve.

Yield: 12 servings.

Cranberry Wine Salad

*(This is lovely for Christmas
with a dollop of mayonnaise
and a mint sprig)*

2   **(3-ounce) packages raspberry
gelatin**
2   **cups boiling water**
1   **(16-ounce) can whole cranberry
sauce**
1   **(8¼-ounce) can crushed pineapple,
undrained**
¾   **cup port wine**
¼   **cup chopped walnuts (optional)**

- Dissolve gelatin in boiling water; stir in cranberry sauce, pineapple, wine and walnuts.
- Pour into individual molds, a Pyrex dish or a larger mold. Refrigerate until congealed.
- When ready to serve, unmold on lettuce leaves and serve with mayonnaise. Chopped walnuts can be sprinkled over top, also.

  Variation: Can add chopped apples, mandarin oranges and/or celery.

  Yield: 8 servings.

Blueberry Salad

*(This always has been and always
will be a favorite)*

2   **(3-ounce) packages grape gelatin**
2   **cups hot water**
1   **(16-ounce) can crushed pineapple,
undrained**
1   **(21-ounce) can blueberry pie filling**

- Stir all salad ingredients together; place in pan and let congeal.

Topping:

1   **(8-ounce) package cream cheese,
softened**
1   **(8-ounce) carton sour cream**
¼   **cup sugar**
1   **teaspoon vanilla**
Chopped pecans

- Blend first 4 topping ingredients together with mixer until smooth. Spread on top of congealed salad and top with pecans.

  Note: For a healthier version of this favorite, use the "sugar-free" and "lite" products when available.

  Yield: 8 servings.

Cherry Salad

*(Serve on a cold plate with chicken
salad and marinated squash)*

1   **(16-ounce) can red sour pitted
cherries, undrained**
½   **cup sugar**
2   **(3-ounce) packages red cherry
gelatin**
1   **teaspoon plain gelatin dissolved in
1 tablespoon cold water**
½   **cup cold water**
1   **(16-ounce) can crushed pineapple,
undrained**
½   **cup chopped pecans**

- Boil cherries and sugar for 5 to 10 minutes. Add gelatins and water, stirring until gelatin is dissolved. Add pineapple with juice and nuts.
- Pour into molds of desired shape and size or a Pyrex dish.
- Refrigerate until congealed.

  Yield: 8 to 10 servings.

Molded Spinach Salad

1 (3-ounce) package lemon gelatin
¾ cup boiling water
1 cup cold water
1½ tablespoons vinegar
½ cup mayonnaise
¼ teaspoon salt
⅓ cup chopped celery
1 tablespoon minced onion
1 cup chopped, frozen spinach, thawed and drained
¾ cup cottage cheese

• Dissolve gelatin in boiling water. Add cold water, vinegar, mayonnaise and salt. Place in freezer and chill about 20 minutes; take out and beat until fluffy.

• Add celery, onion, spinach and cottage cheese. Pour into a 1-quart mold and chill until firm.

Orange and Walnut Salad

(Dressing is best when made a day ahead and refrigerated)

2 small heads Bibb lettuce, torn into bite-size pieces
1 pound fresh spinach, torn into bite-size pieces
2 oranges, peeled, sectioned and seeded
½ medium-size purple onion, sliced and separated into rings
½ cup coarsely chopped walnuts
2 teaspoons margarine, melted

• Combine first 4 ingredients in a large bowl.

• Sauté walnuts in margarine until lightly browned; add to lettuce mixture.

• Toss with Oil and Vinegar Dressing.

Oil and Vinegar Dressing:

1 cup oil
⅓ cup cider vinegar
⅓ cup sugar
1 teaspoon dry minced onion
½ teaspoon paprika
½ teaspoon dry mustard

• Place all ingredients in a blender and blend for approximately 15 minutes; pour half of dressing over the salad and toss well.

• Dressing is enough for 2 salads; use half and refrigerate the remainder for up to one month.

Yield: 6 to 8 servings.

Grapefruit Salad

2 (3-ounce) packages lemon gelatin
1 cup grapefruit juice
1 cup ginger ale
2 grapefruits, peeled and sectioned
1 (8-ounce) can crushed pineapple, drained
1 cup chopped pecans

• Dissolve gelatin in boiling hot grapefruit juice; pour in ginger ale.

• Fold in grapefruit sections, pineapple and pecans.

• Pour into individual molds, single mold or a Pyrex dish. Refrigerate until congealed.

Note: Instead of peeling grapefruits, cut them in half and cut each section out. Pull all of membrane out of each grapefruit half. Pour salad mixture into each half and congeal. When ready to serve, cut each half in half. Top with mayonnaise.

Yield: 8 servings.

Fruit Flow Salad

1	(3-ounce) package lemon or lime gelatin
¼	teaspoon onion salt
1	cup boiling water
½	cup cold water
1-2	tablespoons vinegar or lemon juice
¼	cup mayonnaise or sour cream Dash of black pepper
1	tablespoon grated onion
1½-2½	cups cut-up raw vegetables (cucumbers, tomatoes, celery, onion, green peppers and radishes)

- Mix gelatin and salt in boiling water. Add cold water, vinegar, mayonnaise and pepper. Beat well until blended. Pour into a mold and freeze for 15 to 20 minutes or until firm at edges.

- Remove from freezer and pour in bowl. Whip until smooth. Fold in onion and vegetables of your choice.

- Pour into a 1-quart mold or individual molds. Chill until firm, about 1 hour.

  Yield: 8 servings.

Pear Salad with Warm Brie Dressing

2	(8½-ounce) cans sliced Bartlett pears
½	red bell pepper, cut in strips
2	cups torn salad greens
½	cup coarsely chopped walnuts or toasted pine nuts Warm Brie Dressing

- Drain pears, reserve 4 tablespoons pear liquid.

- Toss pears, pepper strips, greens and nuts. Serve with dressing.

Warm Brie Dressing:

⅔	cup dry white wine
4	tablespoons pear liquid
4-6	ounces Brie cheese
4	tablespoons heavy or sour cream

- Combine white wine and pear liquid in a small skillet; bring to boil and reduce liquid by half.

- Remove crust from Brie and cube.

- Add cream to skillet, stir in Brie until smooth. Cool slightly and serve on salad.

Frozen Cranberry Salad

(Perfect for the holidays)

2	(3-ounce) packages cream cheese, softened
2	tablespoons mayonnaise
2	tablespoons sugar
1	(20-ounce) can crushed pineapple, drained
1	(16-ounce) can whole cranberry sauce
½	cup chopped nuts
1	pint whipping cream, whipped

- Blend cheese and mayonnaise with sugar; add fruit, nuts and whipped cream. Pour into 8½x4½-inch loaf pan; freeze overnight.

- Let stand at room temperature for 15 minutes before removing from pan. Slice and serve on lettuce.

  Yield: 8 to 10 servings.

Fruit Medley

2   tablespoons flour
1   cup sugar
2   eggs, well beaten
    Juice of 2 lemons
½   cup pineapple juice
3   bananas
1   cup pecans, chopped
3   medium apples
3   stalks celery, chopped
1   (8¼-ounce) can pineapple chunks,
    drained

- Combine first 5 ingredients in a saucepan and cook until thick and clear. Chill.
- Slice bananas. Peel apples and cut into pieces. Combine bananas, apples, celery, pineapple chunks and pecans in a bowl. Pour cooked dressing over and mix gently.

Yield: 8 servings.

Spiced Peach Salad

1   (3-ounce) package lemon gelatin
1   (28½-ounce) jar spiced peaches,
    drained, reserving 1 cup syrup
1   cup chopped pecans
1   cup ginger ale, cold
    Mayonnaise

- Boil spiced peach syrup and dissolve lemon gelatin in it; add ginger ale to mixture. Stir in pecans.
- Chop peaches and add to gelatin mixture.
- Pour into molds and refrigerate.
- Top with mayonnaise to serve.

Orange-Pineapple Salad with Boiled Dressing

½   envelope plain gelatin
¼   cup cold water
1   (3-ounce) box orange gelatin
1   cup boiling water
1   cup pineapple juice
2   carrots, grated
1   (8-ounce) can crushed pineapple,
    drained

- Dissolve plain gelatin in cold water and set aside.
- Dissolve orange gelatin in boiling water; add pineapple juice and above gelatin. Chill until it begins to thicken. Add carrots and pineapple.
- Pour into mold or individual molds. Return to refrigerator to congeal.

Boiled Dressing:

½   cup sugar
2   tablespoons flour
    Juice of 1 lemon
1   cup pineapple or orange juice, or
    mixture of both
2   beaten egg yolks

- Mix sugar, flour and lemon juice together in saucepan. Add juice to mixture and heat.
- Add a small amount of egg yolks to the hot mixture and stir well. Add remaining yolks to mixture and cook until thickened.
- Refrigerate until cool.
- Serve over congealed salad.

Yield: 6 to 8 servings.

Holiday Mincemeat Salad

1   **envelope unflavored gelatin**
¼   **cup cold water**
1   **(6-ounce) package cherry-flavored gelatin**
3½ **cups boiling water**
1   **(20½-ounce) jar brandy-flavored mincemeat**
1   **(8-ounce) can crushed pineapple, drained**
1   **small apple, unpeeled and finely chopped**
1   **cup chopped nuts**

- Soften unflavored gelatin in cold water; set aside.
- Dissolve cherry gelatin in boiling water; add unflavored gelatin mixture, stirring until gelatin dissolves. Chill until consistency of unbeaten egg white.
- Stir in mincemeat, pineapple, apple and nuts; pour into individual molds or a single mold. Chill until firm.

Yield: 12 to 15 servings.

Orange Salad Supreme

2   **(3-ounce) packages orange gelatin**
1   **(20-ounce) can crushed pineapple, drained and reserving juice**
1   **cup chopped nuts, divided**
1   **(8-ounce) carton whipped topping**
1   **(8-ounce) package cream cheese, softened**
1   **tablespoon lemon juice**
¾   **cup sugar**
2   **tablespoons flour**
2   **eggs**

- Prepare gelatin as directed on package; add pineapple.
- Pour mixture into a medium-size Pyrex dish. Sprinkle half of nuts over gelatin; chill until congealed.
- Combine whipped topping and cream cheese; spread on congealed salad. Chill.
- Add water to pineapple juice to make 1 cup. Add lemon juice, sugar, flour and eggs.
- Pour into a saucepan and cook over medium heat until thickened. Cool. Spread over the salad; sprinkle remaining nuts on top.

Yield: 15 servings.

Pink Salad

(Easy, colorful and tasty)

1   **(16-ounce) can crushed pineapple, undrained**
2   **(3-ounce) packages strawberry gelatin**
½   **pint whipping cream**
1   **(12-ounce) carton small curd cottage cheese**

- In an uncovered saucepan heat the pineapple with its juice and the gelatin until it bubbles; set aside for 10 minutes to cool. Whip the cream at high speed until it peaks.
- Stir in cottage cheese and add gelatin mixture.
- Pour in any mold and set in refrigerator until congealed.

Yield: 4 to 6 servings.

Raspberry Pretzel Salad

1½   cups finely crushed pretzels
2   tablespoons sugar
¾   cup margarine, melted
1   (8-ounce) bar cream cheese, softened
1   cup sugar
1   (9-ounce) container dessert topping
1   (6-ounce) box raspberry gelatin
2   cups boiling water
1   (20-ounce) package frozen raspberries, thawed and drained

- Mix together the pretzel crumbs, sugar and margarine. Spread in a 9x13-inch pan. Bake at 350° for 10 minutes; cool.
- Combine cream cheese, sugar and dessert topping; blend well. Spread on top of the pretzel crust; chill at least 2 hours.
- Dissolve the gelatin in the water and add the raspberries. Thicken slightly in the refrigerator, then pour over the cream cheese. Congeal and cut into squares.

Yield: 10 to 12 servings.

Pineapple and Cherry Frozen Salad

2   (1.5-ounce) envelopes whipped topping mix
2   (3-ounce) packages cream cheese, softened
¼   cup lemon juice
1   (14-ounce) can sweetened condensed milk
1   cup chopped pecans
1   (15¼-ounce) can pineapple chunks, drained
1   (21-ounce) can cherry pie filling

- Prepare whipped topping according to package directions; set aside.
- Combine cream cheese and lemon juice, heating until smooth; stir in the next 3 ingredients then fold in pie filling and whipped topping.
- Place 24 paper baking cups in muffin tins; spoon mixture into cups then cover and freeze.
- Salads may be removed from muffin tins and stored in plastic freezer bags.

Yield: 24 servings.

Shrimp Tomato Aspic

2   (3-ounce) boxes lemon gelatin
½   teaspoon plain gelatin
4   cups Welch's tomato juice
1   tablespoon dry mustard
1   teaspoon Worcestershire sauce
1   teaspoon salt
½   teaspoon red pepper
1½   cups chopped celery
1   cup stuffed olives, sliced
1   pound small shrimp, cooked, cleaned and cut in half

- Mix lemon gelatin and plain gelatin together.
- Make gelatin following the package directions using tomato juice instead of water; add spices and blend well.
- Allow tomato mixture to cool slightly, then add celery, olives and shrimp.
- Pour into molds and refrigerate to congeal.

Yield: 6 to 8 servings.

Strawberry and Cream Squares

2 (3-ounce) packages strawberry-flavored gelatin
2 cups boiling water
2 (10-ounce) packages frozen strawberries, thawed and drained
1 (13-ounce) can crushed pineapple, drained
2 large ripe bananas, finely diced
1 cup sour cream

- Dissolve gelatin in boiling water; add berries, stirring occasionally until thawed; add pineapple and bananas.
- Pour half the mixture into an 8x8x2-inch pan; chill until firm.
- Spoon sour cream over chilled gelatin spreading in an even layer; pour remaining gelatin on top of cream. Chill until congealed.
- To serve, cut in 9 squares and put touch of sour cream on top with a whole strawberry split in half from top to bottom.

Yield: 9 servings.

Triple Fruit Salad

3 (3-ounce) packages strawberry gelatin
1 cup boiling water
1 (10-ounce) package frozen strawberries, thawed and undrained
1 (15¼-ounce) can crushed pineapple, undrained
3 bananas, sliced
2 cups sour cream, divided
½ cup chopped pecans or walnuts

- Dissolve gelatin in boiling water; stir in fruit. Pour half of gelatin mixture into an 8-inch pan, and refrigerate until firm; store remaining gelatin mixture at room temperature.
- Spread congealed gelatin with 1 cup sour cream. Spoon remaining gelatin over sour cream, and refrigerate until firm. Top with remaining sour cream, spreading evenly; sprinkle with pecans.

Yield: 8 to 10 servings.

White Asparagus Salad

1 #300 can white asparagus, drained
1 (6-ounce) package lime gelatin
½ teaspoon plain gelatin
1 cup boiling water
¼ teaspoon salt
1 cup mayonnaise
½ cup milk
½ cup grated cheese of your choice
1 tablespoon minced onion
1 tablespoon vinegar
Dash hot pepper sauce

- Dissolve gelatins in boiling water and cool until partially congealed.
- Fold remaining ingredients, except asparagus, into gelatin mixture. Gently add asparagus.
- Pour into chosen container or mold and refrigerate until congealed and ready to serve.

Yield: 8 to 10 servings.

Congealed Vegetable Salad

6 tablespoons sugar
1 teaspoon salt
1 (6-ounce) package lime gelatin
3¼ cups boiling water
¼ cup vinegar
2 cups shredded cabbage
1 cup shredded carrot
   Lettuce
   Spiced apple rings

- Combine sugar, salt and gelatin; add boiling water, stirring until gelatin dissolves. Stir in vinegar.
- Chill until partially set; fold in cabbage and carrot.
- Spoon mixture into an 8-cup ring mold or individual molds; chill until firm.
- Unmold salad on lettuce leaves and garnish with apple rings.

Yield: 10 to 12 servings.

Marinated Cucumbers and Onions

(Keeps in refrigerator for several weeks)

7 cups cucumbers, peeled and sliced
1 cup diced onion
1 cup white vinegar
1¼ cups sugar
1 teaspoon salt
1 teaspoon celery seeds

- Combine ingredients.
- Chill and serve.

Yield: 10 to 12 servings.

Asparagus Vinaigrette

2 pounds fresh asparagus, cleaned and trimmed
1 teaspoon salt
2 tablespoons lemon juice
2 tablespoons red wine vinegar
4 tablespoons olive oil
2 tablespoons vegetable oil
1 teaspoon salt
½ teaspoon sugar
2 teaspoons Dijon mustard
   Pepper to taste

- Cook asparagus slowly in salted boiling water for 5 to 7 minutes, being careful not to overcook. Drain and cool.
- Combine remaining ingredients and marinate asparagus in dressing for 1 hour at room temperature.
- Serve on lettuce leaves.

Yield: 8 to 10 servings.

Sauerkraut Salad

1 (27-ounce) can sauerkraut, drained
1 medium onion, chopped
½ cup shredded carrots
1 cup diced celery
1 cup vegetable oil
1 medium green pepper, chopped
1 cup sugar
¼ cup vinegar
½ teaspoon salt

- Combine vegetables in a bowl.
- Blend remaining ingredients together; pour over vegetables.
- Chill for several hours. Drain before serving.
- Will keep for several weeks in the refrigerator.

Yield: 8 to 10 servings.

Country Style Slaw

1   large cabbage, coarsely chopped
1½ cups shredded carrots
1   cup chopped green pepper
¼   cup chopped green onion
1   cup mayonnaise
3   tablespoons sugar
3   tablespoons vinegar
1½ teaspoons salt
¾   teaspoon dry mustard
¼   teaspoon celery seeds
    Leaf lettuce, green pepper rings
    (optional)

- Combine first 4 ingredients; set aside.
- Combine mayonnaise, sugar, vinegar, salt, mustard and celery seeds. Stir well. Pour dressing over cabbage mixture, and toss well. Chill and serve garnished with pepper rings in a lettuce-lined bowl.

Yield: 12 servings.

Marinated Broccoli Salad

2   bunches broccoli, broken into bite-size pieces
½   medium-size red onion, sliced
½   cup raisins (optional)
1   cup shredded Cheddar cheese
1   cup mayonnaise
3   tablespoons vinegar
3   tablespoons sugar
1   pound bacon, cooked and crumbled
¼   cup sunflower seeds (optional)

- Combine first 4 ingredients in a bowl. Mix mayonnaise, vinegar and sugar and pour over ingredients in bowl.
- Marinate for at least 6 hours. Sprinkle with bacon and sunflower seeds before serving.

Yield: 6 to 8 servings.

Marinated Squash Salad

(A nice addition to a cold plate with chicken salad)

3   medium yellow squash, washed and thinly sliced
3   medium zucchini squash, washed and thinly sliced
1   bunch green onions, thinly sliced, some tops included
½   cup thinly sliced celery
½   cup chopped green pepper
⅔   cup cider vinegar
2   tablespoons wine vinegar
¾   cup sugar
⅓   cup salad oil
1   teaspoon pepper
1   (2-ounce) jar diced pimento, drained

- Combine both squash, onion, celery and green pepper in a large bowl.
- Combine remaining ingredients in a bowl, stirring until sugar dissolves. Pour over vegetables.
- Chill, covered, for at least 12 hours, stirring several times. Drain well and serve.

Note: Can use all yellow squash or all zucchini.

Yield: 10 to 12 servings.

When washing lettuce, add lemon juice or vinegar to the rinsing water and it will remove any remaining insects and won't harm the flavor.

Fire and Ice Tomatoes

(Best when you use fresh summer tomatoes)

6   firm ripe tomatoes, peeled and quartered
1   green pepper, seeded and cut in strips
1   red onion, cut in rings
¾   cup vinegar
1½   teaspoons celery salt
1½   teaspoons mustard seed
½   teaspoon fresh ground pepper
¼   cup water
6   teaspoons sugar
   Salt and hot pepper sauce to taste

- Combine first 3 ingredients together in a bowl.
- Mix remaining ingredients together in a saucepan and boil for 1 minute; pour over vegetables and chill well.

Yield: 6 to 8 servings.

Garden Patch Potato Salad

8   cups cubed new potatoes, cooked
2   medium zucchini, sliced and quartered
1   cup sliced celery
¾   cup shredded carrot
3   tablespoons minced onion
1   (16-ounce) carton commercial sour cream
2   tablespoons vinegar
1   tablespoon sugar
1   teaspoon salt
¼-½   teaspoon dillweed
½   teaspoon celery seeds
⅛   teaspoon pepper

- Combine first 5 ingredients in a large bowl; toss lightly and set aside.
- Combine remaining ingredients; stir until blended.
- Add sour cream mixture to vegetables, stirring well. Chill thoroughly before serving.

Yield: 8 to 10 servings.

Fresh Green Bean Salad

1½   pounds fresh green beans, cleaned and left whole
   Water
   Salt
1   garlic clove, minced
3   tablespoons wine vinegar
2   teaspoons dry mustard
   Salt to taste
   Pepper to taste
9   tablespoons vegetable oil
1   teaspoon dry tarragon
1   teaspoon chopped fresh parsley
½   pound Swiss cheese, cubed

- Add green beans to boiling salted water to cover and cook for 7 minutes; drain.
- In wooden salad bowl combine next 6 ingredients; beat with a whisk. Add hot beans, stirring well; add tarragon and parsley.
- Allow to cool for 15 to 20 minutes; add cheese. Refrigerate until serving time.

Yield: 8 servings.

Marinated Vegetables

(Make ahead)

½   cup salad oil
½   cup olive oil
3   cups tarragon vinegar
½-¾ cup sugar
3   cloves garlic
1   tablespoon Dijon mustard
1   tablespoon salt
2   teaspoons tarragon leaves
    Pepper to taste
2   heads cauliflower, cut into bite-sized pieces
1   bunch broccoli, cut into bite-sized pieces
3   yellow squash, sliced
2   pounds carrots, peeled and sliced
1   bunch celery, sliced
1   pound mushrooms, sliced
2   cucumbers, sliced
3   medium green peppers

• Combine first 9 ingredients together in a large bowl or covered container.

• Add all vegetables to marinade except mushrooms. Stir well to coat all vegetables. Marinate for at least 24 hours ahead, preferably two days. Stir several times while marinating.

• Add mushrooms to the other vegetables and marinade the night before serving.

   Note: Can marinate only broccoli or any combination of vegetables.

Yield: 12 to 16 servings.

Two Layer Tomato Aspic

(Great for buffets)

2   (3-ounce) packages lemon gelatin
2   cups small curd cottage cheese
½   cup mayonnaise
¾   cup finely chopped green pepper
1   teaspoon grated onion
1½   teaspoons salt, divided
1⅔   cups tomato juice, divided
1   cup diced celery
1   cup boiling water
1   (6-ounce) jar marinated artichoke hearts, drained and quartered

• Add 1 cup of boiling water to 1 package lemon gelatin; cool.

• In blender, purée cottage cheese until smooth.

• Combine mayonnaise, green pepper, grated onion, cottage cheese and ½ teaspoon salt; mix with cooled gelatin and pour into 7-cup gelatin mold. Refrigerate until set, approximately 2 hours.

• Dissolve the second package of lemon gelatin in 1 cup hot tomato juice; add ⅔ cup cold tomato juice, 1 teaspoon salt and diced celery. Pour on top of first set layer; place artichokes on top. Refrigerate until set.

Yield: 12 to 16 servings.

Save sweet pickle juice to use when preparing salads.

Refrigerator Slaw

*(Serve this with hot dogs,
hamburgers, or any dish)*

4   **pounds green cabbage, shredded**
4   **onions, chopped**
4   **green peppers, chopped**
13   **ounces salt**
1   **pint white vinegar**
6   **cups sugar**
1   **teaspoon celery seed**

- Place vegetables in a large bowl; cover with cold water and salt; let stand overnight.
- Drain and rinse in two cold waters. Squeeze all liquid out of mixture. Make syrup of vinegar, sugar and celery seed. Heat until sugar has melted. Cool.
- Pour over cabbage mixture and refrigerate 24 hours before using.

  Note: Try mixed with tuna for a different salad.

Scandinavian Salad

*(Will keep in the refrigerator
for several days)*

1   **(16-ounce) can French-style green beans, drained**
1   **(16-ounce) can small green peas, drained**
4   **ribs celery, finely chopped**
1   **large green pepper, chopped**
2   **medium onions, chopped**
1   **(2-ounce) jar chopped pimento, drained**

- Combine vegetables in a 2½-quart casserole.

Marinade:

1   **cup vinegar**
½   **cup salad oil**
1   **cup sugar**
½   **teaspoon paprika**
1   **teaspoon salt**
½   **teaspoon pepper**

- Mix marinade ingredients in a bowl. Pour over the vegetables.
- Refrigerate for 24 hours before serving.

Leafy Salad with Garlic Parsley Vinaigrette

3   **small to medium heads of Romaine lettuce**
1   **bunch parsley**
2   **cloves garlic**
2   **tablespoons whole-grain mustard**
2   **tablespoons tamari**
¼   **teaspoon freshly ground pepper**
½   **cup extra-virgin olive oil**

- Wash lettuce; tear into bite-size pieces and set aside.
- Chop the parsley and garlic; place in a large wooden salad bowl. Mix in the mustard, tamari, pepper and oil.
- Add the Romaine to the bowl just before serving. Toss gently to coat evenly with the dressing. Serve immediately.

  Yield: 8 to 10 servings.

Midwest Vegetable Crunch Salad

2 cups broccoli flowerets
2 cups cauliflowerets
1 cup sliced celery
1 cup halved cherry tomatoes
1 cup sliced zucchini
¾ cup sliced green onion
½ cup sliced, pitted ripe olives
¼ cup sliced carrot
1 cup Italian dressing
1 (3-ounce) jar Bacon Bits

- In a large bowl combine all ingredients, except bacon.
- Cover and marinate in refrigerator, turning occasionally, 4 hours or overnight.
- Toss with bacon before serving.

Yield: 8 servings.

Spinach Strawberry Salad

¾ cup sliced or slivered almonds
2 tablespoons butter
1 pound spinach, washed and torn into bite-size pieces
1 pint strawberries, sliced

- In a small skillet, melt butter and sauté almonds until toasted. Remove and set aside to cool.
- Combine spinach, strawberries and almonds in serving bowl.
- When ready to serve, pour dressing over salad and toss lightly.

Dressing:

½ cup sugar
1 tablespoon poppy seeds
1½ teaspoons minced onion
¼ teaspoon paprika
¼ cup cider vinegar
¼ cup wine vinegar
½ cup oil

- Mix dressing ingredients together in a bowl. Whisk to combine thoroughly.

Yield: 6 to 8 servings.

Avocado and Hearts of Palm Salad

1 large ripe avocado, peeled and sliced
1 head Romaine lettuce, torn in bite-size pieces
1 (14-ounce) can hearts of palm, chilled, drained and sliced

- Combine avocado, lettuce and hearts of palm together in a bowl; set aside.

Herb Dressing:

½ cup olive oil
3 tablespoons wine vinegar
⅛ teaspoon powdered thyme
⅛ teaspoon powdered marjoram
¼ teaspoon dried basil leaves
1 tablespoon chopped onion
1 tablespoon water
½ teaspoon salt
1 tablespoon chopped parsley

- Combine dressing ingredients together in a blender and blend until well mixed.
- Pour over salad and toss well. Serve immediately.

Spinach Salad

*(This has an interesting
sweet-hot taste)*

1   pound fresh spinach, washed and
trimmed
½   cup sour cream
½   cup sugar
2   teaspoons horseradish
½   teaspoon dry mustard
3   teaspoons vinegar
¼   teaspoon salt
¼   pound cottage cheese
Pecans, broken into pieces

- Tear spinach into bite-size pieces and place
in a salad bowl; mix next 7 ingredients and
pour over spinach and toss.
- Top with pecan pieces.

Tossed Tar Heel Salad

2   heads Bibb lettuce or 2 hearts
Romaine, washed and dried
½   red apple, unpeeled, cored and
julienned
1   stalk celery, julienned
1   cooked artichoke heart, fresh or
canned, cut into ½-inch cubes
½   avocado, peeled and cut into ½-
inch cubes
½   cup walnuts or pecans, coarsely
chopped
4   medium mushrooms, stems
trimmed, thinly sliced
4   slices bacon, cooked, drained and
broken into pieces

- Tear lettuce into bite-size pieces and place
in a serving bowl; add dressing and toss.
- Fold in remaining ingredients; toss lightly
and serve.

Dressing:
3   tablespoons safflower oil
1-1½   tablespoons white wine vinegar
½   small garlic clove, minced
½   teaspoon salt
½   teaspoon Dijon mustard
½   teaspoon sugar
Freshly ground pepper

- Whisk together all the ingredients in a bowl
or shake them in a jar until blended.

Yield: 4 servings.

Mandarin Orange Salad

1   head iceberg lettuce, cleaned and
broken into bite-size pieces
1   head Romaine lettuce, cleaned and
broken into bite-size pieces
½   cup bacon bits
½   cup sliced green onions
½   cup sliced almonds
3   (11-ounce) cans Mandarin orange
sections, drained

- Toss salad ingredients together.

Dressing:
½   cup oil
4   tablespoons sugar
4   tablespoons vinegar
1   teaspoon salt
¼   teaspoon hot pepper sauce

- Mix dressing ingredients together and pour
over the salad; toss lightly.
- Serve immediately.

Yield: 8 to 10 servings.

Strawberry and Onion Salad with Poppy Seed Dressing

1 head Romaine lettuce, washed
1 pint fresh strawberries, sliced
1 Bermuda onion, sliced

- Pat lettuce dry and refrigerate until serving time.
- Place greens on individual salad plates or in a large salad bowl. Put strawberries and onions on top of greens.

Poppy Seed Dressing:
½ cup mayonnaise
2 tablespoons vinegar
⅓ cup sugar
¼ cup whole milk
2 tablespoons poppy seeds

- Prepare dressing by combining all ingredients in a food processor and blending well. Will keep in the refrigerator for several weeks.
- Drizzle Poppy Seed Dressing over salad. Toss if using large salad bowl.

Yield: 8 servings.

Super Salad

Dressing:
¾ cup salad oil
¼ cup wine vinegar
½ teaspoon salt
¼ teaspoon sugar
¼ teaspoon pepper

- Combine dressing ingredients in a jar; shake well.

Salad:
1 (16-ounce) can artichoke hearts, drained and quartered
2 cups fresh or frozen peas, cooked crisp-tender
1 large red onion, thinly sliced
½ pound spinach leaves, torn into bite-size pieces
1 head Bibb lettuce, torn into bite-size pieces
2 ripe avocados, sliced
1 (11-ounce) can mandarin oranges, drained
½ cup crumbled bleu cheese

- Place artichokes, peas, and onions in a medium bowl. Pour dressing over, cover and marinate overnight.
- When ready to serve, combine lettuce, spinach, avocados and oranges; pour marinated vegetables over and toss. Top with crumbled bleu cheese.

Yield: 10 to 12 servings.

Colonial Honey Dressing

(Serve with fresh fruit)

½ cup vinegar
¼ cup sugar
¼ cup honey
1 teaspoon dry mustard
1 teaspoon paprika
1 teaspoon celery seed
1 teaspoon celery salt
1 teaspoon onion juice
1 cup vegetable oil

- Combine first 5 ingredients together in a saucepan; boil for 3 minutes and cool.
- Add remaining ingredients. Pour into a jar and shake vigorously.

Caesar Salad Dressing

2   cloves garlic
2   teaspoons salt
1   teaspoon pepper
1   teaspoon anchovy paste
¼   teaspoon powdered mustard
¼   teaspoon Worcestershire sauce
2   tablespoons lemon juice
2   tablespoons wine vinegar
½   cup olive oil
2   raw egg yolks
5   tablespoons Parmesan cheese, divided

- Mince garlic in food processor; add rest of ingredients in order given except egg yolks and half of Parmesan cheese. Pulsate until mixed well.
- Pour dressing into bowl; whisk egg yolks into the dressing.
- Serve remaining Parmesan cheese over top of salad.

Yield: 1½ cups.

Creamy Lemon Mayonnaise

1   cup mayonnaise
3   tablespoons lemon juice
1   teaspoon grated lemon peel
⅓   cup whipping cream
3   tablespoons powdered sugar

- Mix together mayonnaise, lemon juice and lemon peel. Whip cream to medium consistency and add powdered sugar. Fold whipped cream mixture into lemon mayonnaise mixture.
- Serve over chef's salad or shrimp salad.

Yield: 1½ cups.

Celery Seed Dressing

(Delicious on any combination of fruit, also cabbage)

1¼   cups sugar
2   teaspoons mustard
2   teaspoons salt
1   tablespoon onion juice
⅔   cup vinegar, divided
2   cups salad oil
2   tablespoons celery seed

- Combine sugar, mustard, salt, onion juice and half of the vinegar; beat well. Gradually add the oil alternately with remaining vinegar; beat well until a stable emulsion has been formed. Fold in celery seed.
- Will keep in the refrigerator for several weeks.

Yield: Approximately 3 cups.

Curried Chutney Dressing

(Delicious over a spinach salad with grapefruit and orange sections topped with chopped peanuts)

⅔   cup plain low-fat yogurt
6   tablespoons chutney, finely chopped
½   teaspoon curry powder
    Dash pepper

- Combine all ingredients in a mixing bowl, blending well.
- Cover and chill for a few hours.

Yield: 1 cup.

Carolina-Blue Dressing

8   ounces bleu cheese
2   cups mayonnaise
¾   cup sour cream
2   tablespoons lemon juice
1½ teaspoons Worcestershire sauce
7   drops hot pepper sauce or to taste

- Crumble bleu cheese and add remaining ingredients; stir until well blended.
- Flavor seems to enhance when chilled at least an hour before serving.

Italian Herbed Vinegar

(This needs to age for 2 weeks before using)

4   cups cider vinegar
2   tablespoons instant minced onion
1   tablespoon dry Italian seasoning
½   teaspoon coarse ground pepper
¼   teaspoon instant minced garlic

- Combine all ingredients in a medium saucepan. Bring to a boil; reduce heat to low and simmer, covered, for 5 minutes.
- Pour mixture into a quart bottle with a tight lid; let stand for two weeks.
- Strain, if desired.
- To store: Pour in smaller bottles with tight lids. Use in salad dressings or as part of a marinade. Great for gift-giving in decorative bottles.

Yield: 4 cups.

Honey-Apple Salad Dressing

(Helen's Restaurant, Seven Springs Resort, Champion, Pennsylvania)

1   quart basic mayonnaise recipe
5   whole eggs
5   egg yolks
6   cups vegetable oil
1¼ cups honey
1½ cups apple cider
     Pinch of cinnamon
1   teaspoon salt
     Pinch of nutmeg
4   ounces vinegar

- Blend first 4 ingredients together in a food processor.
- Whisk in the remaining ingredients.

Honey Dressing II

     Olive oil
     Red wine vinegar
1   dash hot pepper sauce
2   dashes Worcestershire sauce
     Honey
½   teaspoon dry mustard
     Salt and pepper to taste

- Combine equal portions of olive oil and red wine vinegar together.
- Add the next 4 ingredients, blending well. Season to taste with salt and pepper.

Curried Oil and Vinegar Dressing

(Delicious over a spinach salad)

⅔   cup salad oil
¼   cup wine vinegar with garlic
2   tablespoons white wine
2   teaspoons soy sauce
1   teaspoon sugar
1   teaspoon dry mustard
½   teaspoon curry powder
1½ teaspoons salt
    Freshly ground pepper to taste

- Combine all ingredients in a jar with a tightly fitted lid; shake well.

  Yield: 1¼ cups.

French Dressing

⅔   cup salad oil
⅔   cup vinegar
1   cup chili sauce
1   cup sugar
1   small onion, minced
2   teaspoons Worcestershire sauce
2   teaspoons salt
2   teaspoons garlic salt

- Mix ingredients thoroughly in food processor.
- Chill to blend ingredients and mix before using.

  Yield: 3 cups.

Homemade Mayonnaise

6   egg yolks
2   tablespoons cider vinegar
½   teaspoon salt
¼   teaspoon sugar
¼   teaspoon white pepper
1   teaspoon dry mustard or Dijon mustard
4   cups salad oil
¼   cup lemon juice

- Put all ingredients except salad oil in a mixing bowl; mix well with an electric mixer for one minute. Slowly add salad oil; sauce will become thick as you are mixing.
- Store in refrigerator in a tight lidded container.

  Yield: 1 quart.

Poppy Seed Dressing and Dip

(Good on a fruit salad or as a dip for crudités)

1   cup sugar
½   teaspoon salt
1   teaspoon dry mustard
1½ teaspoons paprika
½   cup apple cider vinegar
1   teaspoon grated onion
1½ cups oil
1   tablespoon poppy seeds

- Combine first 5 ingredients together; add onion, stirring in thoroughly. Add oil very slowly, beating constantly until thick.
- Add poppy seeds and beat for a few minutes more; store in refrigerator. Can add a little ketchup to change color.

  Yield: 2½ cups.

Lemon Dressing

2 teaspoons grated lemon rind
2 tablespoons fresh lemon juice
2 tablespoons sugar
¼ teaspoon dried leaf tarragon
1 cup plain or vanilla yogurt
1 cup whipped topping

- Mix first 5 ingredients; then fold in whipped topping; chill until ready to serve.
- Serve with fresh fruit salad or on a congealed salad.

Mayonnaise

(A very delicate and light dressing)

1 egg white
1 teaspoon sugar
½ teaspoon salt
1 tablespoon vinegar
1½ cups vegetable oil

- Beat the egg white until stiff. Add salt, sugar and vinegar to beaten egg white.
- Add oil, 1 tablespoon at a time, until all is beaten in. Keep beater going all the time you are adding. Add more vinegar if mixture gets too thick.

Shallot-Dill Mayonnaise

(Good served with soft shell crabs)

1 small shallot
2 egg yolks
1 teaspoon dry mustard
½ teaspoon salt
2 tablespoons wine vinegar or lemon juice
1 cup vegetable oil
1 tablespoon fresh dill

- Process shallot in food processor until finely minced; add egg yolks and continue processing then add mustard, salt, vinegar or lemon juice.
- Slowly add oil, continuing to process until mixture thickens; drop in dill and pulse to rough chop then chill.

  Note: Can spread mayonnaise on sandwich buns and put 2 soft-shell crabs on bun for a sandwich.

  Yield: 1 cup.

Roquefort or Bleu Cheese Dressing

¼ pound Roquefort or bleu cheese
1 cup mayonnaise
½ cup light cream
2 tablespoons lemon juice
2 tablespoons chopped fresh parsley
1 teaspoon grated onion
¼ teaspoon Worcestershire sauce
¼ teaspoon garlic salt
¼ teaspoon pepper
   Dash cayenne pepper

- In bowl, mash cheese with a fork; gradually add mayonnaise, blending until smooth.
- Add remaining ingredients; mix well.
- Store in refrigerator.

  Yield: 2 cups.

Onion Dressing

2   tablespoons grated onion
1   tablespoon vinegar
1   teaspoon celery seed
    Paprika
2   tablespoons mustard
1   teaspoon salt
½   cup sugar
1   cup salad oil

- Mix first 7 ingredients together in blender; slowly add oil.
- Thin, if necessary, by adding water, one teaspoon at a time.

  Yield: 1½ cups.

The Best Coleslaw Dressing

(Keeps for weeks in the refrigerator)

2   eggs
1½   cups sugar
½   cup white vinegar
¼   teaspoon salt
¼   teaspoon white pepper
1   pint salad dressing
1   (5-ounce) can evaporated milk

- Beat eggs until fluffy; add sugar, vinegar, salt and pepper.
- Cook over medium-low heat, stirring constantly until thickened.
- Remove from heat and cool at room temperature.
- Add salad dressing and evaporated milk, blending until smooth.
- Pour into a quart jar and refrigerate.
- To make slaw, add only enough dressing to cabbage mixture that will be used that day.

Thousand Island Dressing

2   cups mayonnaise
⅓   cup ketchup
1   teaspoon vinegar
3   drops hot pepper sauce
1   teaspoon Worcestershire sauce
1   teaspoon onion juice
2   hard-boiled eggs, chopped
3   strips crisp bacon, cooked and crumbled
3   tablespoons finely chopped green pepper
3   tablespoons pimento, diced

- Combine all ingredients.
- Let stand at least 6 hours before using.

  Yield: 3 cups.

Notes

EGGS, CHEESE & PASTA

Becky Wienges '92

Index for Eggs, Cheese & Pasta

Pasquotank County Court House – 1882

Fifth Courthouse in the county, the Pasquotank County Courthouse was the second on this site. It replaced a wooden building erected about 1799 and burned during the Federal Occupation of the City in 1862. Records dating from about 1700 were saved by Arthur Jones who hid them in a barn until the end of the war.

Breakfast Casserole

(Make the night before using)

½ cup butter, melted
1½ cups milk
¼ teaspoon salt
    Dash pepper
1 cup shredded Swiss cheese
3 eggs, beaten
½ cup buttermilk baking mix
1 cup shredded Cheddar cheese
½ cup bacon, ham or sausage,
    cooked and drained
    Chopped onions
    Sliced mushrooms

- Blend all ingredients together in a blender or processor except meat, onions, and mushrooms.
- Mix together the meat, onions and mushrooms; fold into egg mixture. Pour into greased 13x9x2-inch casserole dish.
- Refrigerate overnight.
- Bake at 350° for 45 minutes or until set.

Brunch Crabmeat and Egg Muffins Topped with Spicy Cream Sauce

1 pound fresh backfin crabmeat,
    flaked
¼ cup margarine
½ teaspoon salt
½ teaspoon white pepper
12 poached eggs
6 English muffins, split
½ cup chopped fresh parsley

- Sauté crabmeat in margarine in a large skillet for about 5 minutes, stirring frequently. Stir in salt and pepper; set aside.

Spicy Cream Sauce:

¼ cup margarine
3 tablespoons all-purpose flour
1½ cups milk
⅛ teaspoon hot pepper sauce
½ teaspoon salt
¼ teaspoon ground nutmeg
2-3 tablespoons brandy

- To make sauce, melt margarine in heavy saucepan over low heat; add flour, stirring until smooth. Cook for 1 minute, stirring constantly.
- Gradually add milk, cook over medium heat, stirring constantly until thickened and bubbly. Stir in hot pepper sauce, salt, nutmeg and brandy. Keep warm on low heat while assembling muffins.

To Assemble Muffins:

- Heat English muffins. (Brunch muffins can be prepared on individual plates or in a large casserole dish to be served on a buffet).
- Spoon a small amount of crabmeat on each muffin half. Top with one poached egg and spoon remaining crabmeat over eggs.
- Spoon Spicy Cream Sauce over eggs; sprinkle with chopped parsley.

When poaching eggs, add a few drops of vinegar to the water. This will hold them together better and won't affect their taste.

Cheesy Ham and Broccoli Brunch Casserole

6-8 **slices bread, crusts removed**
 ¾ **pound shredded ham**
 ½ **pound Swiss cheese, sliced**
 2 **(10-ounce) package chopped broccoli, thawed and drained**
 6 **eggs, beaten**
 2 **cups heavy cream**
 3 **tablespoons chopped chives, fresh if possible**
   Salt and pepper to taste

- Butter a 9x13-inch pan. Place bread slices in the bottom of the pan.
- Layer chipped ham, Swiss cheese and broccoli over the bread.
- Add eggs with cream and spices; pour over the dish. Refrigerate overnight.
- Bake at 375° for 40 minutes, checking after 30 minutes.

Yield: 8 servings.

Creamed Tarragon Eggs on Asparagus

(Also good with broccoli)

 ¾ **cup margarine or butter**
2¼ **cups fresh bread crumbs**
 3 **small onions, chopped**
 ¾ **teaspoon leaf tarragon, crumbled**
 1 **cup milk**
 3 **(10¾-ounce) cans cream of mushroom, celery or chicken soup**
 6 **tablespoons fresh lemon juice**
18 **hard-boiled eggs**
1½ **pounds fresh asparagus or broccoli**

- Melt butter in large skillet. Remove 3 tablespoons and combine with bread crumbs in medium bowl; reserve.
- Sauté onion in remaining butter until soft. Stir in tarragon, milk, soup and lemon juice until well blended.
- Chop eggs coarsely and stir into sauce.
- Arrange asparagus or broccoli in greased oven-proof baking dish. Pour sauce over vegetable and sprinkle with reserved bread crumbs.
- Bake at 350° for 30 minutes or until bubbly and crumbs are browned.

Yield: 12 servings.

Chicken and Bacon Quiche

 1 **deep-dish frozen pie shell**
 2 **cups shredded Swiss cheese dredged in 1 tablespoon flour**
 ½ **cup cooked and diced chicken**
 5 **slices bacon, cooked, drained and crumbled**
 ¼ **cup sliced olives with pimento**
 3 **eggs**
 1 **cup less 2 tablespoons milk**
 2 **tablespoons dry sherry**
   Salt and pepper to taste

- Spread cheese and flour mixture in frozen pie shell; add chicken, bacon and olives.
- Beat eggs with milk and sherry; add salt and pepper to taste.
- Pour over chicken and cheese; bake in 425° oven for 15 minutes.
- Lower temperature to 325° and continue baking for 30 to 40 minutes or until set.

Yield: 6 servings.

Sausage and Cheese Casserole

(A good brunch dish)

1   pound sausage, cooked, drained and crumbled
¼   pound sharp cheese, grated
8   slices white bread, trimmed
6   eggs
2   cups milk
½   teaspoon salt
½   teaspoon pepper
1   tablespoon dry mustard
    Dash hot pepper sauce
    Dash Worcestershire sauce

- Grease 9x13-inch Pyrex dish.
- Place bread in the bottom of dish. Sprinkle cheese on bread, then sausage.
- Mix together eggs, milk, salt, pepper, mustard and sauces. Pour mixture over bread, cheese and sausage.
- Refrigerate overnight.
- Bake at 350° for 35 to 40 minutes.

  Yield: 6 servings.

Seafood Brunch Casserole

Seafood Filling:

½   pound crabmeat or shrimp, cleaned and sliced
1-2 ribs celery, finely chopped
1   green onion, finely chopped
    Juice of 1 lemon
1½ tablespoons mayonnaise
1   teaspoon prepared mustard
½   teaspoon garlic powder
    Pepper to taste

- Mix all ingredients well.

Bread Shells:

8   slices white bread, crusts removed
½   cup butter, softened
1   small jar pasteurized cheese
3   eggs, beaten
2   cups milk

- Trim crusts from bread; spread butter and cheese on one side of each bread slice.
- Place 4 slices in 2-quart casserole dish; mix together eggs and milk.
- Layer half of egg-milk mixture over bread; add all of the seafood filling over the egg-milk mixture.
- Layer remaining bread slices and top with remaining egg-milk mixture.
- Cover and refrigerate 4-6 hours or overnight. Bake uncovered at 350° for 45 minutes.

Cheese-Grits Casserole

4   cups water
1   teaspoon salt
1   cup quick-cooking grits
1   cup shredded Cheddar cheese
¼   cup margarine or butter
2   eggs, slightly beaten

- Heat water and salt to boiling in 3-quart saucepan. Gradually stir in grits; heat to boiling, reduce heat. Simmer uncovered, stirring occasionally for 5 minutes; remove from heat. Stir in remaining ingredients.
- Pour into ungreased 1½-quart casserole. Cover and refrigerate no longer than 24 hours.
- Bake uncovered in 350° oven until top is firm and cracks are dry, about 50 minutes.

Cheese Sauce

2½   tablespoons butter
2½   tablespoons flour
1½   cups milk
1   cup plus 5 ounces Gruyère cheese, grated
¼   cup Parmesan cheese
½   teaspoon salt
¼   teaspoon dillweed
4   English muffins, toasted
8   slices bacon, cooked and crumbled

- Melt butter, stir in flour and milk. When sauce thickens, add cheeses, salt and dillweed.
- Serve over English muffins; crumble bacon on top.

Yield: 8 servings.

Cheese Soufflé

12   slices bread, buttered, cubed, no crusts
1½   pounds sharp Cheddar cheese, shredded
9   eggs, slightly beaten
4½   cups milk
4   teaspoons dry mustard
3   dashes hot pepper sauce
   Salt and pepper to taste
   Paprika

- Place bread in a 9x13-inch baking dish; cover bread with grated cheese.
- Combine eggs, milk, dry mustard, hot pepper sauce, salt and pepper; pour mixture over bread and cheese. Sprinkle paprika over all.
- Let set at least 3 hours or overnight in refrigerator; bake at 350° for 45 minutes to 1 hour or until set.

Yield: 6 to 8 servings.

Chili and Cheese Breakfast Casserole

3   English muffins, split
2   tablespoons butter or margarine, softened
1   pound bulk pork sausage, cooked, drained and crumbled
1   (4-ounce) can chopped green chilies, drained
3   cups shredded Cheddar cheese
1½   cups sour cream or substitute
12   eggs, beaten

- Spread cut side of each English muffin with 1 teaspoon butter and place buttered side down, in a lightly greased 13x9x2-inch baking dish.
- Layer half of sausage, chilies, and cheese over English muffins. Combine sour cream and eggs; pour over layers. Repeat with remaining sausage, chilies and cheese; cover and refrigerate 8 hours.
- Remove from refrigerator and let stand at room temperature 30 minutes.
- Bake uncovered at 350° for 35 to 40 minutes.

Yield: 6 to 8 servings.

Hard-boiled eggs can be sliced and substituted for poached eggs in Eggs Benedict. The results are just as good but not gooey.

Capellini with Lemon-Parsley Clam Sauce

3   tablespoons butter
5   tablespoons olive oil
6   large garlic cloves, chopped
2   (10-ounce) cans baby clams,
    drained, juices reserved, or 35-40
    fresh clams, reserve juices; cut
    larger clams in small pieces
½   cup bottled clam juice
⅔   cup dry white wine
1½ teaspoons marjoram
¼   teaspoon dried, crushed red pepper
2   tablespoons fresh lemon juice
¾   teaspoon grated lemon peel
12 ounces capellini (angel hair) pasta
½   cup chopped fresh Italian parsley
    Salt and pepper

- Melt butter with oil in heavy, large skillet over medium heat. Add garlic and sauté 1 minute.

- Measure reserved clam juices. Add enough bottled clam juice to equal 1½ cups.

- Add the clam juice, wine, marjoram and dried pepper to skillet. Boil until reduced to about 1¼ cups, about 7 minutes.

- Add clams, lemon juice, and lemon peel to skillet; simmer sauce 2 minutes.

- Meanwhile, cook pasta in a large pot of salted boiling water until tender but firm to bite; drain well.

- Add pasta and parsley to sauce, then toss to coat; season with salt and pepper.

Yield: 4 servings.

Cold Shrimp and Pasta Salad

6   cups water
2   pounds unpeeled fresh shrimp
2   cups peeled, chopped tomatoes
1   (14-ounce) can artichoke hearts,
    drained and quartered
¾   pound fresh mushrooms, sliced
1¼ cups frozen snow pea pods, thawed
1½ cups commercial Italian salad
    dressing, divided
1   (12-ounce) package vermicelli,
    broken in half
¾   cup pine nuts
⅓   cup fresh basil or 3 teaspoons
    dried whole basil
¼   cup minced fresh parsley

- Bring water to a boil; add shrimp and cook for 3 minutes. Drain and rinse with cold water; chill, peel and devein.

- Combine tomatoes, artichoke hearts, mushrooms, snow peas and 1 cup salad dressing; chill.

- Cook vermicelli according to package directions; drain. Combine vermicelli and ½ cup salad dressing, toss well and chill.

- Combine vegetable mixture, vermicelli and remaining ingredients in a large bowl, tossing well.

- Serve salad immediately.

    Note: This is great to serve anytime because it can be done ahead of time and put together at the last minute.

Yield: 10 to 12 servings.

Fettuccini with Sun Dried Tomatoes

6 **tablespoons margarine**
1½ **cups whipping cream, divided**
3-4 **cups hot, cooked pasta, such as egg noodles or fettuccini**
1 **cup shredded Parmesan cheese**
    Salt and pepper to taste
    Ground nutmeg
1 **(8-ounce) jar sun dried tomatoes, undrained**

- In a large skillet melt butter until it is lightly browned. Add ½ cup of the cream and tomatoes; boil rapidly stirring occasionally. Reduce heat to medium; add noodles to the sauce.

- Toss vigorously; pour in the cheese and 1 cup of whipping cream, a little at a time.

- Season with salt, pepper and nutmeg; serve immediately.

Yield: 4 to 6 servings.

Eggplant Pasta

(Even those who hate eggplant will love this)

2 **medium eggplants, peeled and cut into large cubes**
    Salt
1 **large onion, chopped**
5 **large garlic cloves, minced**
    Olive oil
2 **large cans whole, peeled tomatoes, drained**
½ **cup chopped fresh basil or ¼ cup dried**
1 **pound ziti**
1 **cup freshly grated Parmesan cheese, or more to taste**

- Salt cubed eggplant and let stand in colander, weighted down for 15 to 20 minutes. This will drain the juices of the eggplant. After draining rinse lightly and pat dry with paper towels.

- Meanwhile sauté onions and garlic in olive oil, add tomatoes and simmer about 10 minutes. Add basil and continue to simmer.

- Sauté eggplant in olive oil in small batches until light brown on all sides. Remove to paper towels to drain. Combine with tomato mixture. You may prepare to this point early in day and set aside until 45 minutes before serving.

- Cook pasta, drain and combine with eggplant mixture. Add Parmesan cheese and stir to mix thoroughly. Place in casserole and reheat in oven to blend flavors at 350° until cheese starts to melt. Serve with green salad and crusty bread.

Note: Eggplant may be omitted and you can substitute 1 cup fresh mushrooms, sliced, for a great tasting plain pasta. You may also add to this sautéed mussels or even chicken pieces.

Yield: 6 generous servings.

Clam and Mushroom Pasta

½ cup butter
5 cloves garlic, minced
1 pound mushrooms, cleaned and sliced
1 pound minced fresh clams, undrained
½ cup chopped fresh Italian parsley
1 teaspoon salt, or to taste
¼ teaspoon ground black pepper
1 pound angel hair pasta, cooked according to package directions

• Melt the butter in a large skillet and sauté the garlic over medium heat for one minute. Add the mushrooms and sauté for about 5 minutes, stirring frequently. Add clams, including any liquid, along with the parsley, salt and pepper. Mix well and simmer for a few minutes, uncovered, to blend flavors.

• Serve over cooked pasta.

Yield: 6 servings.

Fettuccine with Wild Mushrooms and Sun Dried Tomatoes

¼ cup unsalted butter
¼ cup minced shallots
6 ounces fresh wild mushrooms (such as chanterelle, porcini, shiitake) cut into quarter size pieces
6 whole sun dried tomatoes, sliced lengthwise into ¼-inch strips
2 cups whipping cream
Salt and pepper to taste
1 pound fettuccine
2-3 green onions, cut diagonally into ¼-inch slices

• Melt butter in a heavy large skillet over medium heat. Add shallots and stir 1 minute; add mushrooms and tomatoes and stir 3 minutes. Add cream and season with salt and pepper; bring to a boil. Reduce heat and simmer until sauce is thick enough to coat the back of a spoon.

• Cook fettuccine in salted water until al dente; drain and mix with sauce. Garnish with green onions.

Yield: 4 generous servings.

Pasta with Chicken and Sun-Dried Tomatoes

¼ cup olive oil
4 boneless chicken breast halves, cut into 1-inch cubes
1 onion, chopped
1 garlic clove, chopped
½ teaspoon fennel seeds
1 carrot, peeled, julienned
¼ cup finely chopped and drained oil-packed sun-dried tomatoes
12 ounces fettuccine, freshly cooked
1 cup freshly grated Parmesan cheese

• Heat oil in heavy skillet over medium heat; add chicken and sauté until brown and cooked through. Transfer chicken to a bowl; keep warm.

• Add onion, garlic and fennel seeds to skillet and sauté until onion is tender. Stir in carrot and tomatoes and continue cooking until carrot is crisp-tender.

• Combine mixture in bowl with the chicken. Add cheese and pasta; toss well.

Yield: 4 servings.

Porcini Pasta

1 ounce porcini mushrooms
½ cup Madeira wine
4 tablespoons unsalted butter
4 scallions, coarsely chopped
1 clove garlic, minced
1 pound mushrooms, sliced thick
¼ cup Italian parsley
½ cup heavy cream
  Pasta

- Rinse porcini in cold water until grit-free. Combine porcini and Madeira. Heat just below simmer. Let sit for ½ hour.

- Melt butter; add scallions and garlic. Cook over medium heat for 5 minutes. Add mushrooms and cook for an additional 5 minutes.

- Remove porcini; coarsely chop and add to mushrooms with parsley. Cook for 5 minutes.

- Add Madeira and cream; simmer while pasta cooks.

Linguine with Broccoli and Bay Scallops

1 pound fresh broccoli
1 pound linguine
1 teaspoon salt
¼ teaspoon pepper
½ cup butter, divided
2 teaspoons fresh garlic
1 pound bay scallops
1 teaspoon salt
¼ teaspoon pepper
⅓ cup freshly grated Parmesan cheese

- Cut broccoli into flowerets and ¼-inch pieces. Blanch in water for 2 minutes; drain well; refresh under cold water and set aside.

- Cook linguine to al dente, according to package directions; drain well. Toss with salt, pepper and ¼ cup butter. Cover and keep warm while preparing scallops.

- Heat remaining ¼ cup butter until very hot, add garlic and salt, being careful not to burn. Add broccoli and heat through. Add scallops, salt and pepper and sauté three minutes or until done. Spoon seafood mixture over pasta. Sprinkle with Parmesan cheese. Serve at once.

Yield: 4 servings.

Spaghetti and Shrimp Toss

(Very easy and great tasting)

1 (8-ounce) package thin spaghetti
3 tablespoons butter or margarine
3 tablespoons olive oil
½ pound medium shrimp, shelled and deveined
1 clove garlic, minced
⅓ cup grated Parmesan cheese
¼ cup chopped fresh dill
1 teaspoon salt
½ teaspoon coarsely ground pepper

- Prepare spaghetti according to package directions; drain.

- In large skillet, heat butter and olive oil. Add shrimp and garlic; cook and stir until shrimp are opaque. Combine hot cooked spaghetti, shrimp mixture, Parmesan cheese, dill, salt and pepper. Toss to mix.

- Serve immediately.

Yield: 4 servings.

Shrimp and Broccoli Pasta

1½ pounds shrimp, peeled and deveined
1 (12-ounce) package spaghetti
1 tablespoon Old Bay seasoning
1 cup broccoli flowerets
1 clove garlic, minced
3 tablespoons olive oil
1 bunch green onions, chopped
1 (4-ounce) can sliced mushrooms, drained
1 (4-ounce) can sliced water chestnuts, drained
½ cup sour cream
1½ cups grated Parmesan cheese

- Cook spaghetti according to package directions, omitting salt and adding Old Bay seasoning; drain and return to saucepan, keeping warm.

- Sauté broccoli and garlic in olive oil in a large skillet for 3 to 4 minutes then add green onions; sauté 1 minute. Add shrimp and cook 4 minutes, stirring constantly; stir in mushrooms and water chestnuts, cooking until heated through. Stir in sour cream, heating thoroughly.

- Serve over spaghetti; sprinkle generously with Parmesan cheese.

Yield: 6 servings.

Garlic Spaghetti

(An island favorite)

12 garlic cloves, peeled
¼ cup top quality olive oil
4 quarts water
1½ tablespoons salt
1 pound spaghetti
1½ cups chicken broth
1 cup finely chopped Italian parsley
Freshly ground pepper
Freshly grated Parmesan cheese

- Mince 6 of the garlic cloves and set aside. Slice remaining garlic. Heat the oil in a small skillet. Add sliced garlic and cook over medium heat, stirring occasionally, until golden.

- Bring water to a boil in a large pot. Stir in salt, add spaghetti and cook until tender but still firm; do not overcook. Drain and transfer to a pot.

- Add chicken broth to the pasta and simmer until most of the broth has been absorbed, about 5 minutes. Stir in the heated olive oil and sliced garlic, then add the minced garlic and parsley. Toss thoroughly.

- Divide pasta evenly among heated plates or shallow soup bowls. Pour any remaining broth over pasta and serve at once, accompanied by lots of pepper and Parmesan cheese.

Yield: 6 first course portions.

Linguine with Scallops in Parchment

1	pound sea scallops
2½	cups whipping cream
1	large tomato, peeled, seeded and chopped
1	cup chopped sun dried tomatoes
2	tablespoons minced fresh rosemary
	Salt and pepper to taste
	Baking parchment
¾	pound linguine
½	cup unsalted butter, room temperature
	Dried red pepper flakes

- Cut six 10x14-inch parchment rectangles; generously butter one side of each. Cut scallops into ⅓-inch thick rounds. Simmer cream, fresh tomato, dried tomatoes and rosemary in a saucepan until reduced to 1½ cups, stirring frequently, about 20 minutes. Season with salt and pepper.

- Cook linguine in salted water until al dente; drain and add butter. Stir until melted and pasta is coated. Mix in sauce and scallops.

- Divide pasta mixture among parchment rectangles, placing on half of each. Fold top over and fold edges over a few times to seal. Place on baking sheet. These may be kept in refrigerator at this point for up to three hours. Bake in preheated 400° oven until scallops are opaque, about 15 minutes. Unwrap individual portions, place on plate and sprinkle with pepper flakes.

Yield: 6 servings.

Perfect Pasta Alfredo

(Great, fast, last minute dinner)

1	(8-ounce) package noodles or other pasta
1	envelope Good Seasons Italian Dressing mix
½	cup cream
4	tablespoons butter, melted
1	tablespoon chopped, fresh Italian parsley
½	cup, freshly grated, Parmesan cheese

- Cook pasta and drain well.

- Add remaining ingredients to pasta and toss to blend. Serve immediately.

- Can add: cut-up shrimp, crab, or chicken.

Yield: 4 generous servings.

Put leftover egg yolks in a jar of cold water and refrigerate for several days. Can be used to make sauces or simmer yolks in water until hard. Crumble and use over salads and vegetables.

ENTRÉES

Index for Entrées

Baked Spaghetti

1 medium onion, minced
1 clove garlic, minced
1 pound ground beef
3 (8-ounce) cans tomato sauce
1 cup Burgundy wine
¼ teaspoon dried oregano
¼ teaspoon rosemary
¼ teaspoon basil
¼ teaspoon marjoram
1 tablespoon sugar
½ teaspoon salt
¼ teaspoon pepper
½ pound spaghetti, broken into
   2-inch lengths
1 cup shredded sharp Cheddar
   cheese

- In large skillet, sauté onion, garlic and beef until brown; add tomato sauce.
- Add next 8 ingredients and simmer covered for 1 hour; stir occasionally.
- Meanwhile cook spaghetti; add to sauce with ½ cup grated cheese.
- Put into a 3-quart casserole; refrigerate.
- Remove casserole 1½ hours before serving. Preheat oven to 325°.
- Top casserole with remaining cheese. Bake covered for 45 minutes; uncover and bake an additional 30 minutes.

Yield: 6 servings.

Beef Neapolitan

(A different version of pot roast with pasta)

3-4 pounds sirloin tip or rolled rump
   roast
3 tablespoons lard or drippings
1½ teaspoons salt
¼ teaspoon pepper
1 clove garlic, minced
1 teaspoon parsley flakes
½ teaspoon basil
¼ teaspoon oregano
1 large onion, sliced
1 (16-ounce) can tomatoes
1 (4-ounce) can mushrooms, sliced
½ pound spaghetti, cooked

- Brown meat in lard or drippings in a Dutch oven; pour off drippings. Add salt, pepper, garlic, parsley flakes, basil, oregano, onion and tomatoes.
- Cover tightly and simmer 3 to 4 hours or until tender.
- Remove meat from pan and add water if necessary to make 2½ cups of liquid. Add mushrooms; stir in spaghetti and heat.
- Slice pot roast and serve with spaghetti.

Yield: 6 servings.

Boeuf Bourguinon

2 **pounds lean beef cubes**
10 **small white onions**
2 **tablespoons flour**
1 **cup Burgundy or claret wine**
½ **cup beef bouillon or consommé**
½ **pound fresh or canned mushrooms**
Salt and pepper to taste
Marjoram and thyme to taste

- Cut up onions and fry until brown in bacon fat. Remove onions to separate dish and brown beef (cut into 1-inch cubes) in same fat. After beef is browned, sprinkle with flour and generous pinch of all seasonings.

- Add wine and consommé. Simmer for 3¼ hours as slowly as possible.

- At end of that time, add browned onions and mushrooms which have been sliced.

- Cook about 1 hour longer; serve with cooked rice.

Beef Shish Kebobs

Marinade:
½ **cup Burgundy**
1 **clove garlic**
½ **cup salad oil**
2 **tablespoons ketchup**
1 **teaspoon sugar**
1 **teaspoon Worcestershire sauce**
½ **teaspoon salt**
½ **teaspoon monosodium glutamate**
1 **tablespoon vinegar**
½ **teaspoon marjoram**
½ **teaspoon rosemary**

- Mix marinade ingredients in a deep bowl. Add the beef cubes, pepper quarters and mushrooms overnight in refrigerator or 3 hours at room temperature, covered.

Skewer Ingredients:
1 **pound sirloin, cut into cubes**
12 **small fresh parboiled white onions**
3 **green peppers, quartered**
10-12 **fresh large mushrooms**
10-12 **fresh cherry tomatoes (optional)**

- Fill skewers, alternating meat cubes with vegetables.

- Broil over grill for about 30 minutes, rotating skewers. Brush often while turning frequently.

Yield: 4 servings.

Marinated Flank Steak

(May substitute sirloin, chuck or shoulder roast)

¾ **cup vegetable oil**
¼ **cup soy sauce**
¼ **cup honey**
2 **tablespoons vinegar**
2 **tablespoons finely chopped green onions**
1 **large clove garlic, minced**
1½ **teaspoons ginger, ground**
1½ **pounds flank steak**

- Combine oil, soy sauce, honey, vinegar, onions, garlic and ginger.

- Pour over flank steak and marinate overnight.

- Barbecue over hot coals, turning once, until done to your preference, about 5 minutes on each side for medium rare. Baste occasionally with marinade.

- Carve in thin slices, cutting on the diagonal from top to bottom of steak.

Yield: 4 servings.

Marinated Eye of the Round

1   **(5-pound) eye of the round roast**
¼   **cup salad oil**
2   **tablespoons lemon-pepper seasoning**
½   **cup wine vinegar**
½   **cup lemon juice**
½   **cup soy sauce**
½   **cup Worcestershire sauce**

- Marinate roast in mixture of remaining ingredients for 1 to 2 days, turning at least once a day.
- Cook uncovered with marinade at 250° for 3 hours; refrigerate overnight.
- Slice thin and serve with heated marinade. Can reheat the roast.

Yield: 8 to 10 servings.

Rib Eye Roast

(An easy but elegant main course, perfect for the holiday rush)

1   **(8-12) pound boneless rib eye roast or Spencer roast, room temperature**
    Freshly ground pepper
    Garlic powder

- Preheat oven to 500°. Rub generous amounts of pepper and garlic powder into roast. Set roast on rack in baking pan. Pour in enough water to come ½ inch up sides of pan.
- Roast meat 5 minutes per pound. Turn off heat; do not open oven.
- Let meat stand in oven 2 hours. Cut into slices and serve.

Yield: 12 to 20 servings.

Beef Stroganoff

(Great over rice or buttered noodles)

1½-2   **pounds sirloin tip roast (chuck will do)**
1   **tablespoon cornstarch**
1   **teaspoon salt**
¼   **teaspoon black pepper**
¼   **teaspoon garlic powder**
4   **tablespoons butter**
½   **cup chopped green onion**
2   **tablespoons powdered mushrooms or 1 cup fresh mushrooms, sliced**
1   **chicken bouillon cube in ¾ cup water**
¼   **cup dry white wine**
1   **cup sour cream**
2   **tablespoons sherry**

- Cut meat in 1-inch cubes.
- Combine cornstarch, salt, pepper and garlic powder.
- Roll meat in cornstarch mixture; brown in butter. Add onions and mushrooms; mix thoroughly. Pour in chicken seasoned stock base and white wine.
- Cover and simmer 1 hour or until meat is very tender. Stir occasionally.
- Just before serving, stir in sour cream and sherry.

Yield: 4 servings.

Marinated London Broil

2-3 pounds aged London broil
1½ cups salad oil
¾ cup soy sauce
¼ cup Worcestershire sauce
2 tablespoons dry mustard
2¼ teaspoons salt
⅓ cup fresh lemon juice
1 teaspoon freshly ground black pepper
½ cup wine vinegar
1½ teaspoons dried parsley flakes
2 crushed garlic cloves (optional)

- Combine all ingredients except meat, mixing well.

- Pour marinade over meat and marinate overnight or all day; remove from marinade.

- Cook over hot coals, grilling approximately 10 minutes per side (depending on thickness of meat and desired doneness).

- Marinade can be reused; store in a tightly covered jar in freezer indefinitely or in refrigerator for 1 week.

Yield: 4 to 6 servings.

Oven Barbecued Beef Ribs

(A Southern treat)

1½-2 pounds beef ribs

- Wipe ribs with damp paper towel. Place single layer in shallow roasting pan. Roast at 450° about 30 minutes; drain off fat.

Basting Sauce:

4 green onions, chopped
2 tablespoons butter or margarine
1 tablespoon all-purpose flour
1 tablespoon Dijon mustard
½-1 cup beef broth
2 tablespoons lemon juice
3 tablespoons chili sauce
   Dash ground black pepper

- Prepare sauce by sautéing onions in butter until tender. Blend in flour and mustard; cook about 2 minutes longer.

- Stir in beef broth, lemon juice, chili sauce and pepper. Cook 5 to 7 minutes until sauce is smooth and thick; brush sauce over ribs.

- Bake about 1 hour or until tender, basting occasionally with sauce.

Note: Delicious served with baked potato, buttered cauliflower and a lettuce and tomato salad.

Yield: 4 servings.

Marinated Tenderloin of Beef

1 cup ketchup
2 teaspoons prepared mustard
½ teaspoon Worcestershire sauce
1½ cups water
2 envelopes Italian salad dressing mix
1 (4-6 pound) beef tenderloin, trimmed

- Combine first 5 ingredients. Spear meat in 10 places and place in a large zip-top plastic bag. Pour marinade over meat and seal bag tightly. Place bag in a pan and refrigerate for at least 8 hours, turning several times.

- Drain marinade and reserve.

- Place meat on a rack in a baking pan; insert meat thermometer. Bake at 425° for 30 to 45 minutes or until thermometer registers 140° for rare, 150° for medium-rare and 160° for medium. Baste occasionally with reserved marinade.

- Remove to serving platter and serve with remaining marinade.

Yield: 12 to 16 servings.

Oriental Flank Steak

1 (1½ pound) flank steak
5 green onions, chopped
¾ cup vegetable oil
½ cup soy sauce
1½ teaspoons ginger
1½ teaspoons garlic powder
3 tablespoons honey
2 tablespoons vinegar

- Place steak in a large, shallow dish. Combine remaining ingredients, mixing well. Pour over steak; cover and marinate in refrigerator 8 hours, turning occasionally.

- Drain steak, reserving marinade. Grill over hot coals 5 to 10 minutes on each side or until desired degree of doneness, basting with marinade.

- To serve, slice steak across grain into thin slices.

Yield: 6 servings.

Pineapple-Beef Kabobs

2 (20-ounce) cans pineapple chunks, undrained
½ cup firmly packed brown sugar
⅔ cup cider vinegar
⅔ cup ketchup
¼ cup soy sauce
2 teaspoons ground ginger
1½ teaspoons liquid smoke
1 (3 pound) boneless sirloin tip roast, cut into 1½-inch cubes
½ pound fresh mushroom caps
2 small onions, quartered
2 medium-size green peppers, cut into 1-inch pieces

- Drain pineapple, reserving juice. Combine pineapple juice and next 6 ingredients, mixing well; pour into a large, shallow dish. Add meat; cover and marinate overnight in refrigerator.

- Drain meat, reserving marinade. Pour marinade in a saucepan; bring to a boil. Add mushrooms; reduce heat and simmer, uncovered, 10 minutes. Drain, reserving marinade; set mushrooms aside.

- Alternate meat, pineapple chunks, mushrooms, onion and green pepper on 8 to 10 skewers.

- Grill kabobs over medium-hot coals 10 to 15 minutes or until desired degree of doneness, basting kabobs frequently with marinade.

Yield: 8 to 10 servings.

Busy Day Beef Casserole

(A family favorite — even better after freezing)

1 pound ground beef
2 sweet peppers, chopped
1 large onion, chopped
1 clove garlic or dash garlic powder
1 (10¾-ounce) can tomato soup
1 (18¾-ounce) can tomatoes
1 (12-ounce) can tomato paste
½ small bottle ketchup
1 (2.2-ounce) can chopped, black olives, undrained
1 (4-ounce) can of sliced mushrooms, drained
½ pound sharp Cheddar cheese, grated
1 package wide egg noodles, cooked

- Brown first four ingredients. Add soup, tomatoes, paste, ketchup, olives and mushrooms. Simmer 30 minutes.

- Combine the cooked noodles with mixture. Pour into large Pyrex casserole dish (13½x8¾x1¾-inch). Cover with ½ pound grated cheese.

- Bake at 300° until cheese melts.

Yield: 12 servings.

Stir-Fry Beef and Snow Peas

1   **pound boneless sirloin steak**
1   **tablespoon soy sauce**
2   **teaspoons cornstarch**
½   **teaspoon sugar**
2   **carrots, scraped**
¼   **cup peanut or vegetable oil**
1   **(2-ounce) package cellophane noodles**
1   **(6-ounce) package Chinese pea pods, thawed and drained**
2   **tablespoons peanut or vegetable oil**
2   **slices ginger root**
1   **tablespoon peanut or vegetable oil**
1   **(10-ounce) can baby corn cobs, drained**
1   **(15-ounce) can straw mushrooms, drained**
2   **tablespoons soy sauce**
2   **tablespoons rice wine**
2   **teaspoons sugar**
1   **teaspoon cornstarch**

- Partially freeze steak; slice diagonally across grain into 2x¼-inch strips. Combine next 3 ingredients; pour over steak. Marinate 1 hour at room temperature or overnight in refrigerator.
- Cut 4 or 5 lengthwise triangular grooves ⅛-inch deep at even intervals down length of carrots. Slice carrots ⅛-inch thick; set aside.
- Pour ¼ cup oil into preheated wok; heat to 325°. Add noodles, a few at a time; fry 2 to 3 seconds or until noodles expand and turn white. Remove from wok; drain.
- Arrange around border of serving platter.

- Drain oil from wok. Add pea pods to wok; stir-fry 1 to 2 minutes. Remove from wok, and arrange around inside border of cellophane noodles. Pour 2 tablespoons oil around top of wok, coating sides. Add ginger root and steak; stir-fry 4 to 5 minutes. Remove from wok; pour 1 tablespoon oil around top of wok, coating sides.
- Add carrots, corn and mushrooms; stir-fry 2 to 3 minutes.
- Combine next 4 ingredients, mixing well; add to carrot mixture and cook until thickened, stirring constantly. Stir in steak.
- Pour steak mixture into center of platter.

Yield: 6 to 8 servings.

Reuben Brunch Casserole

(Needs to marinate overnight)

10   **slices rye bread, cubed**
1½   **pounds cooked corned beef**
2½   **cups shredded cheese**
1   **cup sautéed onions**
6   **eggs, lightly beaten**
3   **cups milk**
¼   **teaspoon pepper**

- Grease a 13x9x2-inch pan. Line pan with bread cubes. Layer with corned beef, then cheese.
- Add sautéed onions to egg, milk and pepper mixture. Pour mixture over cubes, beef and cheese.
- Refrigerate overnight. Bake covered for 45 minutes at 350°. Uncover and bake 10 more minutes.

Yield: 6 servings.

Crusty Beef, Cheese and Noodle Bake

2   tablespoons oil
1   onion, chopped
2   pounds ground beef
3   (15½-ounce) cans meatless,
     mushroom spaghetti sauce
1   teaspoon salt
1   pound fine noodles, cooked and
     drained
1   pound sharp Cheddar cheese,
     shredded
     Seasoning salt

- Heat oil; add onion and cook until golden. Add beef and brown. Add mushroom sauce and salt and heat.

- Arrange in casserole dish half of noodles, half of sauce, half of cheese. Sprinkle with seasoning salt. Make another layer of noodles, sauce and cheese.

- Bake in preheated oven at 325° for one hour. Top should be nicely browned.

  Yield: 8 to 10 servings.

Greek Meat and Cheese Moussaka

2   pounds potatoes (may substitute
       eggplant or zucchini)
2   medium onions, diced
¼   cup olive oil
1-1½   pounds lean ground beef
2-3   cloves garlic, chopped
8   ounces regular tomato sauce
1   teaspoon ground cinnamon
       Salt and pepper to taste
1   cup milk
2   eggs, beaten
⅓   cup Romano cheese, grated

- Peel potatoes or scrub well and slice with skins on. Brown in oil in skillet and drain.

- Place one layer potatoes in 7x11-inch loaf pan sprayed with non-stick spray.

- Sauté onions and beef in skillet until onions are soft and redness is gone from meat. Add garlic and tomato sauce, cinnamon, salt and pepper.

- Pour mixture over potato layer and top with remaining potatoes.

- Beat eggs and milk and pour over mixture.

- Sprinkle with cheese.

- Bake in preheated oven at 350° for 45 minutes.

  Yield: 4 servings.

Meatloaf

1   pound ground beef
¼   cup chopped onion
¼   cup chopped green pepper
1   (8-ounce) can tomato sauce;
     reserve 2 tablespoons
½   cup bread crumbs
1   egg, slightly beaten
1   teaspoon pepper
1   teaspoon garlic salt

- Preheat oven to 350°.

- Mix all ingredients together. Shape firmly into loaf.

- Bake in loaf pan for 45 minutes.

- Pour remaining tomato sauce over loaf before serving.

Ladies' "Day Out" Casserole

(A great dish to make ahead for a busy day)

1 pound ground beef, browned
2 medium onions, chopped
¼ cup butter
1½ teaspoons salt
1 (4-ounce) jar sliced pimentos, drained
½ teaspoon oregano
1 cup spaghetti sauce with mushrooms
1 (16-ounce) can tomatoes, undrained
2 cups macaroni, cooked and drained
½ pound extra sharp Cheddar cheese, shredded

- Sauté onions in butter. Add beef, salt, pimentos, oregano, spaghetti sauce and tomatoes. Simmer for 20 minutes.

- Place half of macaroni in a 2-quart or larger casserole. Cover with half of the meat sauce, then half of the cheese; repeat layers.

- Bake uncovered at 350° for 45 minutes.

- Casserole may be made the day before, cooled and refrigerated until ready to bake. May also be frozen for later baking.

Yield: 4 to 6 servings.

Stuffed Cabbage

1 large cabbage
½ pound beef
½ pound pork
½ pound fresh sausage
1 tablespoon oil
1 large onion, chopped
 Salt and pepper to taste
1-2 cups cooked rice

- Using a sharp knife, cut top ¼ of cabbage off. Take a sharp spoon and hollow out cabbage, leaving about four leaves of thickness.

- Chop raw cabbage fine.

- Season and brown meat in a small amount of oil. Add onion and wilt.

- Add ¾ of chopped cabbage to mixture and about 2 cups of water. Cook on medium heat about 1 hour, stirring occasionally.

- Cabbage in meat mixture should mash easily. Stir mixture, mashing larger pieces of cabbage; mixture should be juicy.

- Add enough cooked rice to make a rich, moist but meaty dressing.

- Lightly salt inside of cabbage shell and fill with meat-rice mixture. This can be cooked on the stove or in the oven.

- If on the stove, place stuffed cabbage in a pot a bit larger than the cabbage. Add ½ cup water, cover and steam until cabbage shell is cooked.

- If cooked in oven, put in pan with high sides, adding water; bake at 350° until cabbage is tender.

Yield: 4 servings.

Snow-Capped Meatloaf

(An elegant meatloaf covered with a mashed potato topping)

1   clove garlic, minced
1   teaspoon margarine, melted
1   pound ground round
½   pound ground pork
1   egg, beaten
2   slices rye bread, torn into small pieces
½   cup chopped onion
¼   cup chopped green pepper
¼   cup firmly packed brown sugar
¾   cup ketchup
¼   cup white vinegar
2   teaspoons Worcestershire sauce
1   teaspoon dry mustard
½   teaspoon salt
¼   teaspoon pepper
¼   cup ketchup
    Mashed Potato Topping
½   cup (2 ounces) shredded Cheddar cheese
    Ground nutmeg
    Chopped fresh parsley

- Sauté garlic in margarine; combine with next 13 ingredients. Stir until blended.

- Shape into a 9x5-inch oval loaf and place on a lightly greased rack in a broiler pan. Spoon ¼ cup ketchup on top, cover with foil and bake for 1 hour at 350°. Uncover and bake an additional 15 minutes. Place meatloaf on an ovenproof platter.

- Spread Mashed Potato Topping over entire meat loaf. Can pipe remaining topping around base of meat loaf.

- Bake at 375° for 10 minutes. Sprinkle with cheese and nutmeg and bake an additional 5 minutes. Garnish with chopped parsley.

Mashed Potato Topping:

4   large potatoes, peeled and cubed
½   cup sour cream
¼   cup margarine
1   tablespoon grated onion
    Salt and pepper to taste
    Milk

- Cook potatoes in water to cover until tender; drain well and mash.

- Combine potatoes and next 4 ingredients; stir in enough milk to make potato mixture the right consistency.

Yield: 6 servings.

Working Man's Meat Loaf

1½   pounds ground beef
1   (8-ounce) can tomato sauce, divided
1   cup soft bread crumbs (2 slices of bread chopped in processor)
2   eggs, beaten
1   medium onion, chopped
¾   teaspoon salt
¼   teaspoon pepper
2   teaspoons dried parsley
1   teaspoon Worcestershire sauce

- Combine ground beef, ½ can tomato sauce, and next five ingredients. Mix well.

- Shape into loaf; place on rack of lightly greased broiler pan.

- Bake 1 hour at 350°. Combine remaining tomato sauce with parsley and Worcestershire. Stir well and pour over meat loaf and bake an additional 5 minutes.

Yield: 6 servings.

Osso Buco

Flour
Salt and pepper to taste
6   veal shanks
½   cup olive oil
½   cup sweet butter
2   medium onions, coarsely chopped
6   large garlic cloves, chopped
½   teaspoon basil
½   teaspoon oregano
1   (28-ounce) can tomatoes, drained
2   cups white wine
2   cups beef stock

- Season flour and dredge veal.

- Heat oil and butter in a large oven casserole. Sear veal, brown well and drain on paper towels. Add onion, garlic, basil and oregano to casserole; cook and stir for 10 minutes. Add tomatoes, salt and pepper and cook for 10 minutes. Add wine, bring to a boil and simmer uncovered for 15 minutes.

- Return veal to casserole; add stock to cover. Cover casserole and bake at 350° for 1½ hours. Remove cover; bake ½ hour longer.

Yield: 6 servings.

Valentine Veal

3   tablespoons olive oil
1½   pounds veal scallops, pounded very thin
1   cup heavy cream
⅛   teaspoon hot pepper sauce
2   tablespoons dry sherry
2   teaspoons dried dillweed
¼   teaspoon Worcestershire sauce
1   tablespoon cognac
3   tablespoons butter

- Heat oil and butter in 10-inch skillet. Add veal scallops and sauté on each side until they are lightly browned. Remove veal to a pan and keep warm in oven on very low heat.

- Add cream and dill to skillet; cook over high heat, scraping bottom of pan to loosen drippings until the cream has reduced to the consistency of thick sauce.

- Stir in last four ingredients. Cook until it bubbles.

- Return veal to sauce and serve immediately.

Yield: 6 servings.

Upside Down Pizza

2   pounds ground chuck
1   cup chopped onion
2   (8-ounce) cans tomato sauce
1   (1¼-ounce) package spaghetti sauce mix
1   (8-ounce) carton plain yogurt
2   cups shredded mozzarella cheese
1   (8-ounce) package refrigerated crescent rolls

- Cook beef and onions until meat is brown, stirring until meat crumbles; drain well.

- Stir in tomato sauce and spaghetti sauce mix; cook over low heat 10 minutes, stirring frequently. Spoon into a lightly greased 13x9x2-inch baking dish; top with plain yogurt and sprinkle with cheese.

- Unroll crescent rolls and place on top of cheese; bake, uncovered at 350° for 20 minutes.

Yield: 8 servings.

Veal Paillards with Mustard Sauce and Roasted Potatoes

(Worth the effort to prepare for rave reviews!)

4   **large mustard green leaves or spinach leaves**
2   **(4-ounce) veal cutlets, ¼-inch thick and trimmed**
    Freshly ground white pepper
3-4 **thin slices prosciutto or thin slices boiled ham**
4   **bacon slices**
4   **small red potatoes, halved and unpeeled**
1   **tablespoon olive oil**
    Salt and pepper to taste
    Mustard Sauce

- Bring small saucepan of water to boil.
- Using tongs, dip 1 leaf of greens or spinach in water until just wilted. Set on plate. Repeat with remaining leaves.
- Flatten cutlets to ⅛-inch. Season both sides with pepper.
- Cut stems off mustard leaves.
- Arrange 2 mustard leaves atop each veal cutlet, covering completely.
- Top each with 1 or 2 slices or prosciutto, covering completely. Trim edges to even if necessary.
- Start at one short end, roll veal up jelly roll style.
- Wrap in bacon, covering ends. Tie with string.
- Preheat oven to 400°. Toss potatoes in oil. Season with salt and pepper.

- Arrange potatoes cut side down on heavy, large baking sheet. Bake 10 minutes. Move potatoes away from center of sheet. Turn potatoes over.
- Place veal in center of baking sheet and roast until meat thermometer inserted in center registers 130° for medium and potatoes are golden brown (about 17 minutes).
- Turn veal over; remove string and bacon.
- Coarsely chop 2 pieces of bacon; toss with potatoes.
- Cut veal into thin slices.
- Spoon warm Mustard Sauce onto plates; fan veal atop sauce.
- Spoon potatoes onto sides of plates or thread onto decorative skewers.
- Garnish with fresh mustard leaves.
- When sliced, the rolls reveal a spiral of veal, mustard green and ham; the colors are very appealing.
- Veal rolls can be prepared 1 day ahead and stored in ziplock bag in refrigerator.

Mustard Sauce: *(may be prepared 1 day ahead; store in refrigerator, covered)*

1   **tablespoon unsalted butter**
1   **shallot, minced**
1   **teaspoon dry mustard**
½   **teaspoon ground coriander**
10 **whole black peppercorns**
1   **cup unsalted veal or chicken stock (degreased chicken stock works well)**
¼   **cup unsalted butter, softened**
1   **tablespoon coarse-grained mustard**

- Melt 1 tablespoon butter in heavy, small skillet over medium heat.
- Add shallot, dry mustard, coriander and peppercorns and stir 2 minutes.

- Add stock and boil until reduced to 3 tablespoons, stirring occasionally, about 20 minutes. Strain through sieve. Set over small saucepan, pressing with back of spoon.
- Bring sauce to simmer over low heat. Gradually whisk in ¼ cup butter then mustard; **do not boil**.

Yield: 2 servings.

Chinese Barbecued Spareribs

3   **racks small spareribs**
1   **tablespoon monosodium glutamate**
4   **tablespoons ketchup**
4   **tablespoons soy sauce**
4   **cloves garlic, crushed**
4   **tablespoons hoisin sauce (optional)**
4   **tablespoons dry sherry**
1   **teaspoon powdered ginger**
2   **tablespoons honey**

- Cut spareribs into individual ribs and arrange on rack in baking pan. Sprinkle with monosodium glutamate and bake at 300° for 45 minutes.
- Combine remaining ingredients and brush the ribs with the mixture. Bake 30 minutes longer and turn ribs; brush with sauce. Bake another 30 minutes or until ribs are browned and crisp, brushing again until all sauce has been used.
- Ribs may be kept warm in oven turned to its lowest heat.
- Remove ribs to paper towels to dry and crisp; the towels may remain underneath while ribs wait in the warm oven.

Yield: 8 servings.

Veal Topped with Crabmeat

(An elegant and tasty dish)

3   **tablespoons all-purpose flour**
½   **teaspoon salt**
¼   **teaspoon pepper**
1½   **pounds boneless veal cutlets, ¼-inch thick**
⅓   **cup margarine**
¼   **cup lemon juice**
¾   **pound fresh crabmeat**
1   **tablespoon fresh parsley, chopped**
    Hollandaise sauce
    Paprika

- Combine flour, salt and pepper; dredge veal in flour mixture.
- Melt butter in a large skillet over medium heat; add veal, cooking until lightly browned on both sides.
- Add lemon juice to skillet and cook for 30 more seconds.
- Remove veal to a serving platter.
- Discard all but 1 tablespoon of pan drippings; add crabmeat to drippings in skillet and sprinkle with parsley; sauté until heated.
- Spoon crabmeat evenly over veal cutlets. Top with a hollandaise sauce and sprinkle with paprika.

Yield: 6 servings.

Ham and Potato Casserole

(Quick and easy!)

3   **medium potatoes, peeled and sliced**
¾   **cup cubed ham**
½   **cup chopped onion**
½   **cup chopped green pepper, cut in strips**
1   **can cream of celery soup, undiluted**
1½ **teaspoons salt (optional)**
    Pepper to taste
½   **cup shredded farmer's cheese**

- In 2-quart casserole sprayed with non-stick coating, layer half the potatoes, ham, onions and green pepper. Repeat layers.
- Pour on soup, add salt and pepper and sprinkle with cheese.
- Cover and bake in 350° oven 1 to 1½ hours or until potatoes are done. Uncover last few minutes.

Marinated Pork Roast with Sherried Sauce

2   **tablespoons dry mustard**
2   **teaspoons whole thyme leaves**
½   **cup dry sherry**
½   **cup soy sauce**
2   **cloves garlic, minced**
1   **teaspoon ground ginger**
1   **(4-5 pound) pork loin roast, boned, rolled and tied**
1   **(10-ounce) jar apricot preserves or jelly**
1   **tablespoon soy sauce**
2   **tablespoons dry sherry**

- Combine first 6 ingredients in a shallow dish, stirring well; place pork roast in dish then cover and marinate 3 to 4 hours in refrigerator, turning occasionally. Remove roast from marinade and place on a rack in a shallow roasting pan.
- Insert meat thermometer at an angle into the thickest part of the roast. Bake, uncovered, at 325° until thermometer registers 170°, about 2½ to 3 hours.
- Combine preserves, 1 tablespoon soy sauce and 2 tablespoons sherry in a small saucepan; cook over low heat, stirring occasionally, until preserves are melted.
- Serve sauce with sliced roast.

Yield: 12 to 14 servings.

Marinade for Pork Tenderloin

1   **tablespoon prepared hot mustard**
3   **tablespoons sherry**
2   **tablespoons soy sauce**
½   **clove garlic, crushed**
¼   **teaspoon salt**
2   **teaspoons brown sugar**
½   **teaspoon ground ginger**
1   **teaspoon oil**
1   **tablespoon liquid smoke**
1   **teaspoon lemon pepper**
1   **pork tenderloin**

- Mix all ingredients except tenderloin together, stirring well.
- Marinate one fresh pork tenderloin overnight.
- Bake uncovered at 325° for about 2 hours; baste often while cooking.

Ham Soufflé

12 slices thin sandwich bread, crust removed
  Butter
 2 (10-ounce) packages chopped broccoli, cooked and drained
1½ pounds shaved ham
 3 (4-ounce) packages shredded sharp Cheddar cheese
  Custard Sauce

- Butter one side of each slice of bread.
- Cut bread into triangles and lay half of the buttered slices, buttered side down, in an ungreased flat casserole.
- Over the bread, layer broccoli, shaved ham, cheese and remaining triangle bread slices, buttered side up. Pour custard sauce over bread slices.
- Baked uncovered at 325° for 55 minutes.

Custard Sauce:
 6 eggs, beaten
3½ cups milk
 2 teaspoons minced onion
½ teaspoon salt
¼ teaspoon dry mustard

- Mix eggs, milk, onion, salt and mustard.
- Refrigerate, covered, overnight.

Yield: 6 to 8 servings.

Orange Pork Chops

 4 (1-inch thick) pork chops
  Salt and pepper
  Paprika
 2 tablespoons vegetable oil
⅓ cup water
½ cup sugar
½ teaspoon cornstarch
½ teaspoon ground cinnamon
 1 tablespoon plus 1 teaspoon grated orange rind
 1 cup orange juice
 1 teaspoon whole cloves
  Hot cooked rice

- Sprinkle pork chops with salt, pepper and paprika. Heat oil in a skillet over medium heat and brown pork chops on both sides; add water to skillet. Cover, reduce heat and simmer 45 minutes or until pork chops are tender, turning once.
- Combine sugar, cornstarch and cinnamon in a medium saucepan; stir in orange rind, orange juice and cloves. Cook over medium heat, stirring constantly until mixture is thickened and bubbly.
- Serve pork chops over rice with sauce spooned on top.

Yield: 4 servings.

Quick Sweet and Sour Pork

(Also good with chicken or shrimp)

2 tablespoons oil
2 cups pork, cubed
1 (15¼-ounce) can pineapple chunks, undrained
½ cup dark corn syrup
2 tablespoons ketchup
2 tablespoons soy sauce
1 clove garlic, minced
2 tablespoons cornstarch
2 tablespoons water
½ cup green pepper chunks

- Brown pork in oil. Add ingredients except cornstarch, water and green pepper. Bring to a boil. Reduce heat and simmer 10 minutes.
- Mix cornstarch with water, add to pork with green pepper.
- Boil about two minutes, stirring constantly.
- Serve over rice.

  Yield: 4 servings.

Southern Crockpot Pork Barbecue

(Freezes well; great to have on hand for company)

1 (5-7 pound) fresh pork shoulder
1 tablespoon salt
2 tablespoons sugar
  Pepper to taste
1¼ cups vinegar
½ cup ketchup
½ cup hickory smoked barbecue sauce
1½ tablespoons crushed red pepper
⅛ teaspoon hot sauce

- Trim skin and fat from shoulder; put shoulder in the crockpot. Sprinkle salt, sugar and pepper over shoulder; add vinegar and cover.
- Start cooking at 8 p.m. and cook all night on low heat. Next morning, remove the shoulder from crockpot and remove all the bones; mince meat with a fork.
- Strain the liquid, reserving approximately 2 cups. Add ketchup, barbecue sauce, red pepper and hot sauce. Mix with minced meat and return to crockpot. Cook on low until juice has cooked down to desired moisture.
- Serve on sandwich buns with coleslaw.

  Note: Can be cooked on high for a shorter cooking time.

  Yield: 6 to 8 servings.

Lamb and Beans the French Way

(This will convert even those who normally don't like lamb)

1   **pound dried Great Northern beans**
3   **cloves garlic**
¼   **cup butter or margarine**
2   **pounds onions, thinly sliced**
1   **teaspoon dried rosemary leaves, divided**
1   **teaspoon dried thyme leaves, divided**
3   **teaspoons salt, divided**
¼   **teaspoon pepper**
2   **(1-pound) cans Italian plum tomatoes, drained**
1   **(7-pound) leg of lamb**
    Chopped parsley

- Wash beans and drain. In a large pot combine beans and water, bring to a boil, reduce heat and simmer 2 minutes. Cover; remove from heat and let stand 1 hour. Drain beans, reserving liquid. Measure liquid and add water to make two quarts.

- Return the beans and their liquid to pot; bring to boiling. Reduce heat; simmer gently, covered, 1 hour, or just until beans are tender but not mushy. Drain the beans in colander. Preheat oven to 325°. Peel 1 clove of the garlic, and crush in garlic press.

- In hot butter in large skillet, sauté sliced onion and crushed garlic until golden, about 10 minutes. In shallow roasting pan, combine cooked beans, onion mixture, ½ teaspoon rosemary, ½ teaspoon thyme, 2 teaspoons salt, pepper and tomatoes; mix well.

- Wipe lamb with damp paper towels; trim off most of fat. Using a paring knife make 6 small slits in the flesh. Peel two cloves of garlic; cut into slivers; insert slivers of garlic in each slit in surface. Sprinkle lamb with the remaining rosemary, thyme and salt.

- Place lamb on top of beans; insert meat thermometer into meaty part of leg—be sure not to rest against bone. Roast, uncovered, 3 to 3½ hours, or to 175° on meat thermometer, for well done. Roast 20 minutes less for medium well or pink.

- To serve: Remove lamb to heated platter or carving board. Let stand about 20 minutes before carving, for easier slicing. With a carving knife, cut long, thin, flat slices from leg. Spoon beans around lamb; sprinkle with parsley.

Yield: 10 servings.

Lamb Chops with Mint Sauce

8   **sprigs fresh mint**
¼   **teaspoon rosemary**
1   **clove garlic, minced**
4   **tablespoons white wine**
1   **tablespoon water**
6   **tablespoons sugar**
6   **tablespoons cider vinegar**
    Salt and pepper to taste
8   **(1-inch) thick lamb chops**

- Strip leaves from mint sprigs; finely chop.

- Combine mint with the next 6 ingredients, blending well. Allow mint sauce to stand for 1 hour.

- Salt and pepper the lamb chops. Pour mint sauce over the chops, turning to coat each side. Marinate for 1 hour, turning once.

- Grill lamb chops over hot coals, 9 minutes per side. Baste often with remaining sauce.

Yield: 4 to 6 servings.

Peppercorn Crusted Roast Lamb

3   tablespoons crushed dried peppercorns, equal parts of white, black and green, divided
1   tablespoon fresh rosemary leaves, or 1½ teaspoons dried
½   cup fresh mint leaves
8   garlic cloves, crushed
½   cup raspberry vinegar
¼   cup soy sauce
½   cup dry red wine
1   boned and untied leg of lamb, about 5 pounds (after boning)
2   tablespoons prepared Dijon-style mustard

- Combine 1 tablespoon of crushed peppercorns, the rosemary, mint, garlic, vinegar, soy sauce and red wine in a shallow bowl. Marinate lamb in the mixture for eight hours, turning occasionally.
- Remove roast from marinade and drain; reserve marinade. Roll the roast, tying it with kitchen twine.
- Preheat oven to 350°.
- Spread mustard over meat and pat 2 tablespoons of crushed peppercorns into the mustard. Set roast in a shallow pan just large enough to hold it comfortably and pour reserved marinade carefully AROUND but not over roast.
- Bake 1½ hours or 18 minutes per pound, basting occasionally. Roast will be medium rare. Bake another 10 to 15 minutes for well-done meat. Let roast stand 20 minutes before carving. Serve pan juices along with lamb.

Yield: 6 to 8 servings.

Roasted Leg of Lamb

(Great for that "special" occasion)

1   (5-pound) leg of lamb
6   cloves fresh garlic
    Salt and pepper to taste

- Preheat oven to 450°.
- Remove fell or outer covering from lamb.
- Insert slivers of garlic into as much of the leg as can be penetrated.
- Salt and pepper lamb and place in uncovered pan.
- Reduce heat to 350° and bake 1 hour.

Yield: 10 to 12 servings.

Buttermilk Fried Chicken

1   fryer, cut up
2   tablespoons lemon juice
2   teaspoons Worcestershire sauce
1   teaspoon paprika
2   cups buttermilk
2   cloves garlic, crushed
1½   teaspoons celery seed
1   teaspoon salt
1   teaspoon pepper
1   cup all-purpose flour
      Oil for frying

- Place chicken pieces in a baking dish, one layer deep.
- Combine next 8 ingredients and pour over chicken pieces; cover and refrigerate overnight.
- Drain chicken and roll in flour.
- Pour 1 inch of oil in skillet and heat. Add chicken and fry until golden brown.

Apricot Chicken

1 (8-ounce) bottle Russian dressing
1 envelope dry onion soup mix
1 cup apricot preserves
8 chicken breast halves, boned

- Mix first three ingredients and set aside.

- Grease a 3-quart Pyrex casserole dish. Place chicken breasts in dish. Pour dressing mixture over the chicken and marinate for six hours, turning once or twice.

- Cook at 350° for one hour, covered. Uncover and cook an additional 30 minutes.

- Serve with rice casserole and salad.

  Yield: 8 servings.

Cheesy Chicken

4 whole chicken breasts, boned and split
1 (10¾-ounce) can cream of chicken soup
1 cup shredded sharp Cheddar cheese
1 (8-ounce) jar sliced mushrooms, drained
  Salt and pepper to taste
  Flour
4 tablespoons butter

- Salt and pepper the chicken breasts and roll in flour.

- Brown chicken breasts in butter; remove from pan and place in a casserole dish.

- Mix soup, mushrooms and cheese in pan that chicken was browned in and stir until smooth. Pour sauce over chicken.

- Bake at 300° for 1 hour.

  Yield: 8 servings.

Breast of Chicken with Spinach

2 whole chicken breasts, split
1 (10-ounce) package frozen spinach, chopped and thawed
1 (10-ounce) can chicken stock
1 cup cream sauce
¼ cup shredded Cheddar cheese
  Salt to taste
  White pepper to taste

Cream Sauce:

2 tablespoons flour
2 tablespoons butter, melted
1 cup milk or ½ cup milk and ½ cup chicken stock
  Salt and pepper to taste

- Cook chicken breasts and cut into 1-inch square pieces. Cook spinach in chicken stock about 3½ minutes; drain well.

- Make cream sauce and mix half of cream sauce with cooked spinach. Season with salt and pepper.

- Place spinach in bottom of individual heatproof dishes and put chicken on top. Season with salt and pepper.

- Melt cheese and add to other ½ cup of sauce. Pour on top of spinach.

- Bake at 375° for 10 minutes or until bubbling.

  Yield: 4 servings.

Chicken and Biscuits

1 **(3-4) pound chicken**
2 **cups chicken broth**
1 **(10¾-ounce) can cream of celery soup**
2 **cups buttermilk**
1½ **cups self-rising flour**
6 **tablespoons margarine or butter, melted**

- Cover chicken with water in large pot and cook until tender. Bone and cut into large bite-size pieces; set aside.
- Mix broth and soup in saucepan and heat to boiling point, stirring constantly.
- Place chicken in a 9x13-inch Pyrex dish. Pour broth-soup mixture over chicken. Mix buttermilk, flour and margarine; pour over chicken-broth mixture.
- Bake at 350° for 40 minutes or until crust seems done and brown.

Yield: 8 to 10 servings.

Chicken and Artichoke Casserole

4 **tablespoons margarine**
8 **boneless chicken breast halves, skinned**
  Salt, pepper and chives to taste
1 **(15-ounce) can artichoke hearts, quartered and drained**
1 **(8-ounce) can sliced water chestnuts, drained**
8 **ounces fresh mushrooms, sliced**
1 **(10¾-ounce) can cream of chicken soup**
1 **(8-ounce) package sour cream**
4 **ounces dry white wine**

- Sprinkle chicken breasts with salt, pepper and chives. Brown them in 2 tablespoons margarine. Remove and place in 9x13-inch Pyrex dish.
- Cover with quartered artichoke hearts. Spread water chestnuts on top. Put remaining 2 tablespoons of margarine in pan and sauté mushrooms. Spread them on top.
- In the frying pan, pour the can of chicken soup, sour cream and wine. Stir well and pour over top of casserole. Sprinkle with paprika (optional).
- Bake at 350° for 1 hour.
- Serve over rice.

Yield: 8 servings.

Chicken Breasts with Apricot Glaze

2 **whole chicken breasts, halved**
1 **(20-ounce) can apricot halves, reserving juice**
3 **tablespoons margarine**
1 **tablespoon grated onion**
1 **tablespoon soy sauce**
2 **tablespoons chopped parsley for garnish**

- Place chicken in close fitting baking dish.
- In a small saucepan, melt the margarine and add ½ cup of syrup from the apricots, onions and soy sauce. Heat to boiling and pour over the chicken.
- Bake at 350° for 1 hour, basting often. Place the drained apricot halves around the chicken for the last 10 minutes.
- Serve with rice and sprinkle with parsley if desired.

Yield: 4 servings.

Chicken and Broccoli Delight

2 (10-ounce) packages frozen broccoli, drained
6 chicken breast halves, cooked and cut into bite-size pieces
2 (10¾-ounce) cans cream of mushroom soup
½ cup milk
1 teaspoon lemon juice
¾ cup mayonnaise
½ teaspoon curry powder
1 cup shredded sharp Cheddar cheese
½ cup bread crumbs
½ cup herbed stuffing mix
2 tablespoons margarine, melted

- Preheat oven to 350°.
- Arrange broccoli in lightly greased 12x8-inch baking dish. Spread chicken on top.
- Combine soup, milk, lemon juice, mayonnaise, curry powder and cheese, mixing until smooth and well blended. Pour over chicken.
- Mix bread crumbs, stuffing mix and margarine. Sprinkle on top of casserole.
- Bake for 40 minutes.

Yield: 10 servings.

Chicken and Wild Rice Casserole

(Easy to prepare and very tasty)

1 (6-ounce) box wild rice with herbs
4 cups cooked chicken or turkey, diced
1 (10¾-ounce) can cream of celery soup
1 medium onion, minced
1 (2-ounce) jar pimento, drained
2 (8-ounce) cans sliced water chestnuts, drained
2 (16-ounce) cans French-cut green beans, drained
2 cups mayonnaise
  Parmesan cheese
  Paprika

- Preheat oven to 350°.
- Cook rice according to package directions; combine with remaining ingredients except Parmesan cheese and paprika.
- Pour into a greased 3-quart casserole; sprinkle with the cheese and paprika.
- Bake for 45 minutes and serve.
- Can be prepared one day ahead and refrigerated until ready to bake.

Yield: 12 servings.

Add a teaspoon of vinegar to the water when cooking rice to make it fluffier.

Chicken Breasts and Rice Casserole

1¼ cups long grain rice
1   medium green pepper, finely chopped
1   (4-ounce) jar chopped pimento, drained
1   (8-ounce) can sliced water chestnuts, drained
1   tablespoon Worcestershire sauce
¼   cup sherry
2   (10¾-ounce) cans cream of mushroom soup
1   (6-ounce) can sliced mushrooms, drained
3   cups of chicken stock made from chicken bouillon cubes
6   chicken breast halves

- Preheat oven to 350°.
- Mix all ingredients together in large bowl except chicken. Pour mixture into Pyrex dish which has been sprayed with nonstick vegetable spray. Place chicken breasts over this mixture.
- Bake for 1 hour and 20 minutes.
- Add more stock if needed while baking.

Yield: 6 servings.

Chicken Breasts in Sherry and Sour Cream

(An elegant and easy dish for company)

4   whole chicken breasts, skinned, boned and halved
1   (3-ounce) can sliced mushrooms, drained
1   (10¾-ounce) can cream of mushroom soup
½   soup can sherry wine
1   cup sour cream
     Salt and pepper to taste
     Paprika

- Place chicken breasts in flat baking dish, approximately 7x11 inches. Cover with mushrooms.
- Combine soup, sherry and sour cream. Add salt and pepper, if desired. Pour over chicken breasts and dust with paprika.
- Bake uncovered at 350° for 1 hour and 30 minutes (325° for glass dish).

Note: May be served over spinach fettuccine with sauce portions doubled.

Yield: 8 servings.

Chicken Cacciatore

6   chicken breast halves, boned
¼   cup olive oil
2   medium onions, cut into ¼-inch slices
1½ teaspoons minced garlic
1   (16-ounce) can whole tomatoes
1   (15-ounce) can tomato herb sauce
1   teaspoon salt
1   teaspoon dried basil
½   teaspoon celery seeds
¼   teaspoon pepper
1-2 bay leaves
¼   cup Sauterne wine
     Hot cooked spaghetti or rice
     Parmesan cheese, grated

- In large skillet, brown chicken in olive oil. Remove chicken and set aside. Add onion and garlic to pan drippings, sauté until tender.

- Combine next seven ingredients in a bowl; stir well. Return chicken to pan and add sauce. Cover and simmer 30 to 40 minutes; stir in wine. Cook uncovered 15 to 20 minutes over very low heat, or until chicken is tender; turn chicken occasionally and skim off excess fat.

- Serve over spaghetti or rice sprinkled with Parmesan cheese.

Yield: 6 servings.

Chicken Cutlets Topped with Swiss Cheese

6   thin, boned chicken breast fillets
2   eggs, beaten with a dash of salt
1   cup fine dry bread crumbs
½   cup vegetable oil, divided
3   tablespoons butter
¼   cup all-purpose flour
½   teaspoon salt
¼   teaspoon pepper
2½ cups milk
½   cup dry white wine
1   cup shredded Swiss cheese

- Dip chicken fillets in the beaten eggs, then in the bread crumbs.

- Heat 2 teaspoons oil in skillet. Brown coated fillets in heated oil for 2 minutes on each side, adding remaining oil to skillet as needed. Set the chicken aside.

- Melt the butter in a saucepan. Add flour, salt, pepper and milk, stirring with a wire whisk. Cook over medium heat until thickened; remove from heat and stir in wine.

- Pour half of the sauce into a 9x12-inch glass baking dish. Arrange the chicken in the sauce and cover with the remaining sauce; cover and refrigerate overnight.

- The next day, bake, covered, in a 350° oven for 50 minutes. Remove from oven; sprinkle cheese over all and return to oven for 2 minutes.

Yield: 4 to 6 servings.

Chicken Sauce Piquant

3-4 **pounds chicken, cut up**
    Cooking oil
  2 **small onions, chopped**
 ½ **green pepper, chopped**
  2 **cloves garlic, chopped**
  2 **celery ribs, chopped**
  1 **(12-ounce) can tomato paste**
  1 **(6-ounce) can mushrooms, drained**
    Salt, pepper and cayenne to taste
 ½ **cup white wine**
    Hot cooked rice

- Brown pieces of chicken in oil. Remove the chicken from the pot.
- Add onion, pepper, garlic and celery to oil and cook until transparent. Add other ingredients and chicken.
- Add seasonings and cook over medium heat until tender, approximately 45 to 60 minutes.
- Serve over rice.

Yield: 6 servings.

Chicken Diablo

  3 **cups fresh mushrooms, finely chopped**
 ½ **teaspoon salt**
 ¼ **teaspoon pepper**
 ¾ **cup margarine, divided**
1½ **cups fresh bread crumbs (3 slices), divided**
 ¼ **teaspoon nutmeg**
  4 **large chicken breast halves, skinned and boned**
  1 **cup heavy cream**

- In a large skillet, sauté mushrooms, salt and pepper with ½ cup margarine until all margarine is absorbed and mushrooms are very dark. Remove from heat; stir in ¾ cup crumbs and nutmeg.
- Place each breast in a plastic bag and pound with a meat mallet until each is between ¼- and ⅛-inch thick. Divide stuffing evenly, placing a portion on each breast.
- Roll chicken with stuffing in center, place in 8-inch square baking dish seamside down. Melt remaining ¼ cup margarine; brush on chicken and sprinkle with remaining crumbs. Pour cream around chicken.
- Bake in oven at 350° for 30 to 40 minutes or until tender.

Yield: 4 servings.

Chicken Jambalaya

  3 **cups cooked chicken, diced**
  1 **(14½-ounce) can stewed tomatoes, undrained**
1½ **cups cooked rice**
  1 **onion, chopped**
  1 **bell pepper, chopped**
  3 **ribs celery, chopped**
  1 **cup buttered bread crumbs**
 ¼ **cup Parmesan cheese**

- Preheat oven to 325°.
- Heat chicken, tomatoes and rice in Dutch oven. Add vegetables and heat through.
- Place in a buttered 2-quart baking dish. Cover with buttered bread crumbs mixed with Parmesan cheese.
- Bake for 30 minutes.

Yield: 6 servings.

Chicken Nuggets with Spicy Mustard Sauce

½ **cup fine dry bread crumbs**
¼ **cup grated Parmesan cheese**
¼ **teaspoon salt**
½ **teaspoon diced whole basil**
½ **teaspoon dried whole thyme**
4 **chicken breast halves, skinned and boned**
¼ **cup butter or margarine, melted**

- Combine first 5 ingredients in a plastic bag; shake well.
- Cut chicken into 1-inch pieces. Dip chicken pieces in butter, and shake a few at a time in bread crumb mixture. Place on a lightly greased baking sheet.
- Bake at 400° for 20 minutes or until tender.

Spicy Mustard Sauce:
1 **(12-ounce) jar apple jelly**
¼ **cup spicy Dijon mustard**
¼ **cup horseradish**
2 **teaspoons cracked pepper**

- Mix all mustard sauce ingredients together well.
- Store indefinitely in jar in refrigerator.
  Yield: 4 servings.

Chicken Dijonnaise

1 **(2½-3 pound) chicken, quartered**
⅓ **cup mustard (½ Dijon and ½ coarse Pommery; or any combination of flavored mustards) Fresh ground pepper to taste**
⅓ **cup very dry white wine**
½ **cup crème fraîche or heavy cream Salt to taste**

- Coat chicken with mustard; set in bowl, covered to marinate at room temperature for 2 hours.
- Preheat oven to 350°.
- Arrange chicken, skin side up in baking dish. Scrape out any remaining mustard and spread evenly over chicken. Season lightly with pepper and pour wine around chicken.
- Place dish in center of oven and bake, basting occasionally for 30 to 40 minutes or until chicken is tender.
- Scrape mustard off chicken and back into baking dish; transfer chicken to serving platter and cover, keeping warm. Skim off as much fat as possible from baking juices; pour in saucepan. Bringing to a boil, whisk in crème fraîche and lower heat; simmer sauce 5 to 10 minutes or until reduced by about one third.
- Season lightly with salt and pepper; taste and correct seasonings. Spoon sauce over chicken.
  Yield: 4 servings.

Crème Fraîche
1 **cup heavy cream**
1 **cup sour cream**

- Whisk heavy cream and sour cream together in bowl.
- Cover loosely with plastic wrap and let stand in kitchen overnight or until thickened (in cold weather this may take 24 hours).
- Cover and refrigerate for at least 4 hours; Crème Fraîche will be quite thick. The tart flavor will continue to develop as sauce sits in refrigerator.

Chicken Russo

4   chicken breast halves, boned
¾   cup flour
½   teaspoon garlic powder
⅓   teaspoon celery salt
    Dash of pepper
    Dash of Accent
½   cup vegetable oil
1   cup sliced mushrooms
1   large onion, diced
    Dash of pepper
2   garlic cloves, sliced
½   teaspoon marjoram or basil
⅓   cup green olives, cut up
1   tablespoon all-purpose flour
½   cup dry white wine
⅓   cup water

- Blend together the flour, garlic powder, celery salt, pepper and Accent. Dip each chicken breast in flour mixture.
- Sauté floured chicken in a large open skillet in oil until brown on both sides. Cover and cook for another 20 to 25 minutes.
- Add mushrooms, onion, pepper, garlic cloves, marjoram or basil and olives. Cover and allow to simmer for 30 minutes.
- Remove chicken to a platter and keep warm. Reserve pan drippings in pan.
- Mix together 1 tablespoon flour, wine and water in a covered jar; shake until well-mixed.
- Add mixture to pan drippings and cook slowly. When smooth and somewhat thickened, pour the gravy over the chicken on the platter.
- Serve with buttered-parsleyed noodles, peas and tiny onions and cold sliced beets with a French dressing.

Yield: 4 servings.

Chicken Scaloppine with Lemon Sauce

6   chicken breast halves, skinned and boned
1   cup all-purpose flour
¼   teaspoon pepper
2   eggs, beaten
¼   cup butter or margarine
¼   cup vegetable oil
¾   pound fresh mushrooms, thinly sliced
    Wine
    Lemon juice
    Parsley, minced

- Place each chicken piece between 2 sheets of waxed paper; flatten to ¼-inch thickness, using a meat mallet or a rolling pin.
- Combine flour and pepper, stir well. Dredge chicken in eggs and then in flour mixture, shaking off excess flour mixture; set aside.
- Heat butter and oil in heavy skillet. Cook chicken over medium heat about 4 minutes on each side or until golden brown.
- Remove chicken to serving platter; keep warm over medium heat, stirring often, about 3 minutes. Add mushrooms to skillet and sauté. Spoon mushrooms over chicken.
- Add wine and lemon juice to skillet; heat thoroughly. Pour sauce over chicken; sprinkle with parsley.

Yield: 6 servings.

Lemon Herbed Chicken

4	chicken quarters
⅓	cup olive oil
4	tablespoons melted butter
¼	cup lemon juice
1	tablespoons dried oregano
1	teaspoon parsley
	Salt, pepper and paprika to taste

- Wash and pat dry chicken quarters; place in baking dish.

- Mix remaining ingredients and pour over chicken; marinate overnight or at least 8 hours. Sprinkle with salt, pepper and paprika.

- Bake at 350° for 1¼ to 1½ hours, depending on size of chicken.

Yield: 4 servings.

Chicken Tetrazzini

(Takes a little time to prepare but can be made ahead and freezes great)

3	tablespoons butter, divided
1	cup chopped onion
½	cup diced green pepper
1	clove garlic, minced
¼	cup flour
8	ounces fresh mushrooms, sliced
1	cup chicken broth
1	cup milk
1	teaspoon salt
⅛	teaspoon pepper
1½	cups shredded Cheddar cheese, divided
2	cups cooked and cubed chicken
2	tablespoons sherry
8	ounces spaghetti, cooked

- Preheat oven to 350°. In medium saucepan, melt 1 tablespoon butter. Add onion, green pepper and garlic; sauté until onion is translucent, stirring occasionally. Add mushrooms and sauté 1 minute; remove vegetables and set aside.

- Add remaining butter to saucepan and melt over low heat. Stir in flour until smooth and bubbly. Add broth, milk, salt and pepper, stirring constantly. Cook until thickened; add 1 cup cheese, stirring until melted.

- In large bowl, combine vegetables, chicken, white sauce, sherry and spaghetti. Spoon into greased 2-quart casserole dish; cover and bake 30 minutes. Uncover and sprinkle with remaining cheese. Bake 10 minutes more.

- Can be frozen but do not cook until completely thawed.

Yield: 8 servings.

Chicken Paillards with Herbs

2	tablespoons chopped parsley
1	teaspoon chopped marjoram
1	teaspoon chopped thyme
1	teaspoon chopped savory
½	teaspoon chopped rosemary
1	teaspoon chopped chervil
½	cup olive oil
2	whole boneless chicken breasts, pounded to thickness of ⅜-inch

- Mix herbs and oil. Add chicken and marinate, turning occasionally, for 3 to 4 hours.

- Grill chicken 2 to 3 minutes on each side.

- Use fresh herbs; if using dried herbs, cut quantities in half.

Yield: 4 servings.

Chicken with Cashews

8   **chicken breast halves, skinned and boned**
1   **egg white, slightly beaten**
1   **tablespoon rice wine**
1   **teaspoon cornstarch**
1   **tablespoon peanut or vegetable oil**
½   **cup cashews**
2   **tablespoons peanut or vegetable oil**
½   **teaspoon salt**
1   **(8-ounce) can sliced water chestnuts, drained**
1   **(8-ounce) can sliced bamboo shoots, drained**
4   **green onions, cut into 1-inch pieces**
3   **ribs celery, thinly sliced**
2   **red or green peppers, cut into 1-inch squares**
⅓   **cup chicken broth**
1   **tablespoon cornstarch**
1   **tablespoon rice wine**
1   **tablespoon soy sauce**
1   **teaspoon sesame oil**
    Green onion fans

- Cut chicken into 1-inch pieces. Combine chicken and next 3 ingredients; mix well, and let stand in refrigerator 1 hour or overnight.

- Pour 1 tablespoon oil around top of pre-heated wok, coating sides. Add cashews; stir-fry 30 seconds and remove.

- Pour 2 tablespoons oil around top of wok; add chicken, and stir-fry until lightly browned. Sprinkle chicken with salt.

- Add next 5 ingredients; stir-fry 5 minutes or until vegetables are crisp-tender.

- Combine next 5 ingredients, mixing well. Pour over chicken mixture; cook, stirring constantly, until thickened.

- Spoon onto platter, and sprinkle with cashews; garnish with green onion fans.

Yield: 6 to 8 servings.

Chicken with Orange Sauce

(Sauce is good served over rice)

6   **whole chicken breasts, boned, skinned and halved**
1   **teaspoon salt**
1   **teaspoon pepper**
1   **teaspoon paprika**
1   **cup flour**
¼   **cup vegetable oil**
2   **large onions, sliced**
½   **cup diced green pepper**
1   **pound fresh mushrooms, sliced**
2   **cups orange juice**
1   **cup dry sherry**
2½   **tablespoons brown sugar**
⅛   **teaspoon salt**
⅛   **teaspoon pepper**
2   **tablespoons cornstarch**
3   **tablespoons water**
2   **teaspoons grated orange peel**

- Season chicken with salt, pepper and paprika and dredge in flour. Brown chicken breasts on both sides in vegetable oil. Place chicken in a large casserole dish. Cover chicken with sliced onions, green pepper and mushrooms.

- Combine orange juice, sherry, brown sugar, salt, pepper and cornstarch mixed with 3 tablespoons water. Cook until thickened; add orange rind. Pour over chicken and bake at 375° for 45 to 60 minutes, uncovered.

Yield: 12 servings.

Creamy Company Chicken Crêpes

(Wonderful; don't let all the instructions frighten you!)

Chicken Filling:
2 (10¾-ounce) cans cream of mushroom soup, undiluted
1 (8-ounce) carton sour cream
2½ cups cooked chicken, chopped

- Combine soup and sour cream; stir well.
- Combine half of soup mixture with chicken, stirring well. Reserve remaining soup mixture for Mushroom Sauce.

Yield: About 3⅓ cups.

Mushroom Sauce:
2 tablespoons butter or margarine
1 small onion, finely chopped
1 chicken bouillon cube
2 tablespoons water
1 (2½-ounce) jar sliced mushrooms, drained
  Reserved soup mixture

- Melt butter in a large skillet; sauté onion in butter until tender. Add bouillon cube, water and mushrooms; cook, stirring often, until bouillon cube dissolves. Stir reserved soup mixture into skillet.

Yield: 2½ cups.

Crêpes:
1⅓ cups all-purpose flour
1 teaspoon salt
4 eggs, beaten
2 tablespoons vegetable oil
1⅓ cups milk
  Vegetable oil
  Chicken Filling
  Mushroom Sauce
1 cup shredded Cheddar cheese
  Paprika

- Combine flour, salt and eggs; mix well. Blend in 2 tablespoons oil and milk, beating until smooth.
- Refrigerate batter at least 2 hours (this allows flour particles to swell and soften so crêpes are light in texture).
- Brush bottom of a 10-inch crêpe pan or heavy skillet with vegetable oil; place over medium heat until just hot, not smoking.
- Pour 3 tablespoons batter in pan; quickly tilt pan in all directions so that batter covers pan in a thin film; cook about 1 minute.
- Lift edge of crêpe to test for doneness; crêpe is ready for flipping when it can be shaken loose from pan. Flip crêpe, and cook about 30 seconds on the other side (this side is rarely more than spotty brown and is the side on which filling should be placed).
- Remove crêpe from pan and repeat procedure until all batter is used. Place waxed paper between crêpes to keep them from sticking. Set aside 10 crêpes; freeze remaining crêpes for later use.
- Spoon ⅓ cup Chicken Filling in center of each crêpe; roll up and place seam down in a greased 13x9x2-inch baking dish. Spoon Mushroom Sauce evenly over crêpes.
- Bake at 350° for 15 minutes.
- Sprinkle cheese over crêpes and bake 10 additional minutes. Sprinkle with paprika.

Yield: 10 servings.

Chicken with Curry Sauce

4 **whole chicken breasts, skinned, boned and halved**
1 **(10¾-ounce) can cream of chicken soup, undiluted**
1 **cup mayonnaise**
1 **tablespoon lemon juice**
1½ **teaspoons curry powder**
1 **(8-ounce) can sliced water chestnuts, drained**
⅓ **cup sherry**
½ **cup seasoned dressing mix**
1 **cup shredded Cheddar cheese**

- Preheat oven to 350°. Place chicken in a buttered 13x9-inch baking dish.

- Mix soup, mayonnaise, lemon juice, curry powder, water chestnuts and sherry. Pour sauce over chicken. Top with dressing mix, then with cheese.

- Bake, covered with foil, for 45 minutes.

- Remove foil and bake at 325° for 45 minutes more.

Yield: 8 servings.

Dill Chicken with Stuffing

1¼ **cups water**
5 **tablespoons margarine, divided**
1 **(4.4-ounce) package long grain and wild rice with chicken flavor**
4 **chicken breast halves, boned and skinned**
1 **tablespoon lemon juice**
¼ **teaspoon dillweed**
8 **cherry tomatoes, cut in half**
2 **tablespoons chopped green onion**

- Combine water, 3 tablespoons of margarine and contents of rice and seasoning packets in saucepan. Bring to a boil; cover tightly and simmer 5 minutes. Remove from heat and stir in contents of crumb packet; cover and let stand 5 minutes or until water is absorbed.

- Meanwhile, sauté chicken in remaining 2 tablespoons of margarine in medium skillet over medium heat until cooked through. Sprinkle with lemon juice and dill.

- Stir tomatoes into stuffing; fluff stuffing with a fork. Divide rice among 4 plates; serve chicken over rice. Sprinkle green onions over top of chicken.

Yield: 4 servings.

Company Chicken

16 **split chicken breasts, skinned and boned**
3 **(14-ounce) cans artichoke hearts, drained**
¾ **cup butter, melted**
   Salt and pepper to taste
2 **cups hollandaise sauce**
1 **teaspoon finely chopped parsley**

- Preheat oven to 350°.

- Place artichoke hearts in a generously greased baking dish. Place chicken on top and drizzle with butter; season.

- Bake at 350° for 35 minutes, basting often. Drain off excess juice, if any.

- Just before serving, top with hollandaise sauce; sprinkle with parsley.

- Sauce and chicken may be prepared early in day and reheated.

Yield: 8 to 12 servings.

Cranberry Chicken

(Easy and very tasty)

8 **chicken breast halves, boned and
      skinned**
1 **(8-ounce) bottle French dressing**
1 **envelope dry onion soup mix**
1 **(16-ounce) can whole cranberry
      sauce**

- Preheat oven to 350°.
- Mix last three ingredients together. Place
  chicken breasts in an 11x14-inch casserole
  dish. Pour sauce over chicken.
- Bake for 1 hour uncovered.
- Serve with rice casserole and a green
  vegetable. Serve extra sauce in a gravy boat
  to be served over chicken and rice. Sauce is
  not very pretty but very tasty.

Yield: 8 servings.

Grilled Chicken
Kabobs

⅔ **cup soy sauce**
¼ **cup vegetable oil**
¼ **cup Chablis**
½ **cup onion, minced**
2 **cloves garlic, crushed**
10 **skinned and boned chicken breast
      halves, cut into 1½-inch pieces**
5 **medium green peppers cut into 1-
      inch pieces**
2 **(15½-ounce) cans pineapple
      chunks, drained
      Hot cooked rice**

- Combine first 5 ingredients; stir well. Add
  chicken, turning to coat. Cover and marinate in refrigerator 30 minutes.
- Cook green pepper in boiling water 2
  minutes; drain and cool.
- Remove chicken from marinade.
- Alternate chicken, green pepper and
  pineapple on skewers. Grill over medium
  hot coals 15 minutes or until done, brushing
  frequently with marinade.
- Serve over hot rice.

Yield: 10 servings.

Hot Chicken Salad
Casserole

3-4 **cups cooked chicken, cut up**
1 **medium onion, chopped**
½ **green pepper, chopped**
1 **(2-ounce) jar pimento, drained**
1 **cup celery, chopped**
1 **(10¾-ounce) can cream of chicken
      soup**
½ **cup light mayonnaise**
3 **tablespoons chicken broth**
1 **tablespoon lemon juice**
¼ **teaspoon salt**
¼ **teaspoon pepper**
1 **(5-ounce) can Chinese noodles**

- Preheat oven to 250°.
- Mix all ingredients, except Chinese noodles,
  together and pour into a 3-quart baking
  dish.
- Bake for 30 minutes.
- Top with noodles and bake at 375° for 15
  minutes.

Yield: 6 to 8 servings.

Kung Pao Chicken

(Any meat, seafood or poultry may be cooked this way)

¾ **pound chicken breasts**

Marinade:

1 **teaspoon sesame oil**
2 **teaspoons cornstarch**
¼ **teaspoon salt**
Pinch of white pepper

- Cut the chicken into bits; combine them with the marinade ingredients in a medium bowl and stir to coat; set aside for 30 minutes.

Sauce:

⅓ **cup chicken broth**
3 **tablespoons balsamic vinegar**
2½ **tablespoons soy sauce**
5 **teaspoons sugar**
1½ **teaspoons sesame oil**
1 **small green or red bell pepper, seeded**
1 **small onion**
2 **stalks celery**
1 **(15-ounce) can whole bamboo shoots**
3 **tablespoons vegetable oil**
2 **teaspoons minced ginger**
1 **teaspoon minced garlic**
6 **whole dried chili peppers**
¼-½ **teaspoon crushed red pepper**
1½ **teaspoons cornstarch dissolved in 1 tablespoon water**

- Combine sauce ingredients in another bowl.
- Cut the bell pepper and onion into 1-inch squares; cut the celery diagonally into ½-inch slices. Cut the bamboo shoots into 1-inch cubes. Add 2 tablespoons of oil to a wok which has been heated; swirl to coat all sides.

- Add the chicken and stir-fry until opaque, about 2 minutes; remove chicken to a bowl. Add the remaining tablespoon oil to the wok. Add the ginger, garlic, whole red peppers and crushed red pepper; cook, stirring for about 10 seconds.
- Add the bell pepper, onion, celery and bamboo shoots to stir-fry for 30 seconds.
- Pour the accumulated juices in the chicken into the wok and add the sauce. Cover and cook for 1 minute. Return the chicken to the wok; add the cornstarch solution and cook, stirring, until the sauce boils and thickens.

Wild Rice and Chicken

1 **cup wild rice**
2 **cups chicken broth**
Butter
Salt and pepper to taste
1 **(3-ounce) can sliced mushrooms, drained**
6 **chicken breast halves**
½ **package dry onion soup mix**
1 **(10¾-ounce) can mushroom soup**
Paprika

- Soak rice overnight; drain.
- Pour chicken broth over rice in a large, flat casserole dish. Dot with butter, salt and pepper. Add mushrooms to casserole; place chicken over rice.
- Sprinkle onion soup mix over all. Dilute mushroom soup with a little water and spoon over each breast. Sprinkle with paprika.
- Cook uncovered at 350° for 1 hour, then cook covered ½ hour longer.

Yield: 6 servings.

Ham and Cheese Chicken Cutlets

2 whole chicken breasts, halved and boned
8 ounces milk, divided
  Bread crumbs
2 tablespoons butter
1 (10¾-ounce) can cream of chicken soup
¼ cup white wine
4 slices ham
4 slices Swiss cheese
  Cooked rice or noodles

- Preheat oven to 350°. Rinse chicken and pat dry. Dip in 2 ounces of milk and roll in bread crumbs. Brown in butter and remove from skillet.

- Add soup, 6 ounces milk and wine to skillet and heat through.

- Place chicken breasts in 2-quart casserole. Pour sauce over breasts.

- Place a slice of ham over each. Top with a slice of Swiss cheese.

- Bake for 15 to 20 minutes until cheese gets bubbly and light brown.

- Serve with rice or noodles.

Yield: 4 servings.

Oriental Chicken with Pineapple

4 chicken breasts, skinned and boned, cut into bite-size pieces
2 tablespoons margarine
1 cup celery, cut into ½-inch diagonal pieces
1 medium onion, sliced
1 medium green pepper, cut into ½-inch pieces
1 (8-ounce) can unsweetened pineapple tidbits, drained, reserving ¼ cup juice
1 (8-ounce) can tomato sauce
1 tablespoon cornstarch
¼ cup soy sauce
¼ teaspoon ground ginger
3 cups hot cooked rice
3 tablespoons sherry

- Allow wok to heat at medium high (325°) for 2 minutes. Melt margarine in wok, add chicken and stir-fry 4 to 5 minutes or until lightly browned. Stir in vegetables, cover, reduce heat and simmer 5 minutes or until vegetables are crisp and tender.

- Combine tomato sauce, cornstarch, soy sauce, sherry, ground ginger and pineapple juice. Pour over chicken mixture and cook until mixture is slightly thickened.

- Combine rice and pineapple, mixing well; serve chicken over pineapple-rice mixture.

Yield: 6 servings.

Sesame Chicken Kabobs

2   whole chicken breasts, skinned and boned and cut into 1-inch pieces
¼   cup soy sauce
¼   cup Russian reduced-calorie salad dressing
1   tablespoon sesame seeds
2   tablespoons lemon juice
¼   teaspoon ground ginger
¼   teaspoon garlic powder
½   pound mushrooms
1   large green pepper, cut into 1-inch pieces and pre-cooked
2   medium onions, cut into eighths and pre-cooked
3   small zucchini, cut into ¾-inch pieces
1   pint cherry tomatoes
     Vegetable cooking spray

- Place chicken in a shallow container and set aside.

- Combine next 6 ingredients in a jar, cover tightly and shake vigorously. Pour over chicken; cover and marinate in the refrigerator for at least 2 hours.

- Remove chicken from marinade, reserving marinade. Alternate chicken and vegetables on skewers. Spray grill with cooking spray.

- Grill kabobs about 6 inches from medium hot coals for 15 to 20 minutes or until done, turning and basting often with marinade.

Yield: 6 servings.

Sweet and Sour Chicken

3   tablespoons soy sauce
1   tablespoon sherry
1   egg
¼   teaspoon pepper
¼   teaspoon garlic powder
¼   cup cornstarch
1   pound boneless chicken breasts, cut into 1-inch pieces
2   cups vegetable oil
1   (15-ounce) can pineapple chunks, drained, reserving juice
2   tablespoons cornstarch
½   cup sugar
¼   cup ketchup
¼   cup vinegar
1   tablespoon soy sauce
1   medium green pepper, cut into 1-inch pieces
     Hot cooked rice

- Combine first 6 ingredients, mixing well; add chicken, stirring to coat. Heat oil to 375°; fry chicken until lightly browned; drain well.

- Add enough water to pineapple juice to make 1 cup. Add 2 tablespoons cornstarch, stirring well. Combine pineapple, juice mixture and next 4 ingredients in a medium saucepan; bring mixture to a boil.

- Stir green pepper and chicken into sauce; serve over rice.

Yield: 4 servings.

Supreme De Poulet Aux Crevettes

(A luxurious dish — chicken breasts on a bed of spinach, lightly coated with a rich shrimp sauce and garnished with butterflied shrimp. Make the sauce ahead to save time)

Sauce:

- ¼ cup diced celery
- ¼ cup diced onion
- ¼ cup diced carrot
- 1 small clove garlic, diced
- 1 tablespoon butter
- 1 bay leaf
- ½ teaspoon leaf basil, crumbled
- ¼ teaspoon leaf thyme, crumbled
- ¼ teaspoon salt
- ⅛ teaspoon white pepper
- 1 tablespoon all-purpose flour
- 2 tablespoons white wine
- ¼ cup sweet port
- ¼ cup heavy cream
- 1 (13-ounce) can cream of shrimp soup *or* lobster bisque

- Prepare the sauce. Sauté celery, onion, carrot and garlic in butter in large saucepan until vegetables are softened. Add bay leaf, basil, thyme, salt and white pepper; toss. Stir in flour and cook, stirring for 2 minutes; stir in wine, port, heavy cream and shrimp soup. Bring to boiling; lower heat and simmer for 40 minutes without stirring. Strain. The sauce should be very thick.
- Preheat the oven to 350°.

Chicken:

- 4 whole chicken breasts, skinned and boned
- ¼ teaspoon salt
- ⅛ teaspoon pepper
  Paprika
- 1 cup dry white wine
- 2 pounds fresh spinach, cleaned and stems removed, *or* 2 (10-ounce) packages frozen leaf spinach, thawed
- 4 large shrimp, peeled but with tails left on, deveined and split in half lengthwise to ¼-inch from tail.

- Prepare the chicken breasts. Season breasts with salt, pepper and paprika. Arrange in shallow glass baking dish; pour wine over and cover with aluminum foil.
- Bake for 30 minutes or until tender.
- Remove breasts from baking dish with a slotted spoon; draining well. Keep warm.
- Pour some of the baking liquid into a large skillet. Add the spinach; toss over medium heat to heat through.
- Transfer the spinach to a warmed platter; quickly sauté the shrimp in the same skillet until pink color of shrimp brightens, 3 to 4 minutes.
- Arrange chicken breasts over spinach; cover lightly with the sauce and arrange shrimp over the top.
- Can offer additional sauce at the table.

  Note: Serve with Rice Casserole, Strawberry and Onion Salad with Poppyseed Dressing and Baked Zucchini.

  Yield: 4 servings.

Stuffed Cornish Hens

8   Rock Cornish game hens
¾   cup butter or margarine, divided
1   cup fresh mushrooms, sliced
½   cup chopped onion
¼   cup chopped green pepper
2   (12-ounce) packages long grain and
  wild rice, cooked according to
  package directions
1   (8¼-ounce) can crushed pineapple,
  drained
1½ teaspoons salt
¼   teaspoon pepper

- Lightly sprinkle cavity of hens with salt.

- Microwave or sauté ¼ cup butter, mushrooms, onion and green pepper until soft. Add rice, pineapple, salt and pepper and mix well; stuff hens with mixture and fasten with skewers.

- Place breast sides up on rack in roasting pan; brush with remaining ½ cup butter. Do not cover; bake 1 hour, cover and bake 1 hour longer.

- Also delicious with savory sausage rice stuffing or with ½ cup golden raisins added to either stuffing.

Yield: 8 servings.

Pigg's Venison Roast

1   venison ham
1   large browning bag
¼   cup flour
1   (10¾-ounce) can of celery or
  mushroom soup, undiluted
1   (10¾-ounce) can of French onion
  soup, undiluted

- Preheat oven to 350°.

- Trim all fat from ham. Coat inside of browning bag with flour. Place ham inside bag. Add the two cans of soup to bag with ham.

- Close bag and cut slits as directed on package. Put bagged ham on broiler pan or in roaster, uncovered. Bake for 2 to 3 hours, depending on the size of the ham. Let rest for at least 30 minutes before opening.

- Remove ham to platter for carving. Reheat ham drippings and skim excess fat from surface. Serve sauce alongside ham in a gravy boat.

Yield: 10 to 12 servings.

Soy Sauce Duck

3   cups soy sauce
1   cup water
4   slices fresh ginger root
4   sprigs of green onions
4   tablespoons of brown sugar
2   small pieces of orange peel
  (optional)
1   duck, any size

- Heat first 4 ingredients in Chinese wok until boiling. Reduce heat to simmer.

- Put duck in sauce; turn every 10 to 15 minutes. Cook until both sides are evenly colored.

- Cooking time is approximately 2½ to 3 hours.

- Serve hot or cold.

Wild Duck

1 whole duck, cleaned
  Liquid detergent
  Bacon grease
  Salt and pepper
  Garlic salt
  Celery
  Orange wedges
  Warm water
  Hot cooked wild rice

- Wash duck inside and out with liquid detergent. This is a must to cut oils from skin and blood from cavity; rinse well.

- Rub inside and out with bacon grease; salt and pepper inside and out. Sprinkle with garlic salt. Stuff duck cavity with celery and orange wedges.

- Heat electric skillet and sear both sides of breast and back. Leave duck on back; add warm water and simmer for 1¼ to 1½ hours, basting several times. Duck should cook until legs separate from body easily. Make sure skillet always has water in it for steam which cooks the duck.

- Serve on back while hot with drippings over a mound of wild rice.

Yield: 1 serving.

Hasenpfeffer Fricassee

¼ cup flour
½ teaspoon salt
⅛ teaspoon pepper
1 (2 to 2½-pound) ready-to-cook rabbit, cut up
1 tablespoon butter
1 cup water
¼ teaspoon marjoram
¼ teaspoon oregano
⅛ teaspoon allspice or 4-5 whole allspice
⅛ teaspoon ground cloves
1 teaspoon lemon juice
2 tablespoons cold water
1 tablespoon flour
  Hot cooked rice

- Mix flour, salt and pepper; coat rabbit pieces and brown them in butter in heavy pan. Reduce heat; add water and spices and cook, covered, until tender, simmering gently about 1 hour. Remove rabbit to warm platter; measure pan juices and skim off fat. Add lemon juice and enough water to make 1 cup; return to skillet.

- Blend the 2 tablespoons cold water into 1 tablespoon flour; stir into cooking liquid and cook and stir until thickened and bubbly; cook 2 minutes more.

- Season to taste and serve gravy over rice.

Yield: 3 to 4 servings.

Baked Quail with Mushrooms

⅓ cup all-purpose flour
½ teaspoon salt
½ teaspoon pepper
8 quail
½ pound fresh mushrooms, sliced
10 tablespoons margarine, divided
¼ cup plus 1 tablespoon all-purpose flour
2 cups canned diluted chicken broth
½ cup dry sherry
    Hot cooked rice

- Combine ⅓ cup flour, salt and pepper. Dredge quail in flour mixture, and set aside.

- Sauté mushrooms in 4 tablespoons butter in a large skillet 4 minutes. Remove mushrooms from skillet; drain and set aside.

- Melt remaining 6 tablespoons butter in skillet; brown quail on both sides. Remove quail to a 1½-quart casserole.

- Add flour to drippings in skillet; cook 1 minute, stirring constantly. Gradually add chicken broth and sherry; cook over medium heat, stirring constantly, until gravy is thickened. Stir in mushrooms. Pour mushroom gravy over quail.

- Cover and bake at 350° for 1 hour; serve over rice.

Yield: 4 servings.

Country Style Quail

6 quail, cleaned and split down back
¼ cup all-purpose flour
1½ teaspoons salt, divided
½ teaspoon pepper
    Vegetable oil
3 tablespoons all-purpose flour
1 cup water
    Hot cooked rice

- Spread quail open; pat dry with paper towels.

- Combine ¼ cup flour, 1 teaspoon salt and pepper; dredge quail in flour mixture.

- Heat ¼ inch of oil in a skillet; place quail in skillet, and brown on both sides, turning once. Remove from skillet.

- Combine 3 tablespoons flour, 1 cup water and ½ teaspoon salt; stir until smooth. Blend into drippings in skillet.

- Place quail in gravy and add enough water to half cover birds.

- Cover; reduce heat to low, and simmer 30 minutes or until tender. Serve quail over hot cooked rice.

Yield: 6 servings.

Quail in Red Wine

6 quail, cleaned
  Brandy
  All-purpose flour
6 tablespoons margarine
2 cups sliced fresh mushrooms
¼ cup melted margarine
1 cup beef consommé
1 cup dry red wine
1 stalk celery, quartered
  Salt and pepper to taste
  Juice of 2 oranges
  Cooked wild rice

- Rub quail with a cloth soaked in brandy and dust with flour.

- Melt 6 tablespoons margarine in a heavy skillet; add quail and sauté 10 minutes. Sauté mushrooms in ¼ cup margarine; pour over quail. Add consommé, wine, celery, salt and pepper. Cover and simmer 20 to 30 minutes or until quail is tender.

- Discard celery, if desired; stir in orange juice. Heat thoroughly.

- Serve with wild rice.

Yield: 6 servings.

Quail in Wine Herb Sauce

12 quail
 3 tablespoons flour
   Salt and pepper to taste
 1 large onion, sliced
 2 slices lean, smoked bacon, diced
 1 clove garlic, crushed
 1 (4-ounce) can sliced mushrooms, drained
 1 bay leaf
 ½ teaspoon thyme
 ½ cup beef broth
 ½ cup dry, white wine
   Chopped parsley
   Flour (optional)

- Coat quail with a mixture of the flour, salt and pepper. Place onion slices in crockpot; top with quail. Cover quail with diced bacon. Add remaining ingredients except parsley.

- Cover and cook on low setting for 6 to 8 hours.

- Remove quail to a heated platter and sprinkle with parsley. Thicken sauce with flour, if desired, and spoon over quail.

Yield: 12 servings.

Barbecue Sauce

(For pork, beef and chicken)

1   (4-ounce) can tomato sauce
1   can water
½   cup cider vinegar (use for pork or beef) *or* 1 cup white wine (use for chicken)
¼   cup Worcestershire sauce
⅓   cup salad oil
2   teaspoons curry powder
½   teaspoon dry mustard
¼   teaspoon basil or rosemary
1   tablespoon minced parsley
1   small clove garlic, minced
1   small white onion, chopped
1   teaspoon salt
¼   cup dark brown sugar
4   drops hot pepper sauce

- Mix all ingredients in saucepan.
- Simmer over very low heat for 8 to 10 minutes; sauce will be thick.
- Baste meat every time it is turned, or every 5 minutes.

Barbeque Sauce II

(For pork ribs and chops, beef or chicken)

1   (12-ounce) can frozen orange juice concentrate
1½ cups water
⅔   cup brown sugar, packed
¾   cup wine vinegar or yellow cider vinegar
½   cup honey
1   tablespoon lemon juice
4   teaspoons prepared mustard
3   teaspoons soy sauce

½   teaspoon salt *or* ¼ teaspoon salt substitute
⅔   teaspoon fresh ground pepper

- Blend above over heat and allow to come to a slow boil for 5 to 10 minutes or it may be stirred and thoroughly mixed together without cooking.
- Can be used on any barbequed dish you like.
- Store in closed jar in refrigerator for up to a week.

Yield: 4 cups.

Barbeque Sauce III

⅓   cup vinegar
3   tablespoons brown sugar
1   tablespoon prepared mustard
½   teaspoon pepper
2   teaspoons salt
¼   teaspoon cayenne pepper
2   lemon slices
1   medium onion, sliced
⅔   cup ketchup
3   tablespoons Worcestershire sauce

- Mix above ingredients together in a saucepan. Cook over medium heat until well blended and heated to boiling point.
- Great over chicken or pork chops. Excellent as a marinade.

Yield: 1 cup.

A Marinade for Beef

1   **cup butter**
½   **(14-ounce) bottle ketchup**
½   **(10-ounce) bottle Worcestershire sauce**
6   **tablespoons Coleman's mustard**

- Combine all ingredients and use to baste meat before grilling. Allow to marinate about 1 hour. Use remaining sauce to baste with while grilling.

- Try with chicken for an interesting flavor.

Fresh Mint Jelly

(Great with lamb)

1½   **cups tightly packed fresh mint with stems**
2¼   **cups water**
2   **tablespoons fresh lemon juice**
    Green food coloring
3½   **cups sugar**
½   **bottle liquid pectin**

- Rinse mint leaves, put in large pot and crush with masher. Add water and quickly bring to a boil. Remove from heat, cover and let set 10 minutes.

- Strain and measure 1⅔ cups liquid. Return to pan, add lemon juice and food coloring. Stir in sugar and cook over high heat; stir constantly until mixture comes to a boil. Add pectin, stirring constantly and boil 1 minute (full rolling boil).

- Remove from heat, skim off foam with large metal spoon and quickly pour into sterilized jars within ½-inch from top. Put on cap; screw band firmly. Process in boiling water bath 5 minutes.

- Let cool; check seals.

Yield: 4 half cups.

Chicken Marinade

2   **(10-ounce) bottles soy sauce**
1¼   **pounds brown sugar**
1   **clove garlic**
1   **whole ginger root or a few teaspoons ground ginger, to taste**
1½   **cups bourbon**
    Honey (optional)

- Combine soy sauce and brown sugar (add enough brown sugar so that the soy sauce is not too salty). Add all remaining ingredients; marinate overnight and entire next day.

- Cook over hot coals for approximately 20 minutes. You may brush with honey just before removing from grill.

- This marinade recipe makes enough for five whole chickens but you may make half or just save in the refrigerator the remainder.

Onion-Buttered Sauce for Beef Roast

(Great on roast beef sandwiches for a cocktail party)

½   **cup butter**
¼   **cup chopped parsley**
¼   **cup minced onion**
2   **teaspoons Worcestershire sauce**
½   **teaspoon dry mustard**
½   **teaspoon freshly ground pepper**

- Blend all ingredients together in a saucepan and heat thoroughly.

- Pour in dish and cool.

- Serve over broiled steak or roast.

Spaghetti Sauce

(Serve with a tossed salad and garlic bread)

1½ pounds ground beef, browned and drained
1 large onion, chopped
1 medium green pepper, chopped
1 garlic clove, chopped
1 (8-ounce) package fresh mushrooms, chopped
2 (6-ounce) cans tomato paste
1 (8-ounce) can tomato sauce
1 (16-ounce) can tomatoes, undrained and chopped
1 cup water
1 tablespoon Italian seasoning
1 tablespoon Worcestershire sauce
2 tablespoons sugar
1 teaspoon salt
   Cooked spaghetti noodles

- Mix all ingredients except noodles together in a Dutch oven; simmer for 1 hour.
- Serve over spaghetti noodles.

Yield: 6 to 8 servings.

Overnight Marinade

(Wonderful for flank steak to be grilled)

¼ cup soy sauce
3 tablespoons honey
2 tablespoons vinegar
1½ teaspoons garlic powder
½ cup salad oil
1 green onion, chopped
¾ teaspoon ground ginger

- Mix all ingredients together thoroughly.
- Marinate steak all day or overnight.

Quick Barbeque Sauce I

1 onion, quartered
1 cup ketchup
¼ cup vinegar
2 large stalks of celery, coarsely chopped
1 tablespoon mustard
2 tablespoons brown sugar
1 teaspoon salt
2 tablespoons Worcestershire sauce
1½ cups water

- Mix all ingredients in blender, adding one at a time.
- Place selected chicken or pork pieces in baking dish.
- Pour the sauce mixture over meat and bake according to your meat recipe.

Yield: 6 servings.

SEAFOOD

Becky Wenger '92

Index for Seafood

Tasty Clams and Broth

½ cup unsalted butter
4 garlic cloves, minced
2 tablespoons minced fresh Italian parsley
½ cup dry white wine
20-30 fresh small to medium clams, scrubbed and debearded
French bread, thickly sliced and heated

- In a large Dutch oven over medium heat melt butter and add garlic, parsley and wine.

- Place cleaned clams in pot and cover; cook until shells have opened. As they cook, the juices from the clams combine with the seasoned butter for a delicious broth.

- To serve: Ladle clams and broth into soup bowls. Serve with a salad and crusty bread to dip in broth.

Yield: 4 servings.

Baked Crabmeat

1 pound crabmeat, lump preferred
4 tablespoons mayonnaise
4 slices toasted bread, cubed
6 tablespoons butter, melted
⅛ teaspoon white pepper
⅛ teaspoon horseradish
Salt to taste

- Preheat oven to 325°.

- Mix all ingredients together. Pour into 1½-quart casserole. Add a little extra liquid butter or margarine on top.

- Bake uncovered for 20 minutes.

Yield: 4 to 6 servings.

Deviled Crabs

1 pound crabmeat
1 egg, slightly beaten
20 butter crackers, crushed
Salt and pepper to taste
3 tablespoons mustard-mayonnaise sauce
Worcestershire sauce
3 tablespoons salad dressing
Hot sauce to taste

- Mix crabmeat, beaten egg and most of the cracker crumbs (reserve some crumbs for placing on top). Add dressings and sauces. Use dash of salt and pepper. Mix well and place into individual cooking shells. Top with remaining crumbs; dot with butter or margarine.

- Bake in oven at 350° for 40 to 45 minutes.

- Good served with baked potato, salad and lemon pie.

Yield: 4 to 6 servings.

Crab Cakes Albemarle

1 pound backfin crabmeat
12 saltine crackers, crushed
1 egg
2 tablespoons mayonnaise
2 teaspoons dry mustard
2 teaspoons Old Bay seasoning
Salt and pepper to taste

- Put crabmeat in bowl and sprinkle with crackers.

- Combine seasonings, egg, mayonnaise and dry mustard; beat all together and pour over crabmeat.

- Shape into cakes and deep fry or pan fry until golden brown.

Yield: 4 to 6 servings.

Crabs in a Chest

(This is also good with shrimp or a combination of both)

1   **(26-ounce) box salt**
1½   **ounces black pepper**
2   **ounces ground red pepper**
1   **ounce garlic powder**
1   **ounce chili powder**
1   **ounce monosodium glutamate**
2   **teaspoons powdered thyme**
2   **teaspoons bay leaf**
2   **teaspoons sweet basil**
4   **dozen live crabs**

- Combine the seasoning ingredients.
- Obtain an ice chest large enough to hold the crabs. If using the same ice chest that the live crabs were in, be sure to clean it out.
- Plunge crabs into boiling water and boil for 11 minutes. Remove and place immediately a layer of boiled crabs in the bottom of the ice chest.
- Sprinkle boiled crabs generously with the seasoning, then place another layer of crabs. Season and repeat process until all crabs are placed and covered with seasoning.
- Cover with newspaper and close top securely. Heat will steam the crabs and melt the seasoning for flavor.
- Crabs are ready to eat after an hour but will remain hot for 5 to 6 hours if the chest remains closed.
- Can add boiled potatoes and freshly cooked corn on the cob to your cooler.
- Cover a table with newspaper and serve with your favorite beverage. This is great to do outside on a nice summer day.

Note: Newspaper may be used between each layer of crabs to seal in heat.

Yield: 8 servings.

Crabmeat Florentine

2   **tablespoons butter, melted**
2   **tablespoons flour**
2   **cups of milk**
     Salt, pepper and a pinch of nutmeg
4   **egg yolks, slightly beaten**
2   **teaspoons chopped parsley**
2   **teaspoons grated onion**
2   **(10-ounce) packages frozen, chopped spinach, cooked and drained dry**
1   **pound of lump or backfin crabmeat**
¼   **cup Parmesan cheese**

- Make a rich cream sauce with melted butter, flour and milk. Add salt, pepper and nutmeg. Carefully add the egg yolks a little at a time.
- Heat to bring to boiling point, but do not boil. Remove from heat and add parsley and onion. Place a layer of the spinach in 8 individual ramekins or shells. Add a small amount of sauce on top, then a layer of crabmeat. Complete with the rest of the sauce. Sprinkle with Parmesan cheese.
- Bake at 400° for 10 minutes.

Yield: 8 servings.

Crab Baked in a Ramekin

1½   **pounds fresh lump crabmeat**
¾   **cup chopped celery**
1½   **teaspoons lemon juice**
½   **teaspoon salt**
½   **cup mayonnaise**
2   **teaspoons melted butter**
1   **cup dry bread crumbs**
2   **hard boiled eggs, chopped**
1½   **teaspoons Dijon mustard**
1½   **teaspoons Worcestershire sauce**
    Dash of cayenne pepper
1½   **cups fresh bread crumbs**

- Preheat oven to 400°.
- Combine all ingredients except fresh bread crumbs and divide among 6 lightly buttered 8-ounce ramekins. Cover lightly with bread crumbs. Top with 2 thin dots of butter.
- Bake 12 to 15 minutes until crumbs are golden brown.

Yield: 6 servings.

Crabmeat Quiche

1   **unbaked, homemade, 9-inch, deep dish pastry shell**
1½-2   **cups lightly packed, shredded, natural Swiss cheese**
1   **pound fresh backfin crabmeat**
¼   **teaspoon onion salt**
3   **extra large eggs, beaten**
1½   **cups of whipping cream**
½   **teaspoon salt**
1   **grated lemon peel (entire lemon)**
¼   **teaspoon dry mustard**
    Dash of mace
½   **cup slivered almonds**

- Preheat oven to 325°.
- Sprinkle shredded Swiss cheese over bottom of pastry shell. Top with crabmeat. Sprinkle with onion salt.
- Combine in a bowl; eggs, cream, salt, dry mustard, mace and lemon peel. Pour over crabmeat and cheese. Top with almonds.
- Bake in a slow oven for 45 minutes or until set. Remove from oven and let stand 10 minutes before serving.

Yield: 6 servings.

Deviled Crabmeat

(A great luncheon dish)

16   **saltine crackers, crumbled**
2   **tablespoons mayonnaise**
2   **tablespoons sherry**
¼   **teaspoon dry mustard**
1   **tablespoon parsley flakes**
1½   **teaspoons Worcestershire sauce**
½   **teaspoon hot pepper sauce**
¼   **teaspoon salt**
⅛   **teaspoon pepper**
1¼   **sticks butter, melted, divided**
1   **pound fresh crabmeat**

- Mix first 9 ingredients together. Melt one stick of butter and add to cracker mixture.
- Fold in crabmeat gently.
- Bake in a greased casserole for 30 minutes at 400°.
- Melt remaining butter and drizzle over casserole just before serving.
- Serve with broccoli and lemon butter and a congealed aspic.

Yield: 4 to 6 servings.

Divine Crab Cakes

3   pounds lump crabmeat
1   cup mayonnaise
2   tablespoons parsley
3   tablespoons Worcestershire sauce
    Dash of hot pepper sauce
2   egg yolks
1   teaspoon dry mustard
2¾ teaspoons Old Bay seafood
    seasoning

- Mix all ingredients together. Make into at least 14 or 15 flat cakes (about 1-inch thick). Put on cookie sheet and freeze.

- When frozen, put in zip-lock freezer bags.

- When ready to serve, place frozen crab cakes on a cookie sheet and put a pat of butter on each cake.

- Cook at 375° for 12 to 15 minutes.

Scalloped Seafood

2-3 pounds lobster tail
1½   pounds king crabmeat or "sea legs"
1   tablespoon flour
2   cups light cream
2   tablespoons butter
½   teaspoon garlic powder
1   dash hot pepper sauce
2   teaspoons lemon juice (optional)
½   cup dry white wine or light sherry
⅓   cup seasoned cornbread crumbs
     Romano cheese
     Butter

- Wash lobster tail before cooking. Cook and clean out of shell. Cut into 1-inch pieces.

- Combine flour, butter and cream in pan and cook until thickened. Add lobster, crabmeat, seasonings and cornbread crumbs to the hot cream sauce and mix well.

- Pour mixture into individual ramekins or large casserole. Sprinkle Romano cheese and place a pat of butter on each.

- For ramekins bake at 350° for 20 to 25 minutes. If using a casserole bake 35 to 40 minutes. Can be microwaved on high for 8 to 9 minutes.

Yield: 6 to 7 servings.

Tangy Deviled Crab

1   pound crabmeat, picked over
¼   cup vinegar
1   teaspoon dry mustard
     Few dashes hot pepper sauce
1   tablespoon Worcestershire sauce
¼   pound package saltine crackers, crushed, divided
3   tablespoons mayonnaise
3   tablespoons butter, melted
     Paprika

- Combine vinegar, dry mustard, hot pepper sauce and Worcestershire sauce; pour over crabmeat. Add ½ saltine crumbs and mix with hands. Add mayonnaise until moist.

- Pack lightly into slightly buttered individual shells. Sprinkle remaining cracker crumbs which have been moistened with butter over top of crabmeat.

- Sprinkle with paprika. Bake at 375° until heated through.

Soft Shell Crabs with Lemon Butter Sauce

(Can serve with Shallot-Dill Mayonnaise instead of Lemon Butter Sauce)

12   **soft shell crabs, cleaned**
     Milk
     Flour
     Cooking oil
¾   **cup dry white wine**
     Juice of ½ lemon
1   **teaspoon Worcestershire sauce**
2   **tablespoon all-purpose flour**
½   **cup butter**
     Salt and pepper to taste
½   **cup chopped green onion, some green tops included**

- Moisten the crabs with milk and dredge in the flour on all sides, shake off excess flour.
- Heat ¼-inch cooking oil in a frying pan, (preferably a black cast iron skillet) to medium heat.
- Place crabs belly down in pan, cooking until crab bellies are golden brown. Turn crabs over and cook tops of crabs until brown.
- Make sauce while crabs are cooking. Combine wine, lemon juice, Worcestershire sauce and flour in a saucepan, stirring to dissolve the flour. Bring to a boil, reduce heat to medium and continue cooking, stirring constantly for 2 minutes.
- Remove pan from heat and stir in butter until melted and sauce is smooth.
- Add salt and pepper to taste and green onions, stirring well.
- Pour sauce over crabs.

Yield: 6 servings.

Soft Shell Crabs Amandine

6   **tablespoons sweet butter**
¼   **cup sliced almonds**
2-3   **small crabs**
     Unbleached flour
     Juice of ½ lemon
2   **tablespoons finely chopped parsley**
     Lemon slices

- Melt 2 tablespoons butter in pan. Sauté almonds until golden.
- Dredge crabs in flour.
- Heat remaining butter in another skillet until hot and foaming. Add crabs. Sauté over high heat turning occasionally until crisp and reddish brown, approximately 5 minutes.
- Transfer crabs to heated platter.
- Squeeze lemon juice into skillet with butter juices. Boil, add parsley and pour over crabs.
- Sprinkle almonds over crabs.
- Garnish with lemon slices.

Put vinegar on your hands to remove the fishy odors.

Baked Flounder with Cheese

2 pounds flounder fillets
2 tablespoons fresh lemon juice
¼ cup mayonnaise
2 tablespoons finely chopped onion
¼ cup Parmesan cheese
¼ cup margarine
½ teaspoon seasoned salt

- Preheat oven to 450°.

- Place flounder on greased cookie sheet. Pour lemon juice over fish.

- Combine rest of ingredients and set aside.

- Bake fish for 6 to 8 minutes until fish flakes with a fork. Remove from oven.

- Spread cheese mixture on top of fish. Put back in the oven and broil until cheese has melted and top is light brown.

Yield: 4 to 6 servings.

Blackened Fish

(Go easy on cayenne pepper if you have timid guests)

Spice Mix:
1 tablespoon paprika
2½ teaspoons salt
1 teaspoon onion powder
1 teaspoon garlic powder
1 teaspoon cayenne pepper
¾ teaspoon white pepper
¾ teaspoon black pepper
½ teaspoon thyme
   Melted margarine

Fish Steaks Recommended:
Redfish, tuna, red snapper, grouper, salmon, shark or swordfish

- Place spices in jar and shake well to blend; keeps well in jar for many future uses!

- Place fish steaks on wire rack. Brush fish with melted butter and sprinkle with spice mix. Repeat on other side; let sit and dry at this point if grill isn't ready.

- Grill over hot coals about 15 minutes, depending on size of fish steak.

- Fish will produce lots of smoke and the more spice mix used, the hotter the fish.

Baked Fish Fillet Vinaigrette

4 flounder or trout fillets
8 tablespoons Italian salad dressing
   Paprika
2 tomatoes, thinly sliced
2 tablespoons minced chives
½ cup shredded Cheddar cheese

- Preheat oven to 450°.

- Arrange fillets in shallow 9x12-inch baking dish which has been sprayed with cooking spray. Spoon salad dressing over fillets; sprinkle with paprika. Arrange two tomato slices over each fillet; sprinkle with chives.

- Bake, uncovered for 10 minutes. Sprinkle with grated cheese and bake an additional 2 to 3 minutes or until fillets flake with a fork.

- Serve with salad and cornbread.

Yield: 4 servings.

Broiled Tuna

2 pounds tuna steaks, cut 1-inch
thick
½ cup cooking oil
2 tablespoons lime juice
¼ cup dry vermouth or dry white wine
1 teaspoon onion powder
1 tablespoon chopped fresh basil or
½ teaspoon dried basil

- Mix oil, lime juice, vermouth, onion powder and basil, and place in a shallow baking dish just large enough to hold the tuna in a single layer.

- Place the tuna in the marinade and turn once to coat. Marinate for 30 minutes, turning the steaks twice.

- Broil about 4 inches from the heat for 5 minutes on each side. Baste with the marinade when the steaks are turned.

- The steaks are ready when the meat flakes easily when probed with a fork.

Yield: 4 servings.

Fresh Tuna Marinade

Fresh tuna
1 cup soy sauce
1 (16-ounce) bottle Italian dressing

- Slice tuna into steaks 1-1¼-inch thick.

- Combine other ingredients and pour over tuna. Marinate at least 1 hour; no more than 3 hours.

- Grill over hot coals; watch carefully. Does not take long, about 5 minutes on each side.

- Be careful not to overcook.

Fresh Tuna, Swordfish or Salmon

(May be served cold)

2-3 pounds fresh fish, steaked
Vegetable oil
Flour
2 large onions, sliced
2 teaspoons basil
⅓ cup dry wine or wine vinegar
2 teaspoons sugar

- Rinse fish carefully and blot dry with paper towels. Heat enough vegetable oil in open skillet to cover bottom of pan.

- Dust each slice of fish with flour and pan fry 5 minutes on both sides. Remove fish and set aside.

- Add onions to the oil with basil, wine and sugar. Cover pan and cook 5 to 7 minutes. Uncover, add the fish steaks and allow to simmer slowly for 7 to 9 minutes, covered.

- Serve warm or prepare early and serve cold.

Yield: 4 servings.

Carolina Boneless Shad

Roe shad, gutted and roe removed
Cooking oil
¼ **cup butter or margarine**
Salt and pepper to taste
Lemon slices
4 **slices bacon**
1 **cup water**
Parsley

- Wash fish and roe and pat dry. Lightly dust roe with cornmeal and sauté in oil until golden brown. Salt and pepper fish and roe. Replace roe in fish cavity. Rub fish with butter or margarine.

- Line bottom of a roaster with foil to enable easy removal of fish when done. Put fish on foil and place bacon strips and lemon slices on top. Put one cup of water in roaster.

- Cover roaster with top and cook for 8 hours at 250°. No need to check while cooking.

- Serve with lemon slices and parsley.

Flounder Fillets Supreme

2 **tablespoons margarine, divided**
4 **fresh flounder fillets**
2 **tablespoons lemon juice**
½ **cup grated Parmesan cheese**
¼ **cup mayonnaise**
3 **tablespoons chopped scallions**
½ **teaspoon salt**
½ **teaspoon pepper**

- Preheat oven to 500°.

- Cut a piece of foil to fit broiler pan; grease one side of foil with margarine and lay fillets on top. Pour lemon juice over fillets and let stand for a few minutes. Sprinkle fish with a few drops of water. Bake in hot oven 8 minutes.

- Combine cheese, margarine, mayonnaise, scallions, salt and pepper. Remove fish from oven and spread mixture on top of fish. Put in broiler and broil 2 to 3 minutes or until lightly browned.

Yield: 4 servings.

Charbroiled Bluefish

(Mayonnaise based sauce makes fish moist and good)

4 **large bluefish fillets, skin left on**
¾ **cup mayonnaise**
1 **teaspoon steak sauce**
1 **teaspoon lemon juice**
2 **tablespoons grated Parmesan cheese**
⅛ **teaspoon dill weed**
Seafood seasoning to taste

- Cover grill with heavy foil, slit at intervals to release heat. Lightly grease foil or spray with cooking spray.

- Place fish skin-side down on grill. Spread on sauce made of remaining ingredients. Cook without turning for 30 to 40 minutes, or until fish is flaky.

- Can also be baked or oven-broiled.

Yield: 4 to 6 servings.

Sicilian Fish

(Excellent with mixed green salad
and crusty bread)

⅓   cup olive oil
1   small onion, minced
2   garlic cloves, minced
1   (35-ounce) can Italian peeled
     tomatoes, chopped
     Salt to taste
     Pepper to taste
20 green Sicilian olives, pitted and
     sliced
3   tablespoons chopped Italian (flat
     leaf) parsley
2   tablespoons chopped fresh basil
1   tablespoon chopped celery leaf
1½-2 pounds white fish fillets, skinned
     (scrod, cod, halibut)
½-¾ pound linguine, cooked

- Heat oil in large deep skillet; add onion and garlic and cook over medium low heat until golden, approximately 10 minutes.

- Add tomatoes, salt, pepper and olives; bring to a boil. Reduce heat to low and simmer for 15 minutes; add parsley, basil and celery then cook for 15 minutes more.

- Add fish fillets, cut to portion size if needed, and simmer until opaque, approximately 20 minutes.

- Serve over linguine.

Yield: 2 servings.

Trout

4   medium sized whole trout, cleaned
¾   cup flour
     Dash of pepper
     Accent
     Garlic powder
2   cups thinly sliced onion
2   cups mushroom caps
2   beef bouillon cubes diluted in ½
     cup hot water
1¾ cups dry red wine or sherry
4   tablespoons butter

- Combine flour, pepper, accent and garlic powder. Roll each fish in mixture. Lay in greased long open pan. Cover with onions and mushrooms.

- Mix wine and diluted bouillon and pour over onions and mushrooms. Top each fish with 1 tablespoon of butter and cover with foil.

- Bake in preheated 350° oven for 35 to 40 minutes. Serve each fish with some of the sauce over it.

Yield: 4 servings.

Bacon-Baked Oysters

2   dozen unshucked oysters
6   slices bacon, quartered
1   cup buttery cracker crumbs
½   cup mayonnaise
2   tablespoons chopped chives
1   teaspoon lemon juice
1   teaspoon hot sauce
½   teaspoon Dijon mustard
1   (4-pound) package rock salt
¼   cup grated Parmesan cheese

- Wash and rinse oysters thoroughly in cold water; shuck oysters, reserving deep half of shells. Place oysters in a colander to drain; set aside.
- Cook bacon until limp, but not brown; drain and set aside.
- Combine the next 6 ingredients; mix well, set aside.
- Sprinkle rock salt in bottom of a jellyroll pan; arrange reserved shells on salt. Place oysters in half shells. Spread crumb mixture over each oyster; top with a piece of bacon and sprinkle with cheese.
- Bake at 400° for 8 to 10 minutes or until bacon is crisp.

Yield: 4 to 6 servings.

Oysters and Ham Casserole

3   pints oysters, drained and reserving ¼ cup liquid
½   cup cream
1   cup dry bread crumbs
1   cup stuffing mix
¾   cup butter, melted
2   cups cooked country ham, cut into bite size pieces

- Preheat oven to 400°.
- Combine ¼ cup liquid with cream; set aside. Combine bread crumbs and stuffing mix. Pour butter over crumbs.
- Grease large casserole; cover bottom with ham pieces. Cover with a layer of crumbs, a layer of oysters, ½ of liquid, a layer of crumbs, a layer of oysters and rest of liquid. Dot with butter.
- Cook for 20 minutes.

Yield: 8 servings.

Oyster Casserole

3   tablespoons chopped green pepper
2   tablespoons chopped onion
2   tablespoons oil
4   eggs, beaten
1   (15-ounce) can whole kernel corn
1   tablespoon dehydrated parsley
1   pint oysters, drained
½-¾   cup grated sharp Cheddar cheese

- Sauté pepper and onion in a little oil in small sauté pan until onion is opaque. Pour into lightly oiled 1½-quart casserole dish. Add corn and parsley to egg. Pour into casserole dish with onion and pepper; stir oysters into casserole.
- Bake at 375° until thickened.
- Top with grated cheese; return to oven until cheese is melted and lightly browned.
- If casserole is "weepy" add 5 or 6 crumbled saltines and stir into hot mixture just before topping with cheese. Always use sharp cheese. Small oysters are better to use.

Yield: 4 servings.

Oysters Isabelle

(May be used as an appetizer also)

1 **pint oysters, drained**
 Sour cream
2 **tablespoons finely chopped celery**
2 **tablespoons finely chopped onions**
¼ **cup bread crumbs**
¼ **cup melted butter or margarine**
¼ **teaspoon dry mustard**
½ **cup Parmesan cheese**

- Preheat oven to 450°.
- Arrange oysters in seafood shells. Put dab of sour cream on each oyster.
- Mix next 5 items and spread over oysters and sour cream. Top with Parmesan cheese.
- Cook for 10 minutes.

Tomato and Scallops

1 **pound scallops**
 Salt and pepper to taste
5 **tablespoons olive oil**
5 **tablespoons chopped scallions**
½ **cup cut and peeled tomatoes**
2 **tablespoons white wine vinegar**
1½ **tablespoons chopped parsley**

- Sprinkle scallops with salt and pepper; set aside to drain well.
- In saucepan combine oil, scallions, tomatoes and vinegar. Cook for 2 minutes. Add scallops to saucepan in single layer. Cook, shaking skillet, for 2 to 3 minutes.
- Do not brown or overcook. Sprinkle with parsley.

Yield: 4 servings.

Oyster Fritters

1 **pint oysters**
 Salt and pepper to taste
1-2 **eggs**
 Flour
 Vegetable oil

- Season oysters with salt and pepper. Add eggs and enough flour to make a thin batter. Stir thoroughly.
- Cover the bottom of a skillet with ½-inch oil. Cook in pan until browned.

Scalloped Oysters or Clams

30 **soda crackers, divided**
1 **pint oysters or clams with juice**
 Butter
 Thyme
1 **cup milk**
 Pepper
 Parsley
 Paprika

- Crumble 15 crackers and spread in bottom of 3-quart casserole that has been greased. Add oysters or clams and juice. Cover with pats of butter, dash of pepper and thyme.
- Crumble remaining 15 crackers and completely cover oysters; add milk. Dot with butter and add remaining seasonings.
- Bake in preheated oven at 350° for 30 to 35 minutes.

Yield: 4 to 6 servings.

Coquilles Saint Jacques

1   pound scallops
½   cup dry white wine
1   small white onion, finely chopped
½   pound mushrooms, sliced
     Juice of one lemon
¼   cup water
2   tablespoons flour
2   tablespoons margarine
⅔   cup cream
     Fine bread crumbs (optional)
     Grated Parmesan cheese (optional)

• Cook scallops in wine with onion for about 5 minutes. Drain and save liquid.

• Cook mushrooms in water and lemon juice. Drain and save juice.

• Melt butter and add flour. Cook until almost dry and stir in cream; add wine juice. Stir until thick and smooth. Add scallops and mushrooms. Pile into shells; may be sprinkled with bread crumbs and Parmesan cheese.

• Bake in oven at 400° until slightly browned.

Yield: 6 to 8 servings.

Scallop and Bacon Kabobs

¼   cup vegetable oil
¼   cup lemon juice
¼   cup Chablis or other dry white wine
¼   cup soy sauce
2   tablespoons chopped fresh parsley
½   teaspoon salt
½   teaspoon pepper
¼   teaspoon garlic powder
1   pound fresh scallops or frozen scallops, thawed
1   small pineapple, cut into 1-inch pieces
18-24 mushroom caps
3   large green peppers, cut into 1-inch squares
18-24 cherry tomatoes
12   slices bacon, cut in half

• Combine first 8 ingredients in a large bowl, mixing well. Add scallops, pineapple, and vegetables; toss to coat, and marinate in refrigerator for 1 to 1½ hours.

• Cook bacon until transparent (not crisp); drain well. Alternate bacon, scallops, pineapple and vegetables on skewers.

• Place kabobs 4 to 5 inches from hot coals; grill 10 to 12 minutes or until bacon is crisp, turning kabobs frequently and basting them with marinade.

Yield: 6 servings.

Artichoke and Seafood Casserole

4   tablespoons margarine
2   tablespoons shallots or green onions, chopped
1   clove garlic, minced
½   pound (or more) sliced fresh mushrooms
¼   cup flour
1   cup milk
⅔   cup dry white wine, fish stock or clam juice
1½ cups grated Swiss cheese, divided
    Salt and freshly ground pepper to taste
1   tablespoon fresh dill weed or 1 teaspoon dried
1   pound cleaned and cooked shrimp
1   pound lump crabmeat
1   package frozen artichoke hearts, cooked and drained
3   tablespoons buttered crumbs

- Preheat oven to 375°.
- Melt margarine in a skillet and sauté the shallots and garlic until tender; add mushrooms and cook 2 minutes more.
- Sprinkle with the flour, stir and cook one minute.
- Gradually stir in the milk and the wine; bring to a boil stirring until thick.
- Off the heat, stir in one cup of the cheese until it melts. Season to taste with salt and pepper; add dill.
- Stir in shrimp, crabmeat and artichoke hearts; pour into buttered casserole. Sprinkle with the remaining cheese and bread crumbs.
- Bake 25 minutes or until bubbly.

Yield: 6 servings.

Curried Shrimp

2   pounds shrimp, cleaned, deveined and cooked
1   medium onion, sliced
3   tablespoons oil
2   cans condensed tomato soup
1   teaspoon sugar
⅛   teaspoon salt
1   tablespoon Worcestershire sauce
1   teaspoon vinegar
3½   teaspoons curry powder
1   tablespoon butter
¾   soup can of water
     Hot cooked rice
     Condiments

- Sauté onion slices slowly in oil until golden and tender, but not brown. Add other ingredients except shrimp. Mix well and simmer uncovered for 10 minutes.
- Add shrimp, reheat and serve. This is even better when made in advance, but do not overcook shrimp.
- Serve with steamed rice and any or all of the following condiments:

Condiments:

Chopped nuts
Sieved, hard-boiled egg yolks
Sieved, hard-boiled egg whites
Raisins, plumped in warm water
Chutney
Chopped, crumbled bacon
Chopped green onions
Fresh pineapple chunks
Banana slices
Fresh grated coconut

Curried Shrimp Rice

(Serve cold)

1½   cups instant rice
1½   cups boiling water
½   teaspoon salt
¼   cup bottled French dressing
¾   cup mayonnaise
¾   teaspoon curry powder, or more
½   teaspoon salt
½   teaspoon dry mustard
½   cup diced celery
½   cup chopped onion
1½   pounds shrimp, cooked and cleaned
     Pepper to taste

- Combine rice, water and salt in saucepan. Cook by directions on rice package. When rice is cool, lightly toss in French dressing. Refrigerate until thoroughly cool.

- Blend together mayonnaise, onion, curry powder, salt, pepper and mustard. Refrigerate until ready to serve; add to rice and shrimp before serving.

- Can be made ahead of time and chilled.

  Yield: 6 servings.

Crab Stuffed Shrimp

Stuffing for Shrimp:
1   pound fresh crabmeat
1   egg
½   cup seasoned bread crumbs
1   teaspoon mustard
1   tablespoon mayonnaise
1   teaspoon chopped parsley
1   teaspoon Old Bay Seasoning
    Cocktail sauce

- Combine all of the stuffing ingredients together; mixing well.

12   large shrimp
12   strips of bacon

- Peel the shrimp but leave the tails on. Split the backs of the shrimp and lay them flat.

- Place one scoop of stuffing in the middle of the shrimp and wrap a slice of bacon tightly around the shrimp several times to hold the stuffing in place. Insert a toothpick through the shrimp to hold the bacon securely.

- Broil until the bacon is done. Serve with the cocktail sauce.

Dilled Shrimp and Rice Casserole

(The dill makes the difference)

1   cup rice, cooked and drained
½   pound sharp Cheddar cheese, grated and divided
2   cups cleaned and cooked shrimp
4   eggs, separated
¾   cup milk
¼   teaspoon pepper
¼   teaspoon onion salt
¼   teaspoon dill weed

- Preheat oven to 375°.

- Mix rice, cheese, and shrimp; reserve some cheese for the top. Mix egg yolks and milk and combine with shrimp mixture. Season with pepper, onion salt and dill weed.

- Beat egg whites until stiff and fold into shrimp mixture. Turn into greased 2-quart casserole dish. Sprinkle reserved cheese on top.

- Bake for 30 minutes.

  Yield: 8 servings.

Sauce for Shrimp Creole

Bacon drippings
4 tablespoons chopped onion
1 green pepper, chopped
3 cups canned tomatoes
½ cup chili sauce
2 teaspoons of brown sugar
Cayenne pepper to taste
2-3 tablespoons of flour
½ cup cooking wine (optional)
12 finely chopped olives (optional)
2 pounds of shrimp, peeled and deveined

- Sauté onions and peppers in bacon drippings. Add tomatoes and chili sauce. Cook or simmer to reduce liquid.
- Season and add 2 to 3 tablespoons of flour to thicken sauce.
- Just before serving, add wine, olives and shrimp. Cook until shrimp are done.

Yield: 6 to 8 servings.

Fried Shrimp

1½ pounds shrimp, cleaned, leaving tails on, deveined
3 cups milk
2 eggs, beaten
1 teaspoon Old Bay Seasoning
1 cup self-rising flour
Oil for frying

- Preheat oil in a deep fryer to 350°.
- Whip together milk, eggs and seasoning, mixing well.
- Roll shrimp in flour, dip in egg mixture and roll in flour again. Shake excess flour off.
- Slowly drop shrimp into hot oil; fry until golden brown.

Fettuccine with Shrimp

(Cooked pears are a nice accompaniment to this special dish)

6 tablespoons butter
5 garlic cloves, minced
1½ quarts whipping cream,
6 tablespoons dry Marsala
1 teaspoon salt
½ teaspoon freshly ground pepper
8 ounces freshly grated Parmesan cheese, divided
1½ pounds fresh spinach fettuccine
3½ cups small cooked shrimp, cleaned and deveined
Parsley for garnish

- Melt butter in a heavy large skillet over medium heat; add garlic and stir until tender but not brown, about 4 minutes.
- Blend in cream, Marsala, salt and pepper; bring to a slow boil. Cook, stirring frequently, until reduced to 3½ cups, about 45 minutes.
- Remove from heat and add 6 ounces Parmesan cheese, stirring constantly until melted.
- Bring large pot of salted water to rapid boil over high heat; add fettuccine and cook until al dente, about 4 minutes. Drain well; return to pot. Add sauce and shrimp; toss to coat.
- Transfer to heated platter; top with remaining cheese. Garnish with parsley and serve immediately.

Yield: 6 servings.

Shrimp and Asparagus Casserole

(Serve with salad and ham biscuits)

¾ cup butter, divided
½ cup all-purpose flour
3 cups half-and-half
1½ cups milk
½ cup sherry
¾ cup grated sharp Cheddar cheese
½ cup grated Parmesan cheese
 Juice of one lemon
1½ tablespoons grated onion
1 tablespoon chopped parsley
1 tablespoon prepared mustard
2½ teaspoons salt
 Pepper to taste
1 cup mayonnaise
¾ pound vermicelli, broken into 2-inch pieces
1 pound fresh mushrooms, sliced
2 pounds shrimp, cooked, peeled and deveined
2 (15-ounce) cans asparagus, drained

- In heavy saucepan, melt ½ cup margarine; blend in flour. Cook for 2 minutes, add half-and-half, milk and sherry. Cook until thickened, stirring constantly.

- Add cheeses, lemon juice, onion parsley, mustard, salt and pepper; heat until cheeses are melted.

- Remove from heat; add mayonnaise.

- Cook vermicelli according to package directions; drain.

- Sauté mushrooms in remaining margarine until tender; set aside.

- Combine sauce, vermicelli and shrimp; mixing well.

- In 2-quart baking dishes arrange layers in the following order — ⅓ shrimp mixture, ½ sautéed mushrooms and ½ asparagus. Repeat layers ending with the shrimp.

- Bake uncovered 350° for 30 minutes or until thoroughly heated.

Easy Shrimp Casserole

(A good "bring a dish" casserole)

1 cup uncooked, regular rice
1 medium size green pepper, finely chopped
1 medium size onion, finely chopped
1 (8-ounce) can sliced mushrooms, drained
½ cup melted butter or margarine
1 (10¾-ounce) can cream of shrimp soup, undiluted
1 teaspoon seasoned salt
½ teaspoon pepper
1 pound shrimp, cooked, peeled and deveined

- Cook rice according to package directions.

- Sauté green pepper, onion and mushrooms in butter in a large skillet. Add rice, soup, salt and pepper; simmer 20 to 25 minutes, stirring frequently. Add shrimp and simmer 3 to 5 minutes.

- Can be prepared 24 hours ahead of time.

- Serve with tossed salad, broccoli and pickled beets.

Yield: 6 to 8 servings.

Shrimp Cheese Puff Casserole

(Superior)

1 **pound uncooked shrimp, cleaned and deveined**
½ **pound sharp Cheddar cheese, grated**
3 **eggs, slightly beaten**
¼ **teaspoon dry mustard**
4 **slices buttered bread**
2 **cups milk**
   Salt and pepper to taste
   Paprika

- If shrimp are large, cut into 2 or 3 pieces.
- Butter bread and slice into ½-inch cubes. Put half the bread into a buttered casserole dish; spread with half the shrimp and sprinkle with half the cheese. Repeat layers.
- Beat the eggs slightly; beat in seasonings and milk.
- Pour mixture over other ingredients and sprinkle top with paprika.
- Bake 50 minutes at 350°.

Yield: 4 to 5 servings.

Shrimp Almandine

1 **pound raw shelled shrimp**
¼ **cup oil**
¼ **cup lemon juice**
3 **tablespoons margarine or butter**
1 **clove garlic, cut in half**
½ **cup chopped almonds**
2 **dashes hot sauce (optional)**
2 **tablespoons dry Vermouth**
   Hot, cooked rice

- Marinate shrimp in oil and lemon for about 2 hours. Remove shrimp and reserve sauce.
- Sauté shrimp in butter and garlic until pink. Remove garlic and place shrimp on warm platter. Add almonds and reserved marinade to butter in skillet. Add hot sauce and Vermouth; let simmer 2 to 3 minutes. Pour over platter of hot shrimp.
- Serve over mounds of rice.

Yield: 4 servings.

Shrimp Coquille

2 **tablespoons butter**
2 **tablespoons flour**
½ **cup ketchup**
1 **cup light cream**
1 **garlic clove, minced**
½ **teaspoon salt**
½ **teaspoon pepper**
1½ **tablespoons Worcestershire sauce**
   Lemon juice to taste
   Red pepper to taste
   Hot pepper sauce to taste
2 **pounds shrimp, cooked and cleaned**
   Buttered cracker crumbs

- Combine first 5 ingredients in a saucepan; cook over medium heat until cream sauce is thickened. Add seasonings and shrimp.
- Pour into a casserole or individual shells; cover with cracker crumbs.
- Bake in a 375° oven for 10 to 12 minutes.

Yield: 4 to 6 servings.

Shrimp Creole

6　slices bacon, cooked and drained, reserving grease
1　medium onion, chopped
2　ribs celery, chopped
2　green peppers, chopped (optional)
1　teaspoon sugar
2　(14½-ounce) cans stewed tomatoes
1　pound shrimp, cleaned and deveined
　　Cooked Saffron rice

- Sauté onion, celery and peppers in bacon grease until golden. Add sugar to caramelize. Add tomatoes and allow to simmer 30 to 60 minutes.
- Add shrimp to Creole sauce approximately 5 to 8 minutes before serving.
- Serve over Saffron rice.

Yield: 4 servings.

Shrimp Creole II

1　teaspoon chopped garlic
2　tablespoons olive oil
3½　cups chicken broth, divided
1　(12-ounce) can tomato paste
1　tablespoon sugar
1　teaspoon tarragon
1　tablespoon Old Bay Seafood Seasoning
1　bay leaf
1　large Spanish onion, sliced in thin wedges
1　large red bell pepper, sliced in strips
½　pound fresh okra, diced or frozen okra, sliced
4　ribs celery, sliced
1½　pounds shrimp, cleaned and deveined

- In large saucepan, sauté garlic in olive oil. Stir in 3 cups chicken broth. Add tomato paste, sugar and seasonings. Simmer for 30 minutes.
- This may be made early in the day or the day before.
- While sauce is simmering, stir-fry fresh vegetables in ½ cup chicken broth until crisp and tender. Add shrimp and toss 2 to 3 minutes over high heat. Add tomato sauce to vegetables after it has finished simmering and continue cooking for 5 more minutes.
- Serve over a bed of fluffy white rice.

Yield: 6 to 8 servings.

Shrimp Manalé

3　pounds jumbo shrimp with heads, *must* have heads on
1　(1½-ounce) bottle coarse ground black pepper
1　(5-ounce) bottle Worcestershire sauce
1　pound butter cut in cubes
　　Warm French bread

- Wash shrimp well and place them in a baking dish. Pour over shrimp the Worcestershire sauce and pepper. Add butter; cover with foil and bake 30 to 40 minutes at 350°.
- This is very messy to eat since everyone peels his own shrimp. This sauce is delicious when "sopped up" with warm French bread.
- Ladle shrimp and sauce into bowls.
- Serve with plenty of paper towels and cold beer.

Yield: 4 to 6 servings.

Shrimp Egg Foo Yung

½ **pound medium shrimp, cleaned, cooked and diced**
3 **eggs, beaten**
¾ **cup bean sprouts**
½ **cup chopped fresh mushrooms**
¼ **cup chopped green onion**
   Peanut or vegetable oil
   Green Pea Sauce

- Combine shrimp, eggs and vegetables. Let stand 10 minutes; mix well.
- Heat small amount of oil in a large skillet. Spoon ¼ cup egg mixture into hot oil, shaping into a 3-inch circle with a spatula.
- Cook until browned on one side; turn and brown other side. Repeat with remaining egg mixture, adding oil to skillet as necessary.
- Serve with Green Pea Sauce.

Green Pea Sauce:

¼ **cup chicken broth**
1 **tablespoon cornstarch**
1 **tablespoon soy sauce**
1 **teaspoon sugar**
¼ **cup frozen English peas**

- Combine chicken broth, cornstarch, soy sauce and sugar in a saucepan; stir until smooth. Cook over low heat until thickened, stirring constantly. Add peas and cook until thoroughly heated.

Yield: 8 servings.

Shrimp and Artichoke Casserole

½ **pound fresh sliced mushrooms**
6 **tablespoons butter**
1½ **pounds cooked shrimp, shelled and deveined**
10 **cooked artichoke hearts, coarsely chopped**
¼ **cup all-purpose flour**
1½ **cups light cream**
½ **cup dry sherry**
1 **tablespoon Worcestershire sauce**
   Salt and pepper to taste
¼ **teaspoon paprika**
½ **cup freshly grated Parmesan cheese**

- Preheat oven to 350°.
- Sauté mushrooms in 2 tablespoons of butter until soft. Layer a 3-quart casserole dish with the mushrooms, shrimp and artichoke hearts.
- Melt remaining butter until foamy; add flour, cook and stir for 3 minutes. Gradually add cream; cook and stir until sauce is well blended and thickened. Add sherry, Worcestershire sauce, salt, pepper and paprika. Pour over casserole ingredients and sprinkle with Parmesan cheese.
- Bake 30 to 40 minutes until bubbly and lightly browned.

Yield: 6 servings.

Shrimp and Wild Rice Casserole

1 (6-ounce) package long grain and wild rice
2 tablespoons oil or butter
1 cup chopped green pepper
1 cup chopped onion
1 cup chopped celery
3 pounds shrimp, cleaned and cooked
1 teaspoon curry powder
1 teaspoon Worcestershire sauce
¾ cup mayonnaise
Salt and pepper to taste
½ cup white wine
Minced parsley (optional)

- Cook rice according to package directions; set aside.

- Sauté green pepper, onion and celery in butter or oil until tender. Combine with rice and remaining ingredients except parsley. Pour into greased 9x13-inch casserole dish.

- Cover and bake in preheated oven at 350° for 45 minutes or until heated through. Sprinkle parsley over top.

Yield: 6 to 8 servings.

Shrimp Harpin

3 pounds peeled shrimp
1-2 tablespoons lemon juice
3 tablespoons salad oil
¾ cup raw rice
2 tablespoons butter
¼ cup finely chopped green pepper
¼ cup chopped onion
1 teaspoon salt
⅛ teaspoon mace
Black pepper to taste
Dash cayenne pepper
1 can tomato soup, undiluted
1 cup whipping cream
½ cup sherry
½ cup toasted almonds
Paprika

- Add shrimp to boiling water; return to boil and boil for 1 minute. Drain.

- Pour lemon juice and salad oil over shrimp and refrigerate.

- Cook rice as directed until not completely done.

- In butter sauté green pepper and chopped onion until soft. Combine with salt, pepper, mace and cayenne pepper.

- 1 to 2 hours before serving, put all of the above ingredients together in a large casserole. Add tomato soup, whipping cream, sherry and almonds; mixing well. Sprinkle top with paprika.

- Bake at 350° until it bubbles, about 15 to 20 minutes.

Yield: 6 to 8 servings.

Zesty Shrimp Creole

3   pounds shrimp, cleaned and
    deveined
1   tablespoon shortening
1   medium onion, chopped
2   cloves garlic, minced
2   strips celery, chopped
1   hot pepper, minced
1   small bell pepper, chopped
1   (16-ounce) can tomatoes,
    undrained
1   (6-ounce) can tomato paste
3   sprigs thyme
1   bay leaf
1   tablespoon chopped parsley
½   tablespoon sugar
½   teaspoon cayenne (optional)
    Salt and pepper to taste
    Cooked white rice

- In a large saucepan, melt shortening over medium heat; add onion, garlic, celery, peppers; simmer 5 minutes.
- Add tomatoes, paste and seasonings; mix in well. Add shrimp and simmer, covered, for ½ hour over low heat.
- Serve hot over cooked rice.

Shrimp Pie

1   large green pepper, finely chopped
1   large onion, finely chopped
3   (16-ounce) cans tomatoes, drained
    well
5   slices white bread, broken into
    bite-size pieces
2   tablespoons Worcestershire sauce
5   drops hot pepper sauce
5   shakes lemon pepper
    Salt to taste
¾   cup grated cheese, divided
2   pounds cleaned, shelled shrimp

- Mix all ingredients together, except cheese.
- Mix a little cheese with other ingredients and save the rest to put on top. Place in shallow baking dish sprayed with non-stick vegetable spray. Sprinkle remaining cheese over top.
- Bake at 350° until warm and cheese bubbles on top.

Shrimp Soufflé

6   slices of bread, broken into small
    pieces
½   pound white cheese, shredded and
    reserving some for the top
2   cups shrimp, cooked and cleaned
3   eggs, beaten
½   teaspoon salt
½   teaspoon paprika
¼   teaspoon dry mustard
2½ cups milk

- Preheat oven to 325°.
- Grease a 1½-quart casserole dish. Alternate layers of bread, cheese and shrimp until all is used. Add salt, paprika, mustard and milk to the eggs. Pour beaten egg mixture over shrimp etc.
- Sprinkle rest of cheese on top.
- Bake for 1 hour.

Yield: 4 to 6 servings.

Lime Butter

(Use with broiled or grilled fish and corn on the cob)

½   **cup unsalted butter**
2   **tablespoons lime juice**
1   **tablespoon minced fresh dill**

- Melt butter and add lime juice and herbs.

  Yield: ½ cup.

Fresh Tuna Marinade

   Tuna steaks
1   **cup oil and vinegar dressing**
3   **tablespoons soy sauce**
3   **tablespoons sour cream**

- Cut tuna into 1-inch steaks and place in a Pyrex dish.
- Mix dressing, soy sauce and sour cream together. Pour over tuna steaks and marinate for at least 1 hours.
- Cook over medium hot grill for 5 to 10 minutes per side. Do not over cook.

  Yield: 1½ cups.

Fish Sauce for the Grill

(Especially good on mackerel steaks)

½   **cup margarine**
1   **bay leaf**
1   **teaspoon celery seed**
1   **tablespoon Worcestershire sauce**
   Salt and pepper to taste
   Garlic to taste (optional)

- Combine all ingredients in saucepan and bring to a low boil.
- Baste fish often as it is grilled.

Shrimp Rémoulade

½   **cup plus 1 tablespoon salad oil**
1   **tablespoon Creole or other prepared mustard**
3   **tablespoons vinegar**
1   **teaspoon salt**
¼   **teaspoon hot pepper sauce**
½   **tablespoon paprika**
1   **hard-boiled egg yolk**
½   **cup minced celery**
2   **tablespoons grated onion**
2   **tablespoons minced parsley**
2   **tablespoons minced green pepper**
1   **hard-boiled egg white, chopped**
1   **pound shelled, cooked shrimp**

- Beat oil, mustard, vinegar, salt, hot pepper sauce, paprika and egg yolk with rotary beater until thick and blended.
- Fold in celery, onion, parsley, green pepper and egg white. Mix with shrimp. Let stand in refrigerator several hours.
- Serve on bed of lettuce.

  Yield: 4 servings.

Hot Flavored Butter

(Good for dipping crabs, clams, mussels or oysters)

1   **cup butter, melted**
2   **teaspoons Worcestershire sauce**
2   **teaspoons prepared mustard**
2   **tablespoons chili sauce**
2   **drops hot pepper sauce**
4   **teaspoons lemon juice**
2   **teaspoons chopped fresh parsley**

- Mix all ingredients together in a saucepan and heat until bubbly.

  Yield: 1¾ cups.

Rémoulade Sauce

(Serve with lump crab, cold boiled shrimp, fish or fried oysters)

1 **cup mayonnaise, preferably homemade**
1 **tablespoon minced onion**
1 **tablespoon minced parsley**
2 **tablespoons Dijon mustard**
1 **tablespoon horseradish**
1 **teaspoon paprika**
½ **teaspoon salt**
1 **tablespoon vinegar**
½ **teaspoon Worcestershire sauce**
¼ **cup salad oil**
   Dash hot pepper sauce

- Combine all ingredients except oil; whisk in oil slowly.
- Refrigerate for several hours or overnight.

  Yield: 1½ cups.

Seafood Sauce for Grilling

¾ **cup chopped onion**
½ **cup salad oil**
¾ **cup ketchup**
¾ **cup water**
⅓ **cup lemon juice**
3 **tablespoons sugar**
3 **tablespoons Worcestershire sauce**
2 **tablespoons prepared mustard**
2 **teaspoons salt**
¼ **teaspoon hot sauce**

- Cook onions in oil until tender but not brown. Add remaining ingredients and simmer uncovered for 15 minutes. Cool.
- Leave tails on shrimp; marinate for 2 hours.
- Cook shrimp or fish on grill, basting with sauce
- Cook shrimp 5 to 8 minutes and fish until flaky.

  Yield: 3 to 4 cups.

Roasted Red Pepper Sauce

(Excellent over blackened fresh tuna with a dollop of sour cream)

3	red bell peppers, 18 ounces total
2	medium garlic cloves
4½	teaspoons brandy
2	teaspoons red wine vinegar
½	teaspoon salt
⅛	teaspoon cayenne pepper
3	tablespoons unsalted butter, cut into 3 pieces

- Char peppers in broiler until blackened on all sides. Transfer to paper bag and let stand 10 minutes to steam. Peel; rinse under cold water and pat dry. Cut peppers lengthwise into 4 pieces each, discarding seeds and cores.

- In a food processor, with machine running, drop garlic through feed tube and mince. Add peppers, brandy, vinegar, salt and cayenne pepper and blend until very smooth, stopping as necessary to scrape sides.

- Strain mixture into small non-aluminum pan. Add butter and stir over low heat until just melted, 3 to 4 minutes. Adjust seasoning before serving.

  Yield: 1¼ cups.

Parsley-Pecan Sauce for Fish

Sauce:

2	cups fresh parsley leaves, tightly packed
½	cup olive oil
½	cup pecans
1	large garlic clove, chopped
½	cup freshly grated Parmesan cheese
½	cup freshly grated Romano cheese
2	tablespoons unsalted butter, cut in pieces
	Salt, to taste

- Coarsely chop parsley in food processor. Add next 6 ingredients and process into a smooth paste. Correct seasoning with salt.

- Store, tightly covered in refrigerator until ready to use. Sauce freezes well.

Fish:

6	5-ounce fillets (flounder, orange roughy or favorite fish)
2	cups seafood breader mix
1	tablespoon cayenne pepper
1	tablespoon salt
2	tablespoons oil
2	tablespoons unsalted butter

- Combine breader, pepper and salt. Dust over fillets until lightly coated. Melt butter and oil in large skillet. Lay fish skin side down in hot oil and cook until golden on bottom. Turn and spread each with one tablespoon sauce. Cover and cook until brown, about another 4 minutes.

ACCOMPANIMENTS

Becky Wienges '92

Index for Accompaniments

Baked Bananas

12 small ripe bananas
6 tablespoons butter
¾ cup sugar
6 tablespoons lemon juice
½ cup orange juice

- Place butter, sugar and juices in pan and melt.
- Spread peeled bananas in a shallow pan. Pour sauce over bananas.
- Bake in oven at 350° for 30 minutes. Baste frequently.

Yield: 12 servings.

Baked Pineapple

(Good with ham dishes)

1 cup butter, softened
1 cup sugar
2 eggs
1 (20-ounce) can chunk pineapple with juice
½ cup milk
5-6 slices bread, cubed

- Cream butter and sugar together; add eggs and beat.
- Stir in by hand the pineapple with juice, milk and bread cubes.
- Bake in a 2-quart casserole dish for 1 hour at 350°.

Yield: 6 servings.

Brandied Fruit Dish

½ cup butter
1 cup sugar
2 teaspoons flour
1 cup sherry
4 (12-ounce) cans fruit, drained

- Melt butter in small saucepan. Add sugar and flour and heat to a creamy consistency. Add sherry.
- Pour over fruit in casserole dish. Heat in oven for 15 minutes at 350° or until bubbly.

Yield: 10 to 12 servings.

Cranberries Jubilee

6 packages whole fresh cranberries, washed and stems removed
12 medium oranges
3 lemons
7 pounds granulated sugar
1 tablespoon salt or less
2 cups orange juice
1 (2-ounce) package sliced almonds

- Put cranberries in large pot.
- Wash oranges and lemons, remove seeds and slice into fine slices.
- Add orange and lemon slices and juice, sugar, salt and additional orange juice to cranberries.
- Cook slowly for 1 hour; add almonds to hot mixture and cook for 10 minutes, stirring frequently.
- Let stand in pot overnight.
- Heat to simmering, stirring frequently and let stand for 15 minutes.
- Pack into hot, sterilized pint jars; process in hot water bath for 10 minutes.

Yield: 14½ pints.

Carrot Marmalade

3 **pounds carrots, peeled and cut into large pieces**
   Rind and juice of 2 lemons, about 5 tablespoons
6 **cups sugar**

- Cook carrots in boiling water until tender; drain and cool.
- Press carrots and lemon rind through the coarse grind attachment of a hand-operated food mill.
- Place carrot mixture in a mixing bowl and add sugar and lemon juice, combining well.
- Pour into a large kettle and simmer for 45 minutes, stirring often.
- Cool, then pour into sterilized jars.

Yield: 2 cups.

Cranberry Chutney

1 **cup fresh orange sections**
¼ **cup orange juice**
1 **pound fresh, washed cranberries**
1½ **cups sugar**
1 **large tart apple, chopped, unpeeled**
½ **cup raisins**
¼ **cup chopped pecans**
1 **tablespoon vinegar**
½ **teaspoon ground ginger**
½ **teaspoon cinnamon**
½ **teaspoon ground cloves**

- Combine all ingredients in saucepan and bring to a boil. Simmer until berries burst.
- Fill jars and chill. Will keep in refrigerator for 4 weeks.

Yield: 4 (8-ounce) jars.

Fresh Cranberry Casserole

(A great side dish for the holidays)

½ **cup white sugar**
½ **cup light brown sugar**
1 **cup quick oatmeal, uncooked**
3 **tablespoons flour**
1 **teaspoon cinnamon**
1½ **cups fresh cranberries**
3 **medium apples, diced**
1 **cup pecans, chopped**
½ **cup margarine**

- Combine the first 5 ingredients; add fruit and nuts, mixing well. Spread in a casserole; top with margarine.
- Bake at 350° for 30 minutes.

Curried Peaches

(Make a day ahead)

½ **cup butter**
¾ **cup brown sugar**
4 **teaspoons curry**
1 **(29-ounce) can peach halves, drained**

- Melt butter in a saucepan and add sugar and curry, stirring to blend.
- Arrange peach halves in a casserole dish; pour sauce over fruit.
- Bake at 325° for 40 minutes.
- Let the flavors marry for 25 hours before serving.

Yield: 8 servings.

Festive Fruit

(A prize winner!)

1 **(15-ounce) can whole cranberries, drained**
1 **(15-ounce) can blueberries, drained**
1 **(15-ounce) can sliced pears, drained**
1 **(15-ounce) can apricots, drained**
1 **(15-ounce) can sliced peaches, drained**
1 **(15-ounce) can chunk pineapple, drained**
1 **(15-ounce) can sweet, pitted cherries, drained**
1 **cup chopped pecans (optional)**
1 **cup brown sugar**
6 **tablespoons butter**

- Preheat oven to 350°.
- Layer fruit (in order given) in a 8x11-inch Pyrex dish. Add pecans if desired.
- Sprinkle brown sugar over all. Cover with thinly sliced butter.
- Bake for 30 minutes.

Yield: 20 to 24 servings.

Peach/Blueberry Jam

(A wonderful combination of two popular summer fruits)

4 **cups blueberries**
2 **pounds ripe peaches**
2 **tablespoons lemon juice**
5 **cups sugar**
1 **(1¾-ounce) box powdered fruit pectin**

- Stem and crush berries. Measure 1 cup into 6- to 8-quart saucepan.
- Peel and pit peaches. Chop very fine or grind. Measure 3 cups, add to berries; add lemon juice.
- Measure sugar and set aside.
- Mix fruit pectin into fruit. Place over high heat and stir until mixture comes to a full boil. Immediately add all sugar and stir. Bring to a full rolling boil; boil hard for 1 minute.
- Remove from heat; skim foam. Ladle into jars to within ¼-inch from top; seal with tops and bands. Process 5 minutes in water bath.

Yield: 7 half pint jars.

Fig Preserves

5 **pounds figs**
5 **cups sugar**
3 **lemons, sliced**

- Wash figs and remove skins if you want to; add sugar and let sit overnight. Add lemons and simmer uncovered for 2½ to 3 hours until cooked down and thickened.
- Pour in hot sterilized jars.

Yield: 4 to 5 pints.

Spiced Peaches

1 **large can peach halves, drained**
1 **teaspoon whole cloves**
1 **teaspoon allspice**
½ **cup brown sugar**
½ **cup vinegar**

- Mix all ingredients in a saucepan except peaches. Bring to a boil; add peaches and simmer for 8 minutes. Let cool and serve.

Yield: 6 to 8 servings.

Watermelon Fruit Basket with Strawberry Dip

1   large watermelon
3   cantaloupes, peeled and cut into 1-inch cubes
2   medium honeydew melons, peeled and cut into 1-inch cubes
2   quarts fresh strawberries
2   pints blueberries
1   pound seedless grapes
3   (8-ounce) cartons strawberry flavored yogurt
1½ cups commercial sour cream
3   tablespoons honey
1½ tablespoons lemon juice

• Cut watermelon into bite-size pieces. Arrange fruit on lettuce on a large tray or platter.

• Combine yogurt, sour cream, honey and lemon juice, stirring with a wire whisk until well blended.

• Serve chilled as an accompaniment to fruit platter.

Yield: 20 servings.

Fruit in Sherry Sauce

2   (20-ounce) cans sliced pineapple, drained
2   (16-ounce) cans peeled apricots, drained
2   (29-ounce) cans peach halves, drained
2   (29-ounce) cans pear halves, drained
2   (15-ounce) jars cinnamon apple rings, drained
2   (11-ounce) cans mandarin oranges, drained
    Green seedless grapes
1   (6-ounce) bottle red cherries, drained

• Alternate fruits in stacks in a 3-quart casserole.

Sauce:
3   cups sherry
1½ cups margarine
1½ cups sugar
6   tablespoons flour

• Combine all sauce ingredients in a saucepan; cook over medium heat, stirring often until a creamy consistency.

• Cook to lukewarm and pour over the fruit; marinate overnight in the refrigerator.

• Remove from the refrigerator 30 minutes before cooking. Bake at 350° for 30 minutes, uncovered.

Yield: 20 servings.

Artichoke Casserole with Spinach

1½   **cups artichoke hearts**
1   **(8-ounce) can sliced mushrooms, drained**
2   **(10-ounce) packages frozen spinach, thawed and drained**
1   **(8-ounce) package cream cheese**
2   **tablespoons margarine**
   Salt and pepper to taste
   Dill weed to taste
½   **cup milk**
   Parmesan cheese

- Butter bottom of 1-quart casserole. Place artichokes in bottom of casserole. Add mushrooms on top of artichokes, then add spinach.
- In separate bowl whip cream cheese, margarine, salt, pepper, dill weed and milk until smooth. Spread mixture over spinach and sprinkle with Parmesan cheese.
- Cover and bake in oven at 350° for 30 minutes. Remove cover and continue to bake for 10 more minutes.

Yield: 4 servings.

Asparagus Gratin

(A quick, delicious way to fix this favorite)

1   **pound asparagus, trimmed and tied together in a bundle**
   Salt
¼   **cup butter, melted**
   Juice of ½ lemon
¼-⅓   **cup freshly grated Gruyère or Parmesan cheese**
   Pepper

- Cook asparagus, uncovered, in boiling salted water for 10 minutes or until tender. Drain the asparagus on a kitchen towel and remove the tie.
- Just before serving, place asparagus in layers in a buttered gratin pan. Pour melted butter and lemon juice over and sprinkle with the cheese. Season with pepper and brown under broiler just until the cheese starts to melt.

Yield: 2 servings.

Asparagus and Peas Casserole

1   **(15-ounce) can asparagus, drained**
1   **(8½-ounce) can peas, drained**
1   **(6-ounce) can mushrooms, drained**
   Juice of ½ a lemon
1   **(10¾-ounce) can mushroom soup**
1   **teaspoon salt**
2   **hard-boiled eggs, sliced**
   Paprika
   Bread crumbs

- Layer in casserole ½ of asparagus, peas, eggs and mushrooms. Repeat layers.
- Mix together lemon juice and soup. Pour over vegetables. Top with bread crumbs and paprika.
- Bake at 350° until bubbly.

Beefy Baked Beans

½   pound ground beef
1   (31-ounce) can pork and beans
1   (16-ounce) can red kidney beans,
    drained
1   medium onion, chopped
½   green pepper, chopped
½   cup ketchup
½   cup dark corn syrup
2   tablespoons prepared mustard
4   slices bacon, cut in half

- Cook ground beef until browned, stirring to crumble meat. Drain well.
- Combine beef and next 6 ingredients; stir well. Spoon mixture into a lightly greased 12x8x2-inch baking dish. Arrange bacon on top.
- Bake at 400° for 40 minutes.

Yield: 8 servings.

Fannie's Beans

(Soul food!)

2   pounds dry pinto beans
½   cup salt pork, cut into small cubes
    Water
1   tablespoon chili powder
4   tablespoons bacon grease
1   tablespoon salt
1   tablespoon sugar
1   teaspoon black pepper
    Salt to taste

- Wash beans several times. Combine all ingredients in a large pot; cover with water. Cover pot and bring to a slow boil.
- Reduce to low heat and simmer all day. Keep beans covered with water at all times.
- The longer they cook, the better.

Yield: 10 to 12 servings.

Three Bean Baked Beans

12   slices bacon, cooked
 3   tablespoons bacon drippings
 3   medium onions, thinly sliced
 2   cloves garlic, chopped
 1   cup brown sugar
 ½   cup vinegar
 ¼   teaspoon dry mustard
 2   (15½-ounce) cans kidney beans,
     drained
 2   (17-ounce) cans small lima beans,
     drained
 2   (15-ounce) cans Northern white
     beans, drained

- Cook onions and garlic in bacon drippings until onions are translucent. Add brown sugar, vinegar and mustard. Simmer for 20 minutes; stir together onion mixture from pan, bacon and beans.
- Pour into a 3-quart casserole and cover with foil.
- Bake at 300° for 1 hour.

    Variation: In place of vinegar and dry mustard, add ⅔ cup ketchup, 2 tablespoons Worcestershire sauce. Add ½ pound sharp Cheddar cheese, shredded and ½ pound Monterey Jack cheese, shredded. Cook at 375° for 1½ hours or 4 hours in slow cooker.

Yield: 16 to 20 servings.

Marinated Fresh Green Beans

¾ pound fresh string beans, left whole with ends snipped
2 cloves of garlic, minced
¼ cup red onion, diced
1½ tablespoons olive oil
¼ teaspoon salt
3 tablespoons lemon juice

- Steam whole string beans for 3 to 5 minutes. Drain but do not rinse.

- Mix next 4 ingredients and toss with drained string beans. Let set for one hour. Just before serving, add lemon juice and toss.

- String beans should be about the same size so they will be crisp and cook at the same rate.

Yield: 3 servings.

Broccoli with Sesame Dressing

(Really jazzes up a favorite vegetable)

2 pounds broccoli cut into 2-inch pieces (or just use florets)
2½ tablespoons sugar
2 tablespoons vegetable oil
2 tablespoons soy sauce
2 tablespoons sesame seeds, toasted
2 tablespoons vinegar

- Cook broccoli approximately 8 to 10 minutes in a steamer; drain.

- Combine the remaining ingredients in a saucepan and bring to a boil over medium heat.

- Pour over broccoli and serve.

Yield: 6 to 8 servings.

Sweet and Sour Green Beans

(Really perks up an old stand-by)

8 strips bacon, fried, drained and crumbled
1½ tablespoons bacon drippings
1 small onion, thinly sliced
3 teaspoons cornstarch
½ teaspoon salt
½ teaspoon dry mustard
2 (16-ounce) can green beans, reserving liquid from 1 can
2 tablespoons brown sugar
2 tablespoons vinegar

- Add the onion to bacon drippings and sauté until lightly browned. Stir in cornstarch, salt and mustard.

- Bring to a boil, stirring constantly. Stir in liquid from 1 can of beans and return to boil. Blend in brown sugar and vinegar; add drained green beans and heat through.

- Garnish with crumbled bacon at serving time.

Yield: 8 servings.

Better Broccoli

1 cup water
1 clove garlic, unpeeled
¼ cup olive oil
1 bunch broccoli, cleaned
Parmesan cheese

- Cook broccoli in boiling water with oil and garlic for 4 to 5 minutes, until crunchy-tender; drain.

- Sprinkle with Parmesan cheese.

Yield: 4 to 5 servings.

Broccoli and Cheese Bake

½   cup finely chopped onion
12   tablespoons of butter or margarine, divided
4   tablespoons of flour
1   cup of water
2   (8-ounce) jars of pasteurized, processed cheese spread
4   (10-ounce) packages of chopped frozen broccoli, thawed and drained
6   eggs, beaten
1   cup bread crumbs

- Sauté onions in 8 tablespoons of butter until soft. Stir in flour. Add water and cook over low heat to make sauce. Blend in the cheese.
- Combine the sauce and broccoli. Add the beaten eggs and mix gently.
- Place mixture in a 3-quart greased casserole dish. Cover with buttered bread crumbs.
- Bake for 45 minutes at 325°, uncovered.

Broccoli with Horseradish Sauce

1   bunch broccoli
    Mayonnaise
    Mustard
    Horseradish

- Steam broccoli for a very short time until stems are just beginning to get tender.
- Cover with a sauce of mayonnaise, mustard and horseradish, mixed according to taste.

Yield: 4 to 6 servings.

Carrot Ring

2   eggs, well beaten
1   teaspoon sugar
2   tablespoons butter, melted
2½   cups coarsely grated carrots
¼   cup blanched almonds
1   (5-ounce) can evaporated milk
1   teaspoon salt
    White pepper, if desired
    Non-stick vegetable spray

- Preheat oven to 375°.
- Add sugar, butter, carrots, almonds, evaporated milk, salt and pepper to eggs.
- Spray a ring mold with non-stick vegetable spray; pour mixture into mold. Place in a pan of hot water.
- Bake for 30 to 40 minutes. Turn out onto a platter; fill the center with peas, beans, asparagus or other vegetable.

Yield: 8 servings.

Dilled Baby Carrots

¾   pound baby carrots
2   cups boiling water
2   tablespoons unsalted butter
½   teaspoon salt
    Fresh dill to taste

- In a large skillet, cook the baby carrots in the boiling water until tender, 10 to 15 minutes. Drain well and return to pan.
- Add the butter and salt and shake over moderate heat until the butter is melted and the carrots are well coated.
- Just before serving snip some fresh dill over the carrots.

Note: Use a combination of baby vegetables: squash, corn, etc., for a nice change.

Honey and Nut Carrots

5 cups carrots, julienned
1½ cups water
½ teaspoon salt
½ cup butter, melted
2 teaspoons honey
1 teaspoon salt
¼ teaspoon coarse ground pepper
2 tablespoons fresh lemon juice
½ teaspoon lemon peel, freshly grated
½ cup walnuts, broken in pieces

- Cook carrots in water with ½ teaspoon salt until just tender; drain thoroughly.
- Combine the remaining ingredients except walnuts and heat.
- Pour sauce over carrots; toss with walnuts.

Corn Custard

2 tablespoons margarine
2 tablespoons flour
½ teaspoon salt
¼ teaspoon sugar
1 (17-ounce) can cream-style golden sweet corn
2 eggs, beaten
¾ cup milk, scalded

- In saucepan, melt margarine; blend in flour, salt and sugar. Add corn, eggs and scalded milk and mix well.
- Place in a 1½-quart dish; set in shallow pan of hot water.
- Bake at 325° to 350° for 45 minutes or until knife comes out clean.

Yield: 6 servings.

Elegant Cauliflower and Peas

1 medium head cauliflower, broken into florets and cooked
2 tablespoons butter
2 tablespoons flour
1½ cups sour cream
1 (10-ounce) package frozen peas
2 teaspoons curry powder
1 teaspoon onion salt
Curried Almonds

- Melt butter, blend in flour and sour cream; cook until bubbly.
- Combine remaining ingredients. Mix well and put into a buttered 2-quart casserole. Top with Curried Almonds.
- Bake at 325° for 30 minutes.

Curried Almonds:

1 tablespoon butter
1 teaspoon curry powder
½ cup slivered almonds

- Melt butter and stir in curry.
- Mix and then add almonds; cook until brown.

Yield: 6 to 8 servings.

Celery Supreme

6 **cups diced celery**
½ **cup water**
1 **teaspoon salt**
1 **(8-ounce) can sliced water chestnuts, drained**
1 **(2-ounce) jar chopped pimento, drained**
½ **green pepper, diced**
1 **(10-ounce) can cream of celery soup**

- Simmer celery in water and salt for 10 minutes; drain.
- Combine celery, water chestnuts, pimento, green pepper and soup; mix gently.
- Place in greased 9x9-inch casserole.

Topping:
¼ **cup melted butter**
1 **cup coarse bread crumbs**
½ **cup sliced almonds**

- Combine butter, crumbs and almonds; spread over celery mixture.
- Bake at 350° for 30 minutes.

Yield: 8 servings.

Creamed Eggplant

(A favorite childhood dish)

1 **large eggplant, peeled and cubed**
2 **medium onions, peeled and sliced paper thin**
   White Sauce
½ **cup bread crumbs**
2 **tablespoons butter, melted**

- Combine eggplant and onions in large saucepan. Cover with water to about ½ to top of vegetables. Bring water to a boil, then lower to medium and cook until vegetables are soft; drain completely.

White Sauce:
6 **tablespoons butter**
6 **tablespoons flour**
1 **cup light cream**
1 **cup whole milk**
1½ **teaspoons salt**
   Black pepper to taste
   Hot sauce to taste

- Melt butter in saucepan. Add flour and stir until smooth. Slowly add cream and milk.
- Stir continuously until mixture comes to a boil over medium heat; season with salt, pepper and hot sauce. Mix well; gently fold in eggplant and onion.
- Toss bread crumbs with butter. Pour eggplant mixture into casserole; cover with bread crumbs.
- Cook in 350° oven until hot and bubbly.

Eggplant Casserole

1 **large eggplant, peeled**
1 **large onion, diced**
½ **pound ground beef**
1 **(6-ounce) jar mushrooms, drained**
1 **(15½-ounce) jar spaghetti sauce**
   Parmesan cheese
   Mozzarella cheese

- Parboil eggplant in salted water and slice. Brown meat with onions.
- In 1½-quart casserole, layer ½ of eggplant, meat, onions, mushrooms, sauce and cheeses. Continue to layer and top with cheeses.
- Bake at 350° for 30 to 45 minutes.

Yield: 3 to 4 servings.

Eggplant Parmigiana

2 tablespoons butter
½ cup chopped onion
1 clove garlic, minced
1 pound ground chuck
1 (17-ounce) can Italian tomatoes, undrained
1 (6-ounce) can tomato paste
2 teaspoons oregano
1 teaspoon basil
1 tablespoon brown sugar
2 eggs, beaten
1 tablespoon oil
1½ teaspoons salt
¼ teaspoon pepper
1 cup water plus 1 tablespoon
1 large eggplant, unpeeled and cut into ½-inch thick slices
1¼ cups freshly grated Parmesan cheese, divided
½ cup bread crumbs
⅓ cup salad oil
1 (8-ounce) package sliced Mozzarella cheese, divided

- In hot butter sauté onion, garlic and chuck for about 5 minutes; add tomatoes, tomato paste, oregano, basil, salt, pepper, sugar and 1 cup water. Bring to a boil; reduce heat and simmer uncovered for 20 minutes.

- Preheat oven to 350°. Lightly grease a 13x9x2-inch baking dish.

- In a pie plate combine eggs and 1 tablespoon water, mixing well.

- On a sheet of waxed paper combine ½ cup Parmesan cheese and bread crumbs, mixing well.

- Dip eggplant slices into egg mixture, coating well. Dip into crumb mixture, coating evenly.

- Sauté eggplant slices, a few at a time, in 1 tablespoon hot oil until brown and crisp on both sides.

- Arrange half of the eggplant slices in the bottom of prepared baking dish. Sprinkle with half of the remaining Parmesan cheese; top with half of Mozzarella cheese. Cover with half of the tomato sauce. Repeat layers.

- Bake uncovered for 25 minutes or until cheese is melted and slightly brown.

Yield: 8 to 10 servings.

Mushroom Soufflé

1 (10¾-ounce) can mushroom soup
4 eggs, separated
1 medium onion, grated

- Beat egg yolks. Add mushroom soup and grated onions.

- Beat egg whites until stiff. Fold into egg yolk and soup mixture. Pour into small greased soufflé dish.

- Bake at 250° for 20 to 30 minutes.

Yield: 4 to 5 servings.

Mystery Mushrooms in Tomatoes

8 firm, ripe tomatoes
1½ pounds fresh mushrooms, sliced
½ cup butter or margarine, melted
4 teaspoons all-purpose flour
1 (8-ounce) carton sour cream
1 (3-ounce) package Roquefort cheese
¼ teaspoon ground oregano
1 teaspoon chopped parsley
2 tablespoons dry sherry or white wine
    Salt and pepper to taste
    Paprika

• Cut a slice from top of each tomato; scoop out pulp, leaving shell intact. Invert tomatoes and drain.

• Sauté mushrooms in butter until tender; drain. Combine sour cream, flour, cheese, oregano, parsley and sherry over low heat until smooth and thickened, stirring constantly. Add mushrooms, salt and pepper; stir well.

• Spoon mixture into tomato shells and place in shallow baking pan. Sprinkle with paprika.

• Bake at 375° for 15 to 20 minutes.

Yield: 8 servings.

Baked Vidalia Onions

4 large Vidalia onions
4 tablespoons margarine
1 teaspoon salt
⅛ teaspoon pepper
    Parmesan cheese

• Trim and peel each onion; cut each onion as if quartering but do not cut all the way through.

• Press 1 tablespoon of margarine into each onion; sprinkle with salt and pepper and a generous amount of Parmesan cheese.

• Wrap each onion in aluminum foil; bake at 400° for 1 hour.

Yield: 4 servings.

Vidalia Onion Casserole

5 large Vidalia onions, peeled and coarsely chopped
1 stick butter or margarine
¼ cup milk
24 Ritz crackers, crumbled
½ cup Parmesan cheese, freshly grated

• Sauté onions in butter for 15 to 20 minutes or until clear. Stir in milk.

• Put half of the onion mixture into a 1½-quart casserole dish. Cover with half of the crackers and sprinkle the cheese over the cracker crumbs. Repeat layers.

• Bake at 325°, uncovered, for 30 minutes.

Yield: 5 servings.

Blackeyed Peas

1 (16-ounce) package frozen
   blackeyed peas
2 cups water or chicken stock
¾ cup chopped onion
1 cup chopped green pepper
2 teaspoons chopped garlic
2 tablespoons olive oil
1 (16-ounce) can stewed tomatoes
½ teaspoon dried thyme
½ teaspoon dried basil

- Bring frozen blackeyed peas and water to a boil; reduce heat and cook about 40 minutes on medium.
- Sauté onion, green pepper and garlic in olive oil in sauté pan.
- Add tomatoes and seasonings and cook for 7 to 10 minutes.
- When peas are done, drain, reserving 1 cup liquid. Return peas to pot, add the tomato mixture. Bring to a boil and check seasoning; simmer for 15 minutes.
- Can use blackeyed peas, field peas or crowder peas.
- Adjust your own amount of salt.

  Note: Easily made ahead and reheated or frozen.

  Yield: 8 servings.

Spinach with Cheese Sauce and Bacon

2 tablespoons butter
3 tablespoons flour
½ teaspoon salt
2 cups milk
1 cup shredded Cheddar cheese
2 (10-ounce) packages frozen
   spinach, cooked and drained
6 slices crisp, cooked bacon

- Melt butter, blend in flour and salt. Add milk, stirring constantly.
- Cook and stir until sauce is smooth and thickened. Add cheese and stir until melted.
- Place cooked spinach in 1½-quart shallow baking dish and cover with cheese sauce. Top with bacon.
- Bake at 350° for 20 minutes or until thoroughly heated.

  Yield: 6 servings.

Spinach Casserole

(Perfect for holiday menus)

4 (10-ounce) packages frozen,
   chopped spinach, cooked and
   drained well
1 package onion soup mix
1 pint sour cream
1 package seasoned stuffing mix

- Mix spinach with soup and sour cream; pour into shallow casserole and cover with stuffing mix.
- Bake at 350° for 30 minutes.
- This recipe can be doubled or tripled to serve a crowd.

  Yield: 6 to 7 servings.

Baked Squash

2 **pounds squash, sliced, cooked and drained**
2 **tablespoons margarine**
¼ **cup evaporated milk**
2 **eggs, beaten**
 Salt to taste
 Pepper to taste
1 **small onion, grated**
 Pinch of sugar
¼ **cup finely chopped celery**
¼ **cup slivered almonds or finely chopped pecans**
 Sharp Cheddar cheese, grated
 Seasoned croutons, crushed
 Melted butter

- Mash squash and combine with margarine, milk, eggs, salt, pepper, sugar, onion, celery and nuts.
- Pour in lightly greased casserole and top with cheese and crushed croutons that have been mixed with a small amount of melted butter.
- Bake at 350° for 25 to 30 minutes.

Yield: 4 to 6 servings.

Squash Soufflé

2 **pounds crookneck squash, cubed**
1 **medium onion, sliced**
1 **teaspoon salt**
 Water
½ **teaspoon sugar**
3 **tablespoons butter, melted**
3 **tablespoons flour**
2 **eggs, slightly beaten**
1 **cup milk**
½ **pound grated cheese, Gruyère or Parmesan**
 Salt and pepper to taste

- Combine squash, onion, salt and sugar. Simmer in small amount of water for 20 minutes. Drain well and mash. Add butter, flour, eggs, milk, cheese, salt and pepper and mix well.
- Bake in a 2-quart casserole, uncovered, for 40 minutes at 350°. Center should be firm when removed from the oven.
- May be prepared ahead and frozen. When prepared ahead, bring to room temperature before cooking or increase time by about 25 minutes.

Yield: 6 servings.

Baked Tomatoes with Curry Topping

(Very good when tomatoes are fresh and plentiful)

4 **firm tomatoes, cut into very thick slices**
½ **cup mayonnaise**
¼ **cup freshly grated Parmesan cheese**
½ **teaspoon curry powder**
 Dash paprika

- Preheat oven to 375°.
- Place tomato slices in a shallow baking pan. Mix together the mayonnaise, cheese and curry powder. Spread mixture over tomatoes. Sprinkle with paprika.
- Bake for about 12 minutes or until tomatoes are just tender, but not mushy. Broil for a few seconds to brown tops.
- Serve hot.

Yield: 4 servings.

Broiled Tomatoes with Herbs

4 large tomatoes, halved
  Salt and pepper to taste
1 teaspoon basil
½ teaspoon grated lemon rind
4 tablespoons bread crumbs
2 tablespoons chopped fresh parsley
2 tablespoons olive oil
1 clove garlic, crushed

- Arrange tomatoes cut side up on baking sheet. Sprinkle with salt and pepper.
- Combine remaining ingredients in a food processor or blender and pulse until well blended. Spread over tops of tomatoes.
- Cook at 400° for 15 minutes.

Yield: 8 servings.

Fried Green Tomatoes

1 cup cornmeal
½ cup all-purpose flour
1 tablespoon sugar
  Oil for frying
4-5 firm green tomatoes, sliced
  Salt and pepper to taste

- Mix first 3 ingredients together in a shallow bowl.
- Dredge both sides of tomatoes in flour mixture, pressing firmly to coat well.
- Heat ¼-inch oil in heavy skillet over medium high heat.
- Fry tomatoes, about 2 minutes on each side, until golden brown.
- Remove and drain on paper towels; season with salt and pepper. Serve hot.

Yield: 4 servings.

Sausage Stuffed Tomatoes

(Great for breakfast)

4 large, ripe tomatoes
½ cup soft bread crumbs
½ teaspoon seasoned salt
¼ teaspoon black pepper
¼ cup chopped onion
¼ cup finely chopped green pepper
½ pound mild bulk pork sausage
½ cup shredded Cheddar cheese

- Remove tops from tomatoes and scoop out pulp, reserving pulp. Turn upside down on paper towels and drain.
- Cook sausage until done. Drain well and crumble; set aside.
- Chop tomato pulp. Add bread crumbs, onion, green pepper and sausage.
- Sprinkle inside of tomato shells with salt and pepper. Fill with sausage mixture. Place tomatoes in an 8-inch baking dish and bake for 20 to 25 minutes at 350° or until tomatoes are soft.
- Remove; sprinkle cheese on top and broil for a few seconds until cheese has melted.

Yield: 4 servings.

Tomato Bonnets

2   (10-ounce) packages frozen,
    chopped spinach, cooked and
    drained well
¾   cup bread crumbs
6   green onions, chopped and sautéed
3   eggs, beaten
⅓   cup butter, melted
⅓   cup grated Parmesan cheese
½   teaspoon thyme
1   teaspoon pepper
½   teaspoon cayenne
    Salt to taste
8   thick tomato slices

- Mix all ingredients together well except tomato slices.
- Place tomato slices in buttered casserole dish without tomato slices overlapping. Top with mounds of spinach mixture.
- Bake at 350° for 15 minutes.

    Yield: 8 servings.

Tomatoes and Okra

*(A yummy variation on a good basic
Southern recipe)*

1½   cups fresh okra, cut into ½-inch
     slices
½   cup chopped onion
½   cup chopped green pepper
2   tablespoons salad oil
1   tablespoons sugar
1   teaspoon flour
¾   teaspoon salt
⅛   teaspoon pepper
1   teaspoon sweet basil
3   tomatoes, peeled and quartered

- Cook okra in small amount of water for 10 minutes, covered; drain. Sauté onion and pepper in oil until tender but not brown.
- Blend in sugar, flour, salt, pepper and basil. Add tomatoes and okra. Cook over low heat until hot; stirring as little as possible.

    Yield: 4 servings.

Tomato Pie

*(A nice, light lunch with a fresh green
salad or serve with hamburgers)*

2   cups buttermilk baking mix
⅔   cup milk
4   large tomatoes
¾   cup mayonnaise
1   cup sharp cheese, grated
    Salt and pepper to taste
    Grated onion to taste
    Italian seasoning to taste

- Mix together baking mix and milk and spread in a lightly greased 9-inch pie pan.
- Cover tomatoes with boiling water and let stand a few minutes; drain. Peel and slice thinly. Layer tomatoes in pie shell with salt, pepper, grated onion and Italian seasoning until pie is level.
- Mix together cheese and mayonnaise. Spread over top of pie.
- Bake at 400° for 20 to 25 minutes until nicely browned.
- Let set for a few minutes before slicing.

Veg-All-Vegetable Casserole

(Don't pass this up, it's superb)

2 (16-ounce) cans Veg-All vegetables, drained
1 cup grated extra sharp Cheddar cheese
1 cup mayonnaise
1 cup sliced water chestnuts
1 large onion, chopped
  Buttered bread crumbs

- Preheat oven to 350°.
- Mix all ingredients together. Put in a 2-quart casserole dish. Top with buttered bread crumbs.
- Cook for 40 minutes.

Yield: 6 servings.

Zucchini and Tomatoes

¼ cup margarine, melted
1 small onion, chopped
1 green pepper, chopped
1 rib of celery, chopped
1 clove of garlic, chopped
2 (15-ounce) cans of zucchini and tomatoes
  Salt and pepper to taste
½ cup Parmesan cheese

- Sauté onion, green pepper, celery and garlic in butter. Add zucchini and tomatoes. Heat through and season with salt and pepper to taste.
- Place in a baking dish and sprinkle Parmesan cheese on top.
- Bake at 325° until the cheese is browned.

Yield: 6 servings.

Versatile Vegetables

(With a few simple steps this can be a soup, casserole or a side dish)

1 onion, sliced
4 cups sliced tomatoes
4 cups okra
1 cup chicken stock
2 cups water
  Salt and pepper
1 cup rice, cooked
½ teaspoon basil, thyme or parsley
1 teaspoon filé seasoning
2 ribs celery, chopped
1 small can corn or 1 medium potato

- Sauté onion, tomatoes and okra. Add stock, water, salt and pepper and simmer ½ hour or until tender. Add water as needed; add rice, seasonings, celery and corn or potato.
- For soup: Add 2 cups water and simmer ½ hour longer.
- For casserole: Add cooked chicken, ham, beef, shrimp or oysters.
- Freezes well.

Yield: 6 servings.

Vegetable Casserole

(Great over your favorite pasta)

1   **small eggplant, diced**
1   **onion, sliced**
1   **green pepper, diced**
    Fresh mushrooms, sliced
1   **tomato, sliced**
1   **small squash, sliced**
1   **zucchini, sliced**
    Garlic powder
    Salt and pepper to taste
    Butter
    Mozzarella cheese

- In microwaveable casserole dish, layer vegetables; season. Dribble melted margarine on top. Cover with plastic wrap; cook 10 minutes on high.
- Uncover, spread grated Mozzarella cheese generously on top. Allow to melt or put back in microwave a few seconds.
- Can mix leftover pork, beef or ham in with the vegetables and serve over your favorite pasta.

Baked Zucchini

6   **medium zucchini, ends cut off**
¼   **cup creamy French salad dressing**
2   **tablespoons prepared mustard**
¼   **cup butter or margarine, melted**
1   **cup dry bread crumbs**
1   **teaspoon dried basil leaves**
1   **teaspoon salt**

- Heat 1 inch salted water (½ teaspoon salt to 1 cup water) to boiling. Add whole unpared zucchini; cover and heat to boiling. Reduce heat; simmer until tender, 12 to 15 minutes. Drain; cool slightly.
- Preheat oven to 350°.

- Cut each zucchini lengthwise in half; place cut sides up in buttered baking dish.
- Stir together salad dressing and mustard; spread on zucchini.
- Mix remaining ingredients and sprinkle on top. At this point zucchini can be covered and refrigerated no longer than 24 hours.
- Bake zucchini uncovered until hot, about 20 to 30 minutes.

Yield: 6 to 8 servings.

Baked Potatoes

(A hit with your favorite grilled meat)

6   **baking potatoes**
1   **teaspoon salt**
1   **tablespoon chopped chives**
2   **tablespoons finely crumbled, cooked bacon**
½   **cup butter**
3½ **tablespoons Parmesan cheese, grated**
½   **teaspoon black pepper**
1   **tablespoon sour cream**

- Grease and bake potatoes at 400° for 45 minutes to an hour.
- Cut potatoes in half lengthwise; spoon out the pulp while potatoes are hot. Reserve shells.
- Combine remaining ingredients with the potato pulp; spoon mixture back into the shells.
- Return to oven and brown for a few minutes.

Yield: 12 servings.

Carrot and Sweet Potato Purée

4 large sweet potatoes, about 2 pounds
1 pound carrots
2½ cups water
1 tablespoon sugar
12 tablespoons sweet butter, softened
   Salt and pepper to taste
¼ cup sour cream
¼ cup whipping cream
½ teaspoon nutmeg
   Dash of cayenne

- Scrub potatoes and cut a small deep slit on the top of each. Bake in a preheated 375° oven for 1 hour or until tender.

- While potatoes cook, peel and trim carrots and cut into 1-inch lengths. Place in a saucepan and add water, sugar, 2 table-spoons of the butter and salt and pepper to taste. Bring to a boil and cook uncovered until water has evaporated and carrots begin to sizzle in the butter, about 30 minutes. The carrots should be tender. If not, add a little water and cook until done.

- Combine sour cream and whipping cream. Stir until well blended; set aside. Scrape flesh out of the sweet potatoes and combine with the carrots in a food processor. Add remaining butter and the sour cream mixture and process until very smooth.

- Add nutmeg, and season to taste with salt, pepper and cayenne. Process briefly to blend.

- To reheat, transfer to an ovenproof serving dish and cover with foil. Heat in a pre-heated 350° oven for about 25 minutes, or until steaming hot.

- Delicious with roasted lamb and steamed, fresh, whole green beans.

Yield: 6 servings.

Hash Brown Potato Casserole

(A great dish to take to a pot luck dinner)

1 (2-pound) bag frozen hash brown potatoes, crumbled
1 (10½-ounce) can cream of chicken soup
½ cup margarine, melted
1 cup sour cream
¼ cup chopped onion
2 cups shredded sharp Cheddar cheese
1 teaspoon salt
1 package herb dressing or crushed cornflakes

- Combine all ingredients except herb dressing, mixing well.

- Pour into a greased casserole dish; top with herb dressing.

- Bake at 350° for 1 hour or until potatoes are done.

- Freezes well.

Yield: 10 to 12 servings.

Cheesy Potatoes

6 medium potatoes, peeled and sliced
2 cups Cheddar cheese, shredded
¼ cup butter, softened
1½ cups sour cream
⅓ cup chopped onion
1 teaspoon salt
¼ teaspoon pepper
2 tablespoons butter

- Cook potatoes until done; drain and cool.
- Blend together cheese and ¼ cup butter. Add sour cream, onion, salt and pepper. Fold in potatoes.
- Turn into buttered 1½-quart casserole. Dot with 2 tablespoons butter.
- Bake at 400° for 25 minutes.

Yield: 6 servings.

Fluffy Potato Casserole

12 medium potatoes
1 (8-ounce) container sour cream
1 (8-ounce) package cream cheese, softened
1 garlic clove, minced
¼-½ teaspoon pepper
¼ cup chives, minced
1 tablespoon butter
½ teaspoon paprika

- Peel, dice and cook potatoes; drain and mash potatoes. Add sour cream, cream cheese, garlic, pepper and chives.
- Spoon into greased casserole; dot with butter and paprika.
- Bake at 350° for 45 minutes to 1 hour.

Spinach Stuffed Potatoes

(You will like these even if you are not a spinach lover!)

8 medium potatoes
1 cup butter
1-3 teaspoons salt
1 teaspoon dill weed
½ teaspoon pepper
½ teaspoon chopped chives
½ cup Parmesan cheese
1 (8-ounce) carton sour cream
2 (10-ounce) packages frozen, chopped spinach, thawed and drained well

- Cook potatoes for 1 hour at 400°. Cut potatoes in half and scoop the pulp out; reserve potato shells.
- Mix remaining ingredients except spinach and cheese together with the potato; fold in spinach.
- Stuff the potato shells with the potato-spinach mixture.
- Sprinkle Parmesan cheese on top. Bake at 350° for 20 to 25 minutes.
- Freezes well.

Yield: 16 servings.

Crab Stuffed Potatoes

4 **medium potatoes**
½ **pound fresh crabmeat**
½ **cup butter**
½ **cup light cream**
1 **teaspoon salt**
   Dash cayenne pepper
4 **teaspoons grated onion**
1 **cup grated sharp Cheddar cheese**
½ **teaspoon paprika**

- Bake potatoes in a 325° oven until they can be pierced easily with a fork, approximately 1 hour. Cut potatoes in half and scoop potato pulp out. Reserve potato shells.
- Whip potato pulp with butter; add cream, salt, cayenne, onion and cheese. Fold in crabmeat.
- Sprinkle with paprika and reheat at 450° for 15 minutes.

Yield: 8 servings.

Sweet Potato Soufflé

(Excellent)

Soufflé:

2 **cups cooked and mashed sweet potatoes**
1 **teaspoon vanilla**
½ **cup raisins**
¼ **teaspoon salt**
1¼ **cups sugar**
½ **cup butter, melted**
2 **teaspoons baking powder**
3 **eggs, beaten**
   Topping

- Preheat oven to 400°.
- Blend ingredients together.
- Pour into a baking dish.
- Bake for 20 minutes.

Topping:

3 **tablespoons butter, softened**
¼ **cup brown sugar**
1¼ **cups corn flakes, crushed**
¼ **cup chopped nuts**

- Mix ingredients together.
- Sprinkle topping mixture over the casserole. Return to oven for 10 more minutes.

Yield: 4 servings.

Sweet Potato Casserole

1½ **cups cooked, mashed sweet potato**
¼ **cup orange juice**
¼ **cup skim milk**
¼ **cup sugar**
1 **teaspoon vanilla extract**
2 **tablespoons brown sugar**
1 **tablespoons all-purpose flour**
1 **tablespoon corn oil or margarine**
2 **tablespoons chopped pecans.**

- Combine mashed sweet potato, orange juice, milk, sugar and vanilla in a medium bowl. Beat at high speed of an electric mixer until smooth. Spoon sweet potato mixture into a 1-quart casserole.
- Combine brown sugar and flour in a small bowl; cut in margarine with a fork. Stir in pecans, and sprinkle mixture over potatoes.
- Bake, uncovered, at 375° for 20 to 25 minutes or until lightly browned.

Yield: 5 servings.

Oven Fried Potatoes

6   **large baking potatoes, unpeeled**
½   **cup oil**
3   **tablespoons grated Parmesan cheese**
1   **teaspoon salt**
½   **teaspoon garlic powder**
½   **teaspoon paprika**
½   **teaspoon pepper**

- Wash and scrub each potato; dry with a paper towel. Cut each potato into eight wedges; arrange peel side down in shallow baking pans.

- Mix next six ingredients and brush over potatoes.

- Bake in 375° oven for 45 minutes or until potatoes are golden and tender. Brush occasionally with mixture.

Raw Potato Dumplings

(Especially good with Sauerbrauten)

1   **large potato, cooked and mashed**
6   **medium raw potatoes (2 pounds)**
    Water with lemon juice (1-2 lemons)
½-¾ **cup flour, more as needed**
1   **egg, beaten**
1   **teaspoon salt**
1   **cup slightly dry white bread cubes, sautéed in 2 tablespoons of butter**

- The cooked potato should be freshly cooked, mashed through a ricer or beaten in an electric mixer. Have everything else ready before raw potatoes are peeled.

- Grate the raw potatoes into a bowl of water blended with lemon juice. When all potatoes are grated, put into a cheesecloth bag and expel every bit of liquid. Then mix the cooked potato with flour, egg and salt.

- Mix with raw potatoes until it can be shaped into balls (2 to 3-inch diameter). Into each ball force 2 to 3 pieces of the sautéed bread; seal around it.

- Make a test dumpling by dropping it into rapidly boiling, lightly salted water. If it falls apart add slightly more flour to the dough.

- Cook dumplings until they rise to the top, about 10 minutes. Simmer another 5 minutes.

- Serve with meat and gravy, pouring gravy over dumplings.

Yield: 8 to 10 dumplings.

Garlicky Mashed Potatoes

2½ **pounds medium-sized red potatoes, unpeeled, scrubbed and quartered**
½   **cup olive oil**
10 **cloves garlic, peeled and minced**
2   **teaspoons chopped fresh Italian parsley**
¾   **teaspoon salt**
½   **teaspoon black pepper**

- In large saucepan, boil potatoes in enough water to cover by 1 inch, 10 to 20 minutes or until tender; drain.

- In small saucepan, heat oil over medium heat. Add garlic cloves and cook until tender and golden.

- Mash unpeeled potatoes with parsley, salt and pepper. Stir in garlic and oil until thoroughly mixed. Reheat if needed.

- Spoon into serving bowl. Serve warm.

Yield: 8 servings.

Green Tomato Pickles

7 pounds sliced green tomatoes
2 gallons water
3 cups new lime
5 pounds sugar
3 pints vinegar
1 tablespoon whole cloves
1 tablespoon ginger root
1 tablespoon allspice
1 tablespoon celery seed
1 tablespoon mace
1 stick cinnamon

- Soak tomato slices in mixture of lime and water for 24 hours; make sure lime is dissolved.
- Drain and soak in fresh water for 4 hours, changing water every hour.
- Drain, place in large non-aluminum pot.
- Bring mixture of sugar, vinegar and spices to a boil; pour over tomatoes and let stand overnight.
- Next morning boil for 1 hour; pack into hot sterilized jars and seal.
- Do not put spices in jars.

Yield: 8 pints.

Artichoke Pickles

1 peck Jerusalem artichokes, washed and cut to desired size
10 medium onions, sliced
4 pounds light brown sugar
1 gallon cider vinegar
1 box pickling spices
1 hot pepper
1 (1-ounce) tin dry mustard
Alum

- Sterilize jars; place artichokes in jars, layering artichokes with alternate layer of sliced onion.
- Combine remaining ingredients, except alum, in non-aluminum pot and bring to a boil.
- Pour this liquid over artichoke and onions in packed jars.
- Add a pinch of alum in top of each jar.
- Be sure to leave 1 inch air space between liquid and jar top.
- Screw tops on tightly and let set for two weeks.

Yield: 8 to 10 pints.

Dilly Beans

(Great served in Bloody Marys instead of celery)

Green beans
2 teaspoons red or cayenne pepper
2 garlic cloves
4 tablespoons dill seed
2 cups pure cider vinegar
4 teaspoons sugar
2 cups water
4 tablespoons salt

- Wash and cut stems from beans; pack beans into hot, sterilized jars.
- Add to each jar:

½ teaspoon red or cayenne pepper
½ clove garlic
1 tablespoon dill seed

- Heat vinegar, sugar, water and salt to boiling.
- Pour into beans and seal.

Yield: 4 pints.

Pickled Squash

6 quarts sliced yellow squash
8 small onions, sliced
Salt
Ice
4½ cups sugar
5 cups cider vinegar
2 sweet green peppers, sliced

- Sprinkle a little salt over squash and onions; place in a big pan of ice and soak for 3 hours.
- Dissolve sugar in vinegar in large pot; add sliced peppers and bring to a boil.
- Drain squash and onions and add to peppers, sugar and vinegar.
- Boil combined vegetables in vinegar solution for 3 minutes.
- Pack into hot sterilized jars and seal.

Yield: 10 to 12 pints.

Cantaloupe Pickles

3 quarts cantaloupe balls or cubes (1½-inch)
Lime dissolved in water for soaking, enough to cover
5 pounds granulated sugar
2 quarts white vinegar
3 tablespoons whole cloves
9 (3-inch) sticks of cinnamon
1 lemon, sliced thinly
1 lime, sliced thinly

- Cover with enough water, in which lime has been dissolved, to cover melon; soak overnight.

- Drain and wash all lime off melon; tie cloves and cinnamon sticks in cheesecloth.
- Cook sugar, vinegar and spice bag for 15 minutes; taste for flavor before removing bag of spices.
- Remove bag when spice flavor is strong enough to your taste; add cantaloupe, lemon and lime slices and cook until tender and transparent (about 1 hour).
- Pack into hot sterilized jars; seal.

Green and Red Pepper Chow

1 dozen medium green bell peppers
1 dozen medium red bell peppers
1 dozen medium onions
½ cup salt
Water
1 pint cider vinegar
1 tablespoon cider vinegar
1 tablespoon celery seed
1 tablespoon black pepper
1 tablespoon mustard seed
Dash of red pepper
2 cups sugar

- Grind peppers and onions; add salt to vegetables and enough water to cover.
- Let stand for 1 hour; drain.
- In a large saucepan, place the pepper mixture and the last 6 ingredients; mix well and cook covered for 20 minutes.
- Fill sterilized pint jars with chow and seal; process in hot water bath for 10 minutes.

Yield: 4 pints.

Artichoke Mustard Pickle

(A great accompaniment to roast beef)

1   peck Jerusalem artichokes, scrubbed and chopped
4   pounds cabbage, chopped
2   quarts chopped onions
8-10   green peppers, coarsely chopped
2   gallons water
3   cups plain salt, not iodized salt
1   gallon apple cider vinegar, reserve 2 cups
2   tablespoons mustard seed
2   tablespoons black pepper
5   pounds granulated sugar
1½   cups all-purpose flour
2   tablespoons turmeric
2   small jars mustard

- Mix all chopped vegetables in large pan; dissolve salt in water and pour over vegetables.

- Soak overnight; drain well.

- Combine vinegar, mustard seed, black pepper and sugar in large pot and bring to a boil.

- Add drained vegetables and boil for only 10 minutes.

- Make a paste of flour, turmeric, mustard and the 2 cups of reserved vinegar.

- Add the paste to the cooked vegetables and continue to cook for 5 minutes.

- Pat artichoke mixture in hot, sterilized jars; seal.

- These pickles do not need to age.

Yield: 8 to 10 pints.

Pickled Okra

6   pounds okra
6   hot peppers, red or green
6   garlic cloves
1   quart cider vinegar
1⅓   cups water
½   cup salt
1   tablespoon mustard seeds

- Wash and trim okra; pack in clean hot jars; with one pepper and one garlic clove in each jar.

- Bring all other ingredients to a boil; cover okra with hot liquid.

- Put tops on jars, loosely; process jars of okra with hot liquid for 10 minutes in hot water bath. Remove carefully.

- Let age 4 weeks before using.

Yield: 6 pints.

Sweet Garlic Dills

3   pounds cucumbers, sliced
6   onions, thinly sliced
2   green peppers, cut into thin strips
7½   teaspoons dill seed, divided
5   garlic cloves, divided
3   cups vinegar
1   cup water
2   tablespoons pickling salt
2   cups sugar

- Pack vegetables equally into 5 sterilized pint jars.

- Add ½ teaspoon dill seed and 1 garlic clove to each jar.

- Boil remaining ingredients; pour over vegetables to within 1 inch from top and seal.

- Age one month before using.

Yield: 5 pints.

Garden Couscous with Onion Harissa

Couscous:

¼ cup plus 1 tablespoon olive oil
2 large leeks (white and green parts only), minced
4 large garlic cloves, chopped
2¼ cups chicken stock
1 cup raisins
1 cup butternut squash, peeled and cut into ½-inch cubes
1 large zucchini, cut into ½-inch cubes
1 large yellow crookneck squash, cut into ½-inch cubes
¾ cup frozen limas, thawed
1 teaspoon turmeric (optional)
½ teaspoon ginger
   Pinch of cayenne pepper
1 cup diced, seeded plum tomatoes
¾ cup frozen peas, thawed
½ cup fresh cilantro
1½ cups (10 ounces) couscous

- In large Dutch oven, heat oil over low heat. Add leeks and garlic. Cover and cook until tender, not brown, about 10 minutes.

- Add stock and next 8 ingredients. Season with salt and pepper. Bring to a boil; cover and reduce heat to medium and simmer until veggies are crisp-tender, about 5 minutes.

- Mix in tomatoes, peas, cilantro, and couscous. Remove from heat; cover and let stand 10 minutes. Fluff with a fork and serve, passing Onion Harissa separately.

Onion Harissa:

¼ cup tomato paste
1 tablespoon plus 1 teaspoon dried red pepper
¾ teaspoon cayenne
1 cup olive oil
½ cup red wine vinegar
6 green onions, chopped
1 small red onion, chopped
3 large garlic cloves, minced

- Combine tomato paste, red pepper and cayenne in a bowl. Whisk in oil slowly. Whisk in vinegar.

- Mix in onions and garlic. Season generously with salt and pepper.

- Can be made 8 hours ahead; let stand at room temperature before serving. Stir well.

Yield: 8 servings.

Easy Rice Casserole

(Good with any entrée)

¼ cup butter
1 (10½-ounce) can beef broth
1 (10½-ounce) can consommé
1 (4-ounce) can mushroom pieces, drained
1 medium onion, chopped
1 cup rice

- Melt butter in a 2-quart casserole.

- Combine broth, consommé, mushrooms, onions and rice in the casserole dish.

- Cover and bake for 1 hour at 350°.

- May also add 1 (8-ounce) can water chestnuts, undrained.

Pork Fried Rice

1   pound boneless pork chops, cut in
     thin strips
2   celery stalks, diced
4   garlic cloves, minced
1   medium onion, diced
1   tablespoon sesame oil
3   eggs
4   cups cooked white rice
1   large carrot, diced
½   pound bacon, cooked and crumbled
     (save grease)
1   (8-ounce) can sliced water
     chestnuts, drained
1   (16-ounce) can bean sprouts
     Soy sauce and pepper to taste

- In a large skillet add bacon grease to pan
  and sauté onions, celery and garlic. When
  tender add carrots and simmer 5 minutes.
- Add rice and mix together adding enough
  soy sauce to turn rice a light brown.
  Scramble eggs with sesame oil (may be
  done in microwave). Chop into small pieces
  and add to rice mixture. Add remaining
  ingredients, and simmer for 15 minutes.
  Serve.

  Yield: 5 to 6 servings.

Company Rice Casserole

½   stick melted butter or margarine
½   cup chopped onion
½   cup chopped green pepper
½   cup chopped celery
½   cup water
1   (4-ounce) can sliced mushrooms,
     drained
1   (2-ounce) jar chopped pimento,
     drained

1½   cups long grain rice
1   (13-ounce) can beef consommé
1   (13-ounce) can beef broth

- Preheat oven to 350°.
- Sauté onion, green pepper and celery in
  butter until slightly transparent, but crisp.
- Mix with other ingredients in lightly greased
  3-quart oblong casserole.
- Bake covered with foil for 45 minutes;
  uncover and bake for 10 to 15 minutes until
  dry and slightly crisp on top.

  Yield: 6 to 8 servings.

Oriental Baked Rice

¾   cup butter or margarine
2   cups long grain rice
2   (8-ounce) cans water chestnuts,
     drained and thinly sliced
2   (4-ounce) cans sliced mushrooms,
     drained or sautéed fresh
     mushrooms
1   (8-ounce) can bamboo shoots,
     drained
1   (16-ounce) can bean sprouts,
     drained
2   (10¾-ounce) cans onion soup
1   cup water
1   teaspoon soy sauce

- Melt butter in a 3-quart casserole; add all
  the remaining ingredients and stir well.
- Cover and bake at 350° for 1 hour and 15
  minutes.
- Uncover last 15 minutes to dry a little.

  Yield: 12 servings.

Wild Rice

2½ cups chicken stock
1½ cups wild rice
   Salt and pepper
 2 tablespoons unsalted butter
 1 medium onion, minced
 2 stalks celery, minced
⅔ cup dry white wine

- Heat stock to boil in 2½-quart saucepan.

- Heat 2 inches of water in the bottom half of double boiler. Combine hot stock and rice in top half. Season, cover and cook over medium heat for one hour.

- As rice starts to cook, heat butter in sauce-pan over medium heat; when hot add onion, celery, and season. Sauté 3 minutes and add wine.

- Reduce heat to low and simmer until all liquid has evaporated, 45 to 50 minutes. Combine rice and vegetables; adjust season-ings.

Yield: 8 servings.

Cabbage Dressing

 1 pound lean ground meat
½ cup raw rice
 1 teaspoon oil
 1 (8-ounce) can of tomato sauce
 3 cups shredded cabbage
 1 large onion, chopped
 1 large green pepper, chopped
½ cup water
   Salt and pepper

- Mix meat and rice with ½ of tomato sauce.

- Cover bottom of a Dutch oven with 1 teaspoon of oil.

- Press ½ of meat and rice mixture into Dutch oven and season with salt and pepper. Cover with a layer of cabbage, a layer of onion and a layer of green pepper. Repeat layers.

- Pour the rest of the tomato sauce mixed with ½ cup of water over the layers. Add more salt and pepper to taste.

- Cover and bake at 350° for 1 to 1½ hours. Do not stir while the dish is cooking.

Yield: 6 servings.

Sweetened Condensed Milk

(Make a day ahead)

 1 cup dry milk
⅔ cup sugar
⅓ cup hot water
 3 tablespoons butter

- In blender container, combine all ingredi-ents; blend until smooth.

Chinese Spring Rolls

(Don't be alarmed, it's not as hard as it seems and you'll never want store-bought again!)

¼	cup shiitake mushrooms
1	cup boiling water
4	medium boneless pork chops
8	scallions or green onions
3	tablespoons soy sauce, divided
2½	teaspoons sesame oil, divided
1	tablespoon cornstarch
¼	head of cabbage
3	eggs
¼	cup peanut oil plus 1 teaspoon
1	teaspoon salt
½	teaspoon coarsely ground pepper
1	egg
	Egg roll wrappers
2	cups peanut oil

- Put mushrooms in a small bowl and pour boiling water over them. Let soak about 15 minutes. Slice pork into very thin slivers, about the size and shape of a wooden matchstick. Place in a bowl and set aside.

- Clean the onions and cut into 2-inch lengths. Slice these lengths into shreds about the same size as pork. Add one third onions to the pork, along with 2 tablespoons sauce, 1 teaspoon sesame oil and cornstarch. Mix and set aside.

- Cut cabbage into shreds the same size as the meat. Set aside. Drain the mushrooms and chop into shreds the same size as others.

- Beat the eggs with 1 teaspoon sesame oil. You may scramble in frying pan using 1 teaspoon peanut oil or omit the peanut oil and scramble in the microwave. When eggs are firm chop into shreds and set aside.

- Heat pan you usually use for Chinese cooking over high flame for about 15 seconds and add ¼ cup peanut oil. When oil is ready add the meat shreds. Stir-fry for 10 seconds using your cooking shovel to scrape off the sides. Remove meat from pan after 10 seconds even though it will still be pink.

- Now add the shredded cabbage to the pan and stir-fry 15 seconds before adding the mushrooms and the rest of the onions. Cook these vegetables together for another minute, stirring occasionally. Return meat to pan and cook about 15 seconds before adding egg shreds. Finally add the salt, 1 tablespoon soy sauce, pepper and ½ teaspoon sesame oil. Let mixture cool before stuffing egg roll skins.

- Beat egg. Separate egg roll skins and lay on a flat surface. Take about 2½ tablespoons of mixture on one end of roll and roll up as tightly as you can, folding sides over to make sure filling doesn't spill out. Seal with egg mixture.

- Fry in wok in small batches using about 2 cups peanut oil. After they have turned a golden brown, remove and drain on a paper towel. Serve with your favorite sauce.

- Spring rolls can be prepared early in the day up to the point of cooking. Refrigerate, covered, till ready to fry.

Yield: 15 to 16 spring rolls.

Hot Dog Chili

½ cup chopped onion
1 tablespoon butter
2 pounds ground beef
⅔ cup ketchup
½ cup water
¼ cup chopped celery
2 tablespoons lemon juice
1 tablespoon brown sugar
1½ teaspoons Worcestershire sauce
1½ teaspoons salt
1 teaspoon vinegar
¼ teaspoon dry mustard
½ cup tomato juice
3 teaspoons chili powder

- Sauté onions in butter until translucent.
- Cook and drain ground beef. Combine onion and beef. Add the rest of the ingredients to skillet. Cook on simmer, stirring occasionally, for 1 to 2 hours.
- Freezes well.

Yield: 2 to 3 pints.

Yorkshire Pudding

(Easy and wonderful)

¼ cup hot drippings from roast beef
2 eggs, well beaten
1 cup milk
1 cup flour, sifted
  Dash of salt

- Put drippings in 11x7-inch pan. Keep hot; add milk, flour and salt to beaten eggs. Beat until smooth. Pour in pan over hot drippings.
- Bake at 400° 30 to 40 minutes, until puffed and golden brown.

Yield: 6 to 8 servings.

Rockefeller Dressing

2 cups fresh mushrooms, chopped
1 large onion, chopped
½ cup shredded carrot
½ cup chopped celery
1 clove garlic, minced
¼ cup butter
1 pint oysters
8 cups bread cubes (11 slices)
2 tablespoons minced parsley
1 teaspoon dried basil
½ teaspoon salt
½ teaspoon poultry seasoning
¼ teaspoon pepper
1 (10-ounce) package frozen chopped spinach, cooked and drained
¼-½ cup milk

- In skillet cook first 5 ingredients in butter until tender.
- Drain oysters and save liquid; chop large ones.
- In bowl mix bread cubes and next 5 ingredients. Stir in vegetable mixture, oysters and spinach. Add oyster liquid to moisten. If necessary add milk.
- This will make enough to stuff a 10 to 12-pound turkey. Instead of stuffing the turkey, you may put dressing in a baking dish and bake at 325° for approximately 30 to 45 minutes.

Granola

*(Lasts a long time in
sealed container)*

4   cups rolled old-fashioned oats
½   cup raw sunflower seeds
½   cup chopped walnuts or pecans
½   cup raisins (optional)
¼   cup safflower oil
¼   cup maple syrup or honey
1½ teaspoons vanilla
      Vanilla yogurt

- Preheat oven to 350°.
- Mix oats, seeds, raisins and walnuts together.
- Mix wet ingredients together and pour over dry ingredients.
- Pour in baking pan, being careful not to pile too high or it won't brown.
- Brown for 20 minutes, stirring after 10 minutes. Cool completely; store in airtight container.
- Serve over vanilla yogurt.

Yield: 8 to 10 servings.

Mustard Sauce for Broccoli

4   tablespoons butter, melted
2   egg yolks
2   teaspoons prepared mustard
2   tablespoons sugar
½   cup vinegar
¼   teaspoon pepper

- Combine all ingredients and cook in double boiler or over low heat; stir constantly until thick.

Yield: 1 cup.

Hot and Sweet Sauce

*(Great to share with friends
in small gift jars)*

1   cup white vinegar
1   cup dry mustard (3-4 small boxes)
2   eggs, well beaten
1   cup sugar
      Pinch of salt

- Mix vinegar and mustard and let stand overnight.
- On the next day, stir in eggs, sugar and salt. Bring to slow boil, stirring constantly until it coats spoon; cool.
- Put in jars and refrigerate.

Note: This sauce is good with everything from pretzels to cold cuts.

Yield: 3 cups.

Oyster-Mushroom Sauce for Microwave

1   pound fresh mushrooms, capped and sliced
1   pint oysters, drained
      Salt and pepper to taste
¼   cup butter or margarine

- Combine ingredients in microwaveable dish. Cover with plastic wrap. Cook 10 minutes on high.
- Use this to spoon over sage dressing in lieu of cooking oysters in the dressing.
- Many improvisations can be done, such as adding herbs, scallops, shrimp, onions, etc., for a pasta sauce.

Quick Hollandaise Sauce

(Serve over broccoli or asparagus)

4   egg yolks
2   tablespoons lemon juice
¼   teaspoon dry mustard
     Dash hot pepper sauce
1   cup margarine

- Mix first 4 ingredients in a blender or food processor by pulsing on and off quickly.

- Melt margarine to a bubbly stage; add to the mixture in the blender. Blend to mix but be careful not to overblend.

- Can be made ahead of time and reheated over hot water.

Yield: 1½ cups.

DESSERTS

Becky Wienges '92

Index for Desserts

Blueberry Cake with Lemon Filling

3 eggs
1½ cups sugar
1½ cups sifted cake flour
2 teaspoons baking powder
1½ cups heavy cream
2 teaspoons vanilla
¼ teaspoon salt
1 cup fresh or frozen blueberries

- Butter three 8-inch layer pans, line with waxed paper and butter again.

- In large bowl, beat eggs until thickened. Beat in sugar, 2 tablespoons at a time, until mixture is light and fluffy.

- Sift flour and baking powder together; reserve.

- Beat cream, vanilla and salt in a chilled bowl to stiff peaks. Fold whipped cream into egg mixture, alternating with flour mixture.

- Divide batter among pans. Sprinkle each layer with ⅓ cup blueberries.

- Bake at 350° for 30 to 35 minutes; cool 5 minutes on rack. Remove from pans and cool.

Lemon Filling:

½ cup butter, softened
2 cups confectioners sugar
1 tablespoon lemon juice
½ teaspoon vanilla
2 egg yolks, beaten

- Prepare lemon filling by beating butter, sugar, lemon juice and vanilla until light and fluffy. Beat in yolks until well combined.

- Invert 1 cake layer on serving plate.

- Spread with half the lemon filling; add a second layer and spread with remaining filling. Top with last layer and sprinkle top of cake with confectioners sugar.

- Garnish with fresh blueberries and lemon leaves.

Yield: 12 servings.

Chocolate Fudge Cake

(This makes a serve-while-hot pudding-cake dish)

1 cup sifted all-purpose flour
2 teaspoons baking powder
1 teaspoon salt
⅔ cup sugar
6 tablespoons cocoa, divided
⅔ cup milk
1 teaspoon vanilla
4 tablespoons melted shortening
½ cup chopped pecans
1 cup packed brown sugar
1¼-1½ cups boiling water

- Sift flour, baking powder, salt, granulated sugar and 2 tablespoons cocoa. Add milk, shortening and vanilla; mix only until smooth. Add pecans and put in greased shallow 1-quart baking dish.

- Mix brown sugar and remaining 4 tablespoons cocoa and sprinkle over mixture in baking dish. Pour boiling water over top.

- Bake 40 minutes at 350°.

- Serve warm or cold, topped with cream or ice cream. This has a chocolate sauce on bottom and cake on top.

Yield: 6 to 8 servings.

Chocolate, Chocolate Cake

2 cups butter
3 ounces chocolate bits, melted
12 eggs, beaten
2 pounds semi-sweet chocolate pieces
1 teaspoon cream

- Melt butter and chocolate in top of double boiler. Add eggs and pour into springform pan.
- Cook 20 minutes at 325°. Cool for 10 minutes.
- Glaze with melted chocolate bits and cream. Cool completely before removing from pan.

Chocolate Cake with Chocolate Icing

(Have an ice cold glass of milk ready for that first slice)

2 sticks butter, softened
2 cups sugar
6 eggs
3 cups self-rising flour
1 cup milk
1 teaspoon vanilla flavoring

- Cream butter and sugar; add eggs and beat together. Slowly add flour and milk to keep batter loose. Add vanilla flavoring.
- Grease 9-inch cake pans; cook 10 to 20 minutes at 350°. Don't overcook as cake will be dry.
- Punch holes in each layer of cake and spread icing over generously so chocolate fills up holes.

Chocolate Icing:

3 cups sugar
¾ cup cocoa
1 cup plus 2 tablespoons margarine
1 cup evaporated milk
3 teaspoons vanilla flavoring

- Mix sugar and cocoa together; add margarine, milk and vanilla.
- Cook slowly over medium-low heat for at least 5 minutes; bring to a boil for at least 5 minutes.
- Ice layers of cake.

Date Nut Cake

(If you dislike fruitcake, try this)

1 pound package dates, chopped
1 pound nuts, chopped
1 cup all-purpose flour
1 teaspoon baking powder
1 cup butter, melted and cooled
1 cup sugar
4 eggs, separated
1 teaspoon vanilla

- Mix the dates and nuts. Sift together the flour and baking powder. Combine the two mixtures, tossing to coat.
- Beat egg yolks until foamy and egg whites until stiff.
- Add butter, sugar, egg yolks and vanilla to the flour/date/nut mixture.
- Gently fold in egg whites.
- Pour into greased and floured, small loaf pans.
- Bake slowly at 250° for 2 hours or until center is done.

Yield: 2 to 3 cakes.

Coconut Sour Cream Layer Cake

1 (18½-ounce) box butter flavored cake mix
2 cups sugar
1 (16-ounce) carton sour cream
1 (12-ounce) package frozen coconut, thawed
1 (8-ounce) container whipped topping, thawed

- Prepare cake mix according to the package directions, making 2 8-inch layers. When completely cool, split both layers horizontally.

- Combine sugar, sour cream and coconut; blend well, folding rather than beating; chill. Reserve 1 cup of the sour cream mixture for frosting; spread remainder between cake layers.

- Combine reserved sour cream with whipped topping, folding gently until smooth. Spread on top and sides of cake.

- Seal cake in an airtight container, and refrigerate for 3 days before serving.

Yield: 1 8-inch cake.

A cake won't stick to its serving plate if the plate is first dusted with confectioners sugar. Juice from frozen juice concentrates can be quick-thawed by putting it in a blender, along with the recommended amount of water and blending for a few seconds.

Chocolate Pound Cake

1 cup butter, softened
½ cup shortening
5 eggs
3 cups sugar
3 cups flour
½ teaspoon baking powder
½ teaspoon salt
4 tablespoons cocoa
1 cup milk
1 tablespoon vanilla
Chocolate Icing

- Cream together margarine and shortening. Add eggs and sugar.

- Sift dry ingredients together.

- Add dry ingredients alternately with milk to creamed mixture. Add vanilla.

- Bake in 9 or 10-inch greased tube pan at 325° for 1 hour and 20 minutes. Cool in pan.

- Ice with Chocolate Icing.

Chocolate Icing:

¼ cup butter
2 squares chocolate
1 (16-ounce) box confectioners sugar
1 teaspoon vanilla
3 tablespoons milk

- Melt butter and chocolate. Add sugar and vanilla; add enough milk to reach desired consistency.

- Spread on cake.

Cream Cheese and Chocolate Cupcakes

1 (18.25-ounce) box Devil's Food cake mix
1 (8-ounce) package cream cheese, softened
⅓ cup sugar
1 egg
1 (6-ounce) package semi-sweet chocolate morsels
   Dash of salt

- Mix cake mix according to package directions.
- Fill paper lined muffin tins ⅔ full with cake mix.
- Combine cream cheese, sugar, egg and salt together; fold in chocolate morsels.
- Drop one large teaspoon of cream cheese mixture on top of cake mix in each muffin cup. Bake according to directions.

Perfect Chocolate Icing:

1 (6-ounce) package chocolate morsels
½ cup light cream
1 cup butter
2½ cups unsifted confectioners sugar

- In saucepan, mix morsels, cream and butter; stir over medium heat.
- With egg beater, beat in confectioners sugar over a bowl of ice. This can be done the night before.
- Ice cupcakes.

   Yield: 24 to 28 cupcakes.

Fig Cake

1½ cups sugar
2 cups all-purpose flour
1 teaspoon baking soda
1 teaspoon salt
1 teaspoon ground nutmeg
1 teaspoon ground cinnamon
½ teaspoon ground allspice
½ teaspoon ground cloves
1 cup vegetable oil
3 eggs
1 cup buttermilk
1 tablespoon vanilla extract
1 cup fig preserves with juice, chopped
1 cup chopped nuts
   Buttermilk Glaze

- Combine dry ingredients in a large bowl; add oil, beating well. Add eggs and beat well; then add buttermilk and vanilla, mixing thoroughly. Stir in preserves and pecans.
- Pour batter into a greased and floured 10-inch tube pan; bake at 350° for 1 hour and 15 minutes. Cool in pan 10 minutes; remove from pan.
- Poke holes in top of cake with a toothpick; pour warm glaze over the warm cake.

Buttermilk Glaze:

¼ cup buttermilk
½ cup sugar
¼ teaspoon baking soda
1½ teaspoons cornstarch
¼ cup margarine
1½ teaspoons vanilla extract

- Combine first 5 ingredients in a saucepan; bring to a boil and remove from heat.
- Cool slightly and stir in vanilla.

   Yield: 1 10-inch cake.

Double Diabolo

(Very rich and irresistible—needs to be made at least one day ahead)

½ **cup raisins**
½ **cup Scotch whiskey**
14 **ounces semi-sweet chocolate**
¼ **cup water**
1 **cup unsalted butter**
6 **eggs, separated**
1⅓ **cups sugar**
9 **tablespoons cake flour**
1⅓ **cups finely ground blanched almonds**

- Soak raisins overnight in the whiskey.
- Preheat oven to 350°. Butter a 12-inch cake pan, line bottom with waxed paper; butter and flour paper.
- In the top of a double boiler, melt the chocolate with the water; stir in the butter in small pieces until mixture is smooth.
- Beat the egg yolks with the sugar until thick and creamy; stir into the chocolate. Add the flour and almonds, then the raisins and whiskey, mixing together gently.
- Beat the egg whites with salt until stiff but not dry; fold by thirds into the chocolate mixture gently.
- Pour the batter into the prepared pan, smooth the top and bake for approximately 25 minutes. The cake should be moist in the center and just beginning to pull from the sides of the pan. Let the cake rest in the pan for 10 minutes before turning out onto a rack to cool.

Rinse a pan in cold water before scalding milk to prevent sticking.

Icing:

8 **ounces semi-sweet chocolate**
1 **cup heavy cream**

- Bring cream to a scald and add the chocolate, whisking until smooth. If too thin, cool slightly over ice.
- Pour over cake, smoothing with a spatula.

Fresh Apple Cake

¾ **cup melted butter or oil**
2 **cups sugar**
3 **large eggs**
2 **teaspoons vanilla**
3 **cups all-purpose flour**
1 **teaspoon baking soda**
1 **teaspoon salt**
3 **cups coarsely chopped, pared, tart cooking apples**
1 **cup coarsely chopped walnuts or pecans**

- Preheat oven to 350°.
- Sift flour, soda and salt. In a large bowl beat with hand mixer sugar and shortening until creamy. Beat eggs one at a time into mixture. Add vanilla and fold the dry and sugar mixtures together. Fold in apples and nuts until well blended.
- Turn into a 9-inch tube pan that has been greased and floured. Bake 1 hour or until a toothpick inserted comes out clean. Do not overbake. Let set 10 minutes before removing from pan.

Exceptional Carrot Cake

(Look no more, this is the best)

2   **cups all-purpose flour**
2   **teaspoons soda**
½   **teaspoon salt**
2   **teaspoons ground cinnamon**
3   **eggs, well beaten**
¾   **cup vegetable oil**
¾   **cup buttermilk**
2   **cups sugar**
2   **teaspoons vanilla**
1   **(8-ounce) can crushed pineapple, drained well**
2   **cups grated carrots**
1   **(3½-ounce) can flaked coconut**
2   **cups chopped walnuts, divided**
    Buttermilk Glaze
    Cream Cheese Frosting

- Combine the first 4 ingredients and set aside.

- Combine the next 5 ingredients, beating until smooth. Stir in the flour mixture, pineapple, carrots, coconut and 1 cup walnuts. Pour batter into 3 greased and floured 9-inch round cake pans.

- Bake at 350° for 35 to 40 minutes or until a wooden pick inserted in center comes out clean.

- Immediately spread Buttermilk Glaze evenly over layers; cool in pans 15 minutes then remove from pans and let cool completely.

- Frost with Cream Cheese Frosting.

Buttermilk Glaze:

1   **cup sugar**
½   **teaspoon soda**
½   **cup buttermilk**
½   **cup butter**
1   **tablespoon light corn syrup**
1   **teaspoon vanilla**

- Combine sugar, soda, buttermilk, butter and syrup in a saucepan; bring to a boil. Cook 4 minutes, stirring often. Remove from heat and stir in vanilla.

Cream Cheese Frosting:

½   **cup butter, softened**
1   **(8-ounce) package cream cheese, softened**
1   **teaspoon vanilla**
2   **cups confectioners sugar**

- Combine butter and cream cheese, beating until light and fluffy; add vanilla and sugar, beating until smooth.

Yield: 1 cake.

When preparing the cake pan, prepare only the bottom of the pan. The sides are left plain without greasing so the batter can cling as it rises. This helps keep the cake light in texture. Grease or grease and flour pans which will be used for mixtures like cakes and cookies which contain both fat and sugar.

Fresh Peach Cake

(A must to try when fresh peaches are available)

1   (18½-ounce) package butter flavor
    cake mix
1½   cups sugar
4   tablespoons cornstarch
4   cups chopped fresh peaches
½   cup water
2   cups whipping cream
2-3   tablespoons confectioners sugar
1   cup commercial sour cream
    Fresh sliced peaches

- Prepare cake mix according to package directions; using two 8-inch cake pans; cool and split each layer.

- Combine sugar and cornstarch in a saucepan; add peaches and water then cook over medium, stirring constantly until smooth and thickened; cool completely. Combine whipping cream and confectioners sugar in a medium mixing bowl; beat until stiff peaks form.

- Spoon one third of peach filling over split layer of cake; spread ⅓ cup sour cream over filling. Repeat procedure with remaining cake layers, peach filling and sour cream, ending with remaining cake layer.

- Frost cake all over with sweetened whipped cream and garnish with fresh peach slices; refrigerate.

Yield: 1 cake.

Fresh Strawberry Nut Cake

1   (18½-ounce) box yellow cake mix
1   (3-ounce) package strawberry Jello
1   cup oil
1   cup strawberries, crushed and
    sweetened
½   cup milk
4   eggs, beaten
1   cup coconut
1   cup chopped nuts
    Strawberry Icing

- Mix first 8 ingredients together, blending well.

- Grease and flour 3 cake pans; pour batter into pans.

- Bake at 350° for approximately 20 to 25 minutes.

- Ice between layers and top of cake with Strawberry Icing.

Strawberry Icing:

1   (16-ounce) box confectioners sugar
½   cup margarine, melted
½   cup strawberries, mashed
½   cup chopped nuts
½   cup coconut

- Blend together sugar and margarine; add the strawberries and nuts to the icing.

- Sprinkle top of cake with coconut.

Yield: 16 servings.

Scripture Cake

1 **cup Judges (5:25) butter**
2 **cups Jeremiah (6:20) sugar**
2 **cups Nakum (3:12) figs, chopped**
6 **Isaiah (10:4) eggs**
½ **cup Judges (4:19) milk**
4½ **cups Kings (4:22) flour**
2 **teaspoons Amos (4:5) baking powder**
2 **tablespoons I Samuel (14:25) honey**
2 **cups I Samuel (30:12) raisins, chopped**
2 **cups Numbers (17:8) almonds Pinch of Leviticus (2:13) salt**
2 **Chronicles (9:9) spices, to your taste**

- Cream butter and sugar; add figs. Beat eggs until frothy; add milk.
- Sift part of flour with baking powder. Add remaining flour and add this mixture alternately to creamed mixture. Beat well and add honey, raisins and almonds; mix well.
- Pour into greased and floured tube pan.
- Bake at 375° for 30 minutes.

Sour Cream Pound Cake

1 **cup butter, softened**
3 **cups sugar**
6 **large eggs**
3 **cups all-purpose flour**
¼ **teaspoon baking soda**
¼ **teaspoon salt**
1 **(8-ounce) container sour cream**
1 **teaspoon vanilla**
1 **teaspoon lemon juice**

- Preheat oven to 325°.
- Cream butter and sugar until fluffy. Add eggs one at a time, beating well after each addition.
- Combine the flour, baking soda and salt; sift together 3 times.
- Fold flour mixture and sour cream into the batter alternately. Use small portions of each, beginning with the flour; do not stir.
- Fold in vanilla and lemon juice.
- Pour into a greased and floured tube or bundt pan.
- Bake ½ hour at 325°; reduce heat to 300° then continue cooking 1 additional hour.

Yield: 1 cake.

Funnel Cakes

2 **eggs**
1½ **cups milk**
2 **cups all-purpose flour, sifted**
1 **teaspoon baking powder**
½ **teaspoon salt**
Cooking oil

- Combine eggs and milk, beating until well blended.
- Sift together flour, baking powder and salt; add to egg mixture and beat until smooth.
- Heat cooking oil 1 inch deep in frying pan, electric skillet or deep fryer to 360°.
- Cover the bottom of a funnel with finger, pour in ½ cup batter and release into hot oil in spiral pattern.
- Fry until golden, turn with spatula and tongs; drain on paper towels.
- Sprinkle with powdered sugar and/or cinnamon.
- May serve with syrup.

Rum Flavored Chocolate Chip Cake

1   package chocolate cake mix
½   cup oil
1   (3¾-ounce) package instant chocolate pudding
8   ounces sour cream
4   eggs
¼   cup rum
1   teaspoon vanilla
6   ounces chocolate chips
1   cup chopped pecans

- Mix first seven ingredients; beat 3 to 4 minutes. Add chocolate chips and pecans and blend well.
- Pour into well-greased tube pan and bake at 350° for one hour. Remove from oven and glaze while in pan and still warm.

Glaze:

1   cup sugar
½   cup margarine
¼   cup rum
¼   cup water

- Combine ingredients in a small pot and heat until sugar is dissolved. With a thin wooden pick, poke holes in cake and drizzle glaze over, using all. Allow to cool completely and settle before removing from pan. This can be frozen and is delicious.

Yield: 20 servings.

Texas Sheet Cake

(Quick and easy — only one pan)

1   cup butter
1   cup water
4   tablespoons cocoa
2   cups flour
2   cups sugar
½   teaspoon salt
½   cup sour cream
1   teaspoon baking soda
2   eggs
½   cup butter
6   tablespoons milk
4   tablespoons cocoa
1   pound confectioners sugar
1   teaspoon vanilla
1   cup chopped nuts

- Bring to a boil: 1 cup butter, water and 4 tablespoons cocoa. Remove from heat and add flour, sugar, salt, sour cream, baking soda and eggs. Mix well and pour into 11x15-inch pan.
- Bake 22 minutes at 375°.
- In same saucepan bring to a boil remaining butter, milk and cocoa. Remove from heat and add confectioners sugar, vanilla and nuts. Spread over warm cake.

Yield: 16 to 20 servings.

To melt chocolate, grease the pan in which it is to be melted.

Triple Chocolate Torte

Cake:

2½ **ounces unsweetened chocolate**
3 **eggs, separated**
⅓ **cup sugar, divided**
½ **cup butter, softened**
1 **teaspoon vanilla extract**
½ **cup cake flour**

- Melt chocolate in microwave or in double boiler; set aside to cool.

- In a small bowl, beat egg whites until foamy; beat until soft peaks form, adding 3 tablespoons sugar, 1 tablespoon at a time.

- In another bowl beat butter; add remaining sugar and egg yolks. Beat until light and fluffy; beat in melted chocolate, vanilla and flour. Fold beaten egg whites into this mixture.

- Divide between two greased and floured 8-inch cake pans; smooth tops.

- Bake at 350° for 14 minutes; cakes will be thin; cool in pans 15 minutes.

- Remove to a rack and cool completely; chill in refrigerator.

- When cool, spoon filling onto cake layer to thickness of about 1¼ inches. Top with second layer, pressing lightly; smooth sides. Chill at least another hour and pour glaze over; chill until glaze sets.

Filling:

8 **ounces semi-sweet chocolate**
2 **ounces unsweetened chocolate**
2 **cups heavy cream**
2 **tablespoons brandy or coffee liqueur**

- Chop semi-sweet and unsweetened chocolate into saucepan; add cream and cook, stirring constantly, until chocolate melts and mixture just comes to a boil. Pour into a deep bowl; stir in liqueur.

- Cool, stirring often; then chill until mixture begins to thicken and set, about 45 minutes.

- Beat on high speed of electric mixer until mixture becomes light and fluffy and double in volume, about 3 to 5 minutes.

- Makes enough to fill center of layer cake.

Glaze:

4 **ounces semi-sweet chocolate**
½ **cup heavy cream**
3-4 **teaspoons water (optional)**

- Melt chocolate and cream in saucepan over low heat, stirring constantly until mixture comes to a boil.

- Remove from heat and cool to lukewarm; add water if too thick.

Yield: 12 to 16 servings.

Pro's Frosting

⅔ **cup vegetable shortening**
1 **(1-pound) box confectioners sugar**
¼ **cup milk**
   Pinch of salt
1 **teaspoon vanilla**
1 **egg white**

- With an electric mixer at medium speed, cream shortening and sugar.

- Add milk, salt and vanilla, combining well; beat 2 minutes.

- Add egg white and beat on high speed for 5 minutes.

- Spread on cake.

Yield: Enough for 1 cake.

Welsh Cakes

(A delicious and unusual offering for guests)

2   cups all-purpose flour
1   teaspoon fresh baking powder
1   teaspoon allspice
¼   teaspoon salt
½   cup sugar
¼   cup butter
¼   cup lard or shortening
1   egg
¼   cup milk
⅓   cup currants

- Sift the flour, baking powder, allspice, salt and sugar together into a bowl; cut the butter and lard into the flour using a pastry blender or 2 knives.

- Blend the egg with the milk; add the egg mixture to the flour mixture and blend well. Blend in the currants.

- Gather the dough into a ball; roll it out on a floured board ¼-inch thick. Cut in 2-inch rounds and cook on a very hot oiled griddle or frying pan until well-browned; turn and cook on other side until browned.

- Best if served hot.

Tipsy Cake

4   eggs, slightly beaten
3   tablespoons sugar
⅛   teaspoon salt
2   cups milk, scalded
½   teaspoon vanilla extract
1   day-old 9-inch sponge cake, cut into pieces
⅔   cup sherry
½   cup slivered blanched almonds, toasted

- Combine eggs, sugar and salt in top of double boiler. Gradually stir in scalded milk. Cook over hot water, stirring constantly, until mixture thickens, about 5 minutes. Cool thoroughly; stir in vanilla.

- Place half of the cake in glass serving bowl and sprinkle on half the sherry. Cover with half the cooled custard sauce; sprinkle with half the almonds. Repeat layering, ending with almonds; chill.

- Top with whipped and cream and almonds.

  Yield: 6 servings.

No-Fail White Icing

2   cups sugar
¼   cup light corn syrup
½   cup water
2   egg whites, room temperature
    Pinch of cream of tartar

- Combine the sugar, corn syrup and water in a saucepan over low heat until thoroughly mixed. Turn heat to medium and cook until mixture boils, stirring often. Cook until just past the soft ball stage; 135° to 140° on a candy thermometer.

- In a separate bowl, beat the egg whites with cream of tartar until they form stiff peaks. Gradually pour hot syrup into beaten whites continuing to beat at high speed until shiny and thick enough to form peaks.

- Spread on cake.

  Note: This icing may not "set up" well on humid days.

White Chocolate Cake

1	cup butter, softened
2	cups sugar
¼	pound white chocolate, melted and cooled
4	eggs
2½	cups cake flour
¼	teaspoon baking powder
¼	salt
1	cup buttermilk
1	teaspoon vanilla extract
1	cup chopped pecans
1	cup flaked coconut

- Cream butter and sugar until light and fluffy. Add white chocolate and blend well. Add eggs one at a time; beat well after each addition.
- Sift together dry ingredients.
- Alternately add dry ingredients and buttermilk to chocolate mixture; beat well after each addition. Fold in vanilla, pecans and coconut.
- Pour into 2 greased and floured 9-inch round cake pans.
- Bake at 350° for 25 minutes or until inserted toothpick comes out clean.
- Cool; frost with White Chocolate Frosting.

White Chocolate Frosting:

¾	cup white chocolate, melted over low heat
3	tablespoons all-purpose flour
1	cup milk
1	cup sugar
1	cup butter
1½	teaspoons vanilla extract

- Stir flour into melted chocolate. Add milk a little at a time and blend well. Cook over medium heat, stirring constantly until very thick; cool.

- In large mixing bowl, beat butter, sugar and vanilla until light and fluffy. Gradually add cooked chocolate mixture. Beat until icing is consistency of whipped cream.

Yield: 12 servings.

Velvety Chocolate Frosting

3	tablespoons butter
2	squares unsweetened chocolate
1½	cups confectioners sugar; sift after measuring
1	egg
3	tablespoons milk

- Melt butter and chocolate in a double boiler over gently simmering water. Remove from heat, add confectioners sugar, egg and milk. Beat with a mixer until well blended.
- Place the double boiler top in a larger bowl filled with ice water. Let stand 5 minutes or until cold, changing water if necessary to keep it icy.
- Beat until fluffy and of desired consistency.

Black Forest Cheesecake

1½ cups chocolate wafer crumbs
¼ cup butter or margarine, melted
3 (8-ounce) packages cream cheese, softened
1½ cups sugar
4 eggs
⅓ cup Kirsch or cherry-flavored liqueur
4 (1-ounce) squares semi-sweet chocolate
½ cup commercial sour cream
Whipped cream
Maraschino cherries with stems

- Combine chocolate wafer crumbs and butter, mixing well; firmly press into bottom and 1 inch up sides of a 9-inch springform pan.
- Beat cream cheese with electric mixer until light and fluffy; gradually add sugar, mixing well. Add eggs, one at a time, beating well after each addition. Stir in Kirsch; mix until well blended. Pour into prepared pan.
- Bake at 350° for 1 hour; let cake cool to room temperature on a wire rack.
- Place chocolate in top of a double boiler; bring water to a boil. Reduce heat to low; cook until chocolate melts and cool slightly. Mix chocolate with sour cream and spread over cooled cake.
- Garnish with whipped cream and cherries.

Crème de Menthe Cheesecake

Crust:

1 (8½-ounce) package chocolate cookie wafers, crumbled in processor
¼ cup butter, melted

- Combine wafer crumbs and butter; press crumbs onto the bottom of a 10-inch springform pan. Chill in the freezer for 2 hours.

Filling:

4 (8-ounce) packages cream cheese, softened
1 cup sugar
4 eggs
1 tablespoon lemon juice
3 ounces bittersweet chocolate
¼ cup crème de menthe

- With an electric beater, cream together the cream cheese, sugar, eggs and lemon juice until smooth.
- Melt chocolate over a double boiler; add crème de menthe. Pour into cream mixture; combine until blended. Pour entire mixture into a springform pan; bake at 350° for 40 minutes.

Topping:

1 pint sour cream
2 tablespoons sugar
1 teaspoon vanilla
1 teaspoon crème de menthe

- Combine all the topping ingredients. Spread onto the hot cheesecake and bake for an additional 10 minutes.
- Chill overnight.

Yield: 10 to 12 servings.

German Chocolate Cheesecake

Crust:
1½ cups chocolate wafers, crumbled
⅓ cup sugar
4 tablespoons butter, melted

- Combine crumbs, sugar and butter; press into the bottom and sides of a springform pan.

Filling:
3 (8-ounce) packages cream cheese
1 cup sugar
3 eggs
2 tablespoons cocoa
1 teaspoon vanilla

- Cream together cream cheese and sugar until well blended; add eggs, one at a time, and cocoa.

- Scrape sides of bowl and mix all ingredients well; pour filling into crust and bake at 350° for 1 hour or until top feels firm.

- Cool and top with Coconut-Pecan Topping; refrigerate overnight.

Coconut-Pecan Topping:
½ cup evaporated milk
½ cup sugar
2 egg yolks
¼ cup butter
1 teaspoon vanilla
⅔ cup coconut
½ cup chopped pecans

- Cook over medium heat milk, sugar, egg yolks, butter and vanilla, stirring constantly until mixture thickens, about 12 minutes.

- Remove from heat; add coconut and pecans.

- Cool and pour over cooled cheesecake.

Yield: 10 to 12 servings.

Oreo Cheesecake

Crust:
25 Oreos
4 tablespoons unsalted butter, melted

- Crumble Oreos in a food processor; add butter and pour into a greased springform pan. Press onto bottom and up sides and refrigerate while preparing cake.

Filling:
4 (8-ounce) packages cream cheese
1½ cups sugar, divided
2 tablespoons flour
4 eggs
3 egg yolks
⅓ cup whipping cream
2 teaspoons vanilla, divided
1¾ cups Oreos, about 15, chopped coarsely
2 cups sour cream

- In a mixer combine cheese and 1¼ cups sugar, cream together and add flour, whole eggs and egg yolks. When thoroughly mixed add in whipping cream and 1 teaspoon vanilla. Pour half on crust and sprinkle with Oreos. Pour remaining batter over and smooth top. Place on a baking sheet and bake in a preheated 425° oven for 15 minutes. Reduce to 225° and bake for another 50 minutes.

- At this time remove cake and increase heat to 350°. Combine sour cream, ¼ cup sugar and 1 teaspoon vanilla. Blend well; ice cake with mixture, return to oven and bake 7 minutes more. cover and refrigerate several hours or overnight.

Yield: 10 to 12 servings.

Heavenly Kahlúa Cheesecake

1¼ cups graham cracker crumbs
¼ cup sugar
¼ cup cocoa
⅓ cup butter or margarine, melted
2 (8-ounce) packages cream cheese, softened
¾ cup sugar
½ cup cocoa
2 eggs
¼ cup strong coffee
¼ cup Kahlúa
1 teaspoon vanilla extract
1 (8-ounce) carton sour cream
2 tablespoons sugar
1 teaspoon vanilla extract
6-8 chocolate curls (optional)

- Combine first 4 ingredients; mix well. Firmly press mixture into bottom of a 9-inch springform pan. Bake at 325° for 5 minutes; cool.

- Beat cream cheese with electric mixer until light and fluffy; gradually add ¾ cup sugar, mixing well. Beat in ½ cup cocoa; add eggs, one at a time, beating well after each addition. Stir in next 3 ingredients; pour into prepared pan.

- Bake at 375° for 25 minutes; filling will be soft but will firm up as the cake stands.

- Combine sour cream, 2 tablespoons sugar and 1 teaspoon vanilla; spread over hot cheesecake.

- Bake at 425° for 5 to 7 minutes; let cool to room temperature on a wire rack then chill 8 hours or overnight.

- Remove sides of springform pan. Garnish with chocolate curls in center of cheesecake; gently spread remaining curls on cheesecake.

Yield: 10 to 12 servings.

Frozen Cheesecake

3 (3-ounce) packages cream cheese
1 cup sugar
3 eggs, separated
½ pint whipping cream, whipped
1 teaspoon vanilla
¼ teaspoon salt
20 graham crackers, crumbed

- Cream cheese and sugar together; beat egg yolks and add to mixture. Add whipped cream, vanilla, salt and stiffly beaten egg whites.

- Place half of graham cracker crumbs on bottom of pan; pour in mixture and cover with remaining crumbs.

- Freeze. Let thaw slightly before serving.

- Place in pan of your choice, a springform may be used.

Yield: 12 to 14 servings from a springform pan.

Glazed Cheese Cake Puffs

2 (8-ounce) packages cream cheese, softened
¾ cup sugar
2 eggs
1 teaspoon vanilla
24 vanilla wafers
2 (21-ounce) cans fruit pie filling
Whipped cream for topping

- Line muffin tins with cupcake liners and place 1 vanilla wafer into each.

- Thoroughly blend together the cheese, sugar, eggs and vanilla; fill baking cups ¾ full.

- Bake 10 to 15 minutes at 375°. Cook until cheese mixture is set, then set aside to cool.

- Cover with pie filling and chill for 6 hours.

- Top with whipped cream.

Yield: 24 servings.

Reesey Balls

1 cup butter, melted
1⅓ cups graham cracker crumbs
1⅓ cups peanut butter
1 (16-ounce) box confectioners sugar
16 ounces semi-sweet chocolate chips
½ block of paraffin

- Mix together the first 4 ingredients and form into small balls.

- Melt chocolate chips and paraffin in a double boiler.

- Dip balls into hot chocolate mixture and put on waxed paper.

- Store in the refrigerator.

Yield: 5 to 6 dozen.

Butter Toffee Candy

1 cup sliced almonds
1 cup butter
1 cup sugar
3 tablespoons hot strong coffee
1 tablespoon corn syrup
2 (10-ounce) milk chocolate bars

- Roast almonds slightly and spread half into the bottom of a 9x13-inch pan.

- Combine butter, sugar, coffee and corn syrup in a saucepan and cook to the soft ball stage. Cool and pour gently over almonds.

- Melt chocolate bars in double boiler over simmering water, then spread over caramel base. Press remaining almonds into chocolate.

- Refrigerate and cut into squares; freezes well.

Yield: 2 to 3 dozen.

Pralines

3 cups sugar
1 cup buttermilk
1 teaspoon soda
1 teaspoon vanilla extract
1 tablespoon butter
2-2½ cups pecan halves

- Combine sugar, buttermilk, soda and vanilla in a heavy Dutch oven. Cook over medium heat to soft ball stage, stirring constantly.

- Remove from heat, stir in butter; beat 2 to 3 minutes, just until mixture begins to thicken; stir in pecans.

- Working quickly, drop mixture by tablespoons onto lightly buttered waxed paper; let cool.

Yield: 24 pralines.

Nutty O's

½ cup packed brown sugar
½ cup dark corn syrup
¼ cup margarine
½ teaspoon salt
6 cups Cheerios cereal
1 cup pecan halves
1 cup slivered almonds

- Heat sugar, corn syrup, margarine and salt in a saucepan until sugar is dissolved, about 5 minutes.
- Grease 15½x10½x1-inch pan with margarine; add Cheerios and nuts. Pour sugar mixture in and stir until cereal and nuts are coated.
- Bake for 30 minutes at 325°, stirring every 10 minutes; cool. Loosen mixture with spatula while cooling.
- Mixture will stick to pan while warm, once it cools it will loosen.
- Store in airtight container.

Butter Pecan Balls

1 cup butter or margarine
½ cup confectioners sugar
2 cups sifted all-purpose flour
1 teaspoon vanilla
½ cup pecans

- Cream butter and sugar then stir in flour thoroughly; add vanilla and nuts. Chill at least 1 hour; form into small balls.
- Bake at 350° for about 10 to 12 minutes until slightly brown. Sift confectioners sugar and roll balls while hot.

Yield: 2 dozen.

Peanut Brittle

1 cup sugar
½ cup light corn syrup
1½ cups raw peanuts
¼ teaspoon salt
1 tablespoon water
½ teaspoon vanilla
2 teaspoons margarine
1 teaspoon baking soda

- Mix together sugar, syrup, peanuts, salt and water. Cook on high power in microwave for 4 minutes; stir well. Cook about 4 minutes longer.
- Add ½ teaspoon vanilla and 2 teaspoons margarine. Cook about 2 more minutes until mixture turns a golden tint. Take out and add baking soda; stir quickly.
- Pour on buttered cookie sheet, spread; break up when cooled.

Butterscotch Haystacks

2 (6-ounce) packages butterscotch bits (can substitute chocolate)
1 (3-ounce) can Chinese noodles
1 (6½-ounce) can salted peanuts

- Melt the chocolate or butterscotch bits in a double boiler over hot water. Transfer to a large bowl and add the Chinese noodles and salted peanuts. Mix well.
- Drop by teaspoonfuls on a lightly greased cookie sheet and chill in refrigerator.

Yield: 36 cookies.

Almond Cookies

2¾ cups all-purpose flour
1 cup sugar
½ teaspoon soda
½ teaspoon salt
½ cup butter
½ cup solid vegetable shortening
1 egg, slightly beaten
1 teaspoon almond extract
⅓ cup whole blanched almonds

- Combine flour, sugar, soda and salt in a food processor and pulse for 30 seconds. Cut butter and shortening into flour mixture until it resembles coarse cornmeal. Add egg and almond extract to form ball.
- Roll out and cut with a 2-inch cutter; put almond in the center then brush with beaten egg.
- Bake at 325° for 15 to 20 minutes.
  Yield: 50 cookies.

Chocolate Chip Melt Aways

1 cup butter or margarine, softened
1 cup vegetable oil
1 cup sugar
1 cup confectioners sugar
2 eggs
4 cups all-purpose flour
1 teaspoon baking soda
1 teaspoon cream of tartar
1 teaspoon salt
1 teaspoon vanilla
1 (12-ounce) package chocolate chips

- Mix all ingredients together.
- Shape into 1-inch balls and roll in sugar.
- Bake at 375° for 10 to 15 minutes.
  Yield: 3 dozen.

Chewy Cheesecake Cookies

¼ cup butter, softened
1 (3-ounce) package cream cheese, softened
1 cup sugar
1 cup all-purpose flour
½ cup chopped pecans

- In a large mixing bowl combine butter, cream cheese and sugar and beat with rotary beater until fluffy. Gradually add flour and nuts; combine well.
- Shape into 1-inch balls and place on a greased cookie sheet 2 inches apart. Dampen fingers with water and flatten cookie until it is 2-inches in diameter.
- Bake at 350° for 9 to 10 minutes; cool 2 to 3 minutes before taking up.

Diet Buster Bars

1 box yellow cake mix
3 eggs, divided
½ cup butter, melted
1 cup chopped pecans
1 (8-ounce) bar cream cheese, softened
1 (16-ounce) box confectioners sugar
1 teaspoon vanilla

- Combine the cake mix, 1 egg, butter and nuts in a 9x13-inch pan.
- Mix the cream cheese, 2 eggs, sugar and vanilla. Spread over the first mixture in the pan.
- Bake at 350° for 35 to 40 minutes. Cool and cut into 1½-inch squares.
  Yield: 48 squares.

Chocolate Drizzled Buttery Delights

Mixture #1:

1 (3-ounce) package cream cheese, softened
1 cup confectioners sugar
½ cup chopped pecans
½ cup coconut
1 teaspoon vanilla
2 tablespoons all-purpose flour

- Thoroughly blend ingredients for mixture #1 and set aside.

Mixture #2:

½ cup butter, softened
½ cup confectioners sugar
¼ teaspoon salt
1 teaspoon vanilla
1½ cups all-purpose flour

- Cream butter and sugar; add salt and vanilla; slowly add flour.

- Shape into small balls and place on an ungreased cookie sheet; indent the middle with thumb.

- Cook at 350° for 10 to 15 minutes; as cookies cool, fill dent with about ½ teaspoon of mixture #1, then cool thoroughly.

Mixture #3:

½ cup semi-sweet chocolate bits
2 tablespoons water
2 tablespoons butter

- Gently melt together ingredients for mixture #3; remove from heat and beat until smooth.

- Drizzle mixture over cooled cookies.

Yield: 55 cookies.

Chocolate Pecan Pie Bars

3 cups unsifted all-purpose flour
2 cups sugar, divided
1 cup butter
½ teaspoon salt
1½ cups corn syrup, light or dark
6 (1-ounce) squares semi-sweet chocolate
4 eggs, slightly beaten
1½ teaspoons vanilla
2½ cups chopped pecans

- Grease the bottom and sides of a 15x10x1-inch baking pan (pan must be 1 inch deep). Preheat oven to 350°.

- Make the crust by combining flour, ½ cup sugar, butter, and salt in a large bowl and beating with an electric mixer at medium speed until mixture resembles coarse crumbs. Press firmly and evenly into pan and bake 20 minutes in the preheated oven.

- Combine corn syrup and chocolate in 3-quart saucepan over low heat, stirring until chocolate melts. Remove the chocolate mixture from heat and add the remaining ingredients in the order listed. Pour filling over hot crust, spreading evenly.

- Bake 30 minutes or until firm around the edges and slightly soft in center.

Yield: 6 dozen.

Choconut Nuggets

(A wonderful combination of oats, chocolate, corn flakes, coconut and nuts makes these nuggets a special treat)

1	cup butter, softened
1	cup packed brown sugar
1½	cups granulated sugar
1	tablespoon milk
1½	teaspoons vanilla
2	eggs
1	cup corn flakes, crumbled
3	cups oats, uncooked
1½	cups unsifted all-purpose flour
1¼	teaspoons baking soda
1	teaspoon salt
½	teaspoon mace
1½	teaspoons cinnamon
¼	teaspoon nutmeg
⅛	teaspoon powdered cloves
4	ounces coconut
1	(12-ounce) package semi-sweet chocolate chips
1	cup chopped walnuts or pecans

- Preheat oven to 350°.
- Cream together the first 3 ingredients; add the milk and vanilla, beating well. Add eggs and stir in corn flakes and oats.
- Sift together the flour, baking soda, salt, mace, cinnamon, nutmeg and cloves. Add to the above mixture and blend well.
- Stir in the coconut, chocolate and nuts.
- Drop batter by well-rounded teaspoonfuls onto a greased cookie sheet. Bake at 350° for approximately 10 minutes.

Yield: 8 dozen.

Cowboy Cookies

1	cup margarine, softened
¾	cup brown sugar, packed
¾	cup granulated sugar
2	eggs
1	teaspoon vanilla extract
2	cups flour
½	teaspoon baking soda
¼	teaspoon salt
1½	cups quick cooking oatmeal
½	cup coarsely chopped nuts
1	(6-ounce) package chocolate chips
1	cup raisins

- Cream margarine; add sugars and beat well.
- Add eggs and vanilla then stir to blend well; add the dry ingredients at one time and mix to blend thoroughly. Stir in oatmeal, nuts, chocolate chips and raisins; mix well. Drop by spoonfuls on cookie sheet and bake for 13 to 15 minutes in 350° oven.
- This dough freezes well and can be sliced later to make fresh cookies.

Yield: 4 dozen.

Icebox Cookies

½	cup butter
2	cups sugar
⅓	cup cocoa
½	cup canned milk
3	cups quick cooking oatmeal
1	cup chopped nuts
1	teaspoon vanilla

- Melt butter; add sugar, cocoa and milk and boil minutes. Remove from heat and add the remaining ingredients.
- Drop by teaspoonfuls onto waxed paper and chill.

Yield: 72 cookies.

Forget-Me-Nots

2 egg whites
Dash of salt
¾ cup sugar
1 (6-ounce) package chocolate bits
½ cup chopped pecans

- Beat egg whites until stiff; add salt then sugar, one tablespoon at a time.
- Fold in chocolate and nuts.
- Drop by the teaspoonful on a foil lined cookie sheet.
- Put in a preheated 350° oven and immediately turn off; leave cookies in oven for 8 hours.
- DO NOT OPEN OVEN.
- Can use mint-chocolate bits and add green food coloring to get mint chip flavor.

Yield: 40 cookies.

Heritage Cookies

2 egg whites, stiffly beaten
2 cups light brown sugar
2 teaspoons all-purpose flour
¼ teaspoon salt
2 teaspoons vanilla
2 cups chopped pecans

- Fold sugar, flour, salt, vanilla and nuts into very stiffly beaten egg whites. Drop on a greased cookie sheet by tablespoonfuls and bake for 10 to 12 minutes at 325°.
- Remove these from oven before they brown.

Yield: 2 dozen.

Chocolate Sugar Plums

1 cup powdered sugar
1 cup chunky peanut butter
1 cup chopped dates
2 tablespoons butter
1 (12-ounce) package semi-sweet chocolate chips

- Mix first four ingredients and shape into teaspoon-sized balls. Melt chocolate bits in a double boiler and dip each of the balls into chocolate to coat.
- Place on waxed paper and chill. Keep in refrigerator.
- Remove 20 minutes before serving.

Lace Cookies

¼ teaspoon salt
½ teaspoon baking powder
4 tablespoons all-purpose flour
2 eggs, beaten
½ cup butter, melted
1½ cups brown sugar
2 cups regular oatmeal
1 teaspoon vanilla

- Sift together salt, baking powder and flour; add eggs and combine well.
- Mix butter and brown sugar and blend into the flour/egg mixture. Add oatmeal and vanilla. Refrigerate at least 30 minutes; this can keep overnight.
- Drop by the half teaspoonful onto foil-lined cookie sheet. Bake in a preheated 325° oven for 7 to 10 minutes.
- Watch closely! Remove from oven when edges are lightly browned. Cool and peel away foil.

Yield: 2 dozen.

Heavenly Honey Brownies

⅓ cup margarine, softened
¾ cup sugar
½ cup honey
2 teaspoons vanilla extract
2 eggs
½ cup all-purpose flour
½ teaspoon salt
⅓ cup cocoa
1 cup chopped pecans
   Honey Chocolate Frosting

- Combine margarine and sugar, cream until light and fluffy; add honey and vanilla; mix well. Add eggs, one at a time, beating well after each addition.
- Combine flour, salt, and cocoa; add to creamed mixture, mixing well; stir in chopped pecans.
- Spoon batter into a greased 8-inch square pan; bake at 350° for 30 to 35 minutes or until done.
- Let cool; spread Honey Chocolate Frosting over top of layer. Cut into squares.

Honey Chocolate Frosting:

3 tablespoons margarine, softened
3 tablespoons cocoa
¾ teaspoon vanilla extract
1 cup powdered sugar
1 tablespoon milk
1 tablespoon honey

- Combine margarine and cocoa; cream well.
- Add remaining ingredients and beat until smooth.

Yield: 3 dozen.

Holly Wreaths

(Children enjoy making these for Christmas)

½ cup butter
30 large marshmallows
½ teaspoon vanilla
1½ teaspoons green food coloring
3½ cups corn flakes
60 cinnamon candies

- In a heavy 2-quart pan melt butter and marshmallows over low heat, stirring constantly; add vanilla and food coloring. Stir until well blended; fold in corn flakes.
- Drop by rounded greased tablespoons onto waxed paper lined cookie sheet. Shape into 2-inch wreaths; decorate with red candies.

Yield: 25 servings.

Lemon Stickies

1 box lemon cake mix
1 stick margarine, melted
3 eggs
1 (8-ounce) package cream cheese, softened
1 box confectioners sugar

- Mix cake mix, margarine and 1 egg. Batter will be thick. Spread in 9x13-inch pan. May need to use back of wet spoon to spread.
- Mix cream cheese, sugar and 2 eggs, mixing well. Spread on top of cake batter.
- Bake at 350° for 40 minutes. Let cool completely and cut into little squares.

Yield: 50 squares.

Oatmeal Chocolate-Nut Cookie

2 cups butter
2 cups sugar
2 cups brown sugar
4 eggs
2 teaspoons vanilla
4 cups flour
5 cups oatmeal, ground fine in processor
1 teaspoon salt
2 teaspoons baking powder
2 teaspoons baking soda
16 ounces mini-chocolate chips
1 (8-ounce) bar chocolate, grated
3 cups chopped nuts

- Cream butter and both sugars; add eggs and vanilla. Mix together with flour, oatmeal, salt, baking powder and soda; add chips, chocolate bar and nuts.
- Roll into balls and place 2 inches apart on cookie sheet.
- Bake at 375° for 6 to 8 minutes or until cookies are light, not browned.

Yield: 10 dozen.

Edenton Shortbread Cookies

1 cup butter, softened
½ cup sugar
2 cups all-purpose flour

- Cream butter and sugar until fluffy; add flour and blend well. Make into balls, place on an ungreased cookie sheet, and flatten slightly.
- Bake for 50 to 60 minutes at 250°.

Yield: 30 cookies.

Peanut Butter Fingers

1 (24-ounce) loaf sandwich bread
1 (12-ounce) jar of peanut butter
½ cup peanut or vegetable oil
Corn flake crumbs or bread crumbs

- Trim the crusts from the bread, cut into finger strips and place on a cookie sheet in 200° oven for 1½ to 2 hours to dry out. (If using bread crumbs, put these in oven at same time to dry out).
- Melt peanut butter and oil in top of double boiler.
- Using slotted spoon, dip the bread fingers in the melted peanut butter; drain in colander.
- Roll in crumbs and store in airtight container.

Yield: 96 fingers.

Potato Chip Cookies

2 cups butter or margarine
1 cup sugar
2 teaspoons vanilla
1 cup crushed potato chips
½ cup chopped nuts
3½ cups flour

- Cream butter and sugar until light and fluffy; add vanilla. Blend in potato chips, nuts and flour.
- Drop by teaspoonfuls on ungreased cookie sheet.
- Bake at 350° for 12 to 15 minutes.
- Let stand a minute before removing from cookie sheet. Let cool.
- Freezes beautifully.

Yield: 100 cookies.

Ranger Cookies

½ cup granulated sugar
½ cup brown sugar
½ cup butter
1 egg
1 teaspoon vanilla
1 cup self-rising flour
2 cups Wheaties cereal
½ cup coconut

- Heat oven to 350°.

- Mix sugars, butter, egg and vanilla thoroughly. Stir in remaining ingredients. Drop dough by rounded teaspoonfuls, about 2 inches apart onto ungreased cookie sheet.

- Bake 10 minutes. Immediately remove from cookie sheet.

Yield: 3 dozen.

Won't Believe 'Ems

40 saltine crackers
1 cup butter
1 cup light brown sugar
1 (11½-ounce) package milk chocolate chips
1 cup chopped pecans

- Grease an 11x15x1-inch jelly roll pan and cover with saltines in single layer; preheat oven to 350°.

- Melt sugar and butter together, remove from heat and beat until foamy. Pour over saltines, spreading to cover and bake at 350° for 10 minutes. Remove from oven; cover with chocolate chips and pecans and gently press into bars with the back of a fork.

- Cool completely; break or cut into serving sized pieces and refrigerate.

Yield: 40 bars.

Charlotte Russe

1 pint whipping cream
1 teaspoon vanilla
½ cup sugar
2 tablespoons sherry
½ teaspoon gelatin
¼ cup cold milk
¼ cup warm milk
5 egg whites
2 packages ladyfingers, split

- Whip cream until stiff; add vanilla, sugar and sherry. Soften gelatin in cold milk, then dissolve in warm milk.

- When cool add to above mixture, beating the cream constantly; add beaten egg whites. Pour in dish lined with split ladyfingers; chill.

Yield: 6 servings.

Cherry Crunch

1 (9-ounce) box yellow cake mix
¼ cup chopped nuts
2 tablespoons firmly packed brown sugar
2 teaspoons cinnamon
1 (21-ounce) can cherry pie filling
½ cup butter, melted
   Vanilla ice cream or whipped cream

- Combine first four ingredients.

- Spread pie filling in the bottom of an 8-inch square pan.

- Sprinkle cake mixture on top of pie filling.

- Drizzle melted butter over top.

- Microwave on high for 12 to 14 minutes; rotate after 7 minutes. Let stand 5 minutes.

- Serve warm topped with ice cream or whipped cream.

Bavarian Cream

1   **envelope unflavored gelatin**
¼   **cup cold water**
4   **egg yolks**
     Dash of salt
½   **cup sugar**
1   **cup milk**
1   **cup whipping cream**
2   **teaspoons vanilla or 2 tablespoons liqueur (any flavor)**

- Soften gelatin in cold water and set aside.
- Mix egg yolks, salt and sugar together in the top of a double boiler. Gradually blend in milk and cook over hot water, stirring constantly, until thick and smooth.
- Add softened gelatin; stir until dissolved, then set aside to cool.
- Whip the cream, add vanilla, and fold in gently.
- Spoon into 1-quart mold or 4 to 5 individual ones; chill.
- Vanilla can be omitted from whipped cream and replaced with liqueur.

Yield: 4 to 5 servings.

Easy Trifle

1   **(3.4-ounce) package instant vanilla pudding**
2   **cups cold milk**
1   **(20-ounce) can crushed pineapple, drained well**
2   **bananas, sliced**
1   **(21-ounce) can blueberry pie filling**
1   **angel food cake**
1   **(8-ounce) container whipped topping**
1   **(2-ounce) package sliced almonds**
     Sherry, optional

- Mix instant pudding with milk and blend with an electric mixer at lowest speed for 2 minutes; chill for 10 minutes.
- Tear angel food cake into bite-size pieces and place in a 3-quart casserole or a large glass bowl; can sprinkle a little sherry over the cake. Pour pudding over the cake and mix lightly. Spread pie filling over the cake mixture.
- Layer the pineapple and banana over the filling. Spread dessert topping on the top, covering to outer edges.
- Sprinkle almonds on top.
- Chill for 2 hours.

Lemon Freeze

1   **box vanilla wafers, finely crushed**
6   **eggs, separated**
½   **cup lemon juice**
2   **teaspoons lemon rind**
1   **cup sugar**
½   **pint whipping cream, whipped**
1   **(8-ounce) container frozen whipped topping, thawed**

- Line the bottom of a 9x13-inch Pyrex dish with all but 4 tablespoons crushed wafers.
- Beat egg yolks until foamy; add lemon juice and rind. Beat egg whites until stiff, gradually adding sugar in small quantities as you do. Beat until all sugar in incorporated and whites are stiff.
- Fold yolk mixture, whipped cream and whipped topping into beaten whites. Pour into dish and sprinkle reserved crushed wafers on top.
- Store in freezer.

Yield: 8 to 10 servings.

Chocolate Eclair Dessert

(Make a day ahead)

2 (4-ounce) packages vanilla instant pudding
3 cups milk
1 (12-ounce) container whipped topping
   Graham crackers
2 (1-ounce) squares unsweetened chocolate
3 tablespoons butter
1 tablespoon light corn syrup
3 tablespoons milk
1½ cups confectioners sugar
1 teaspoon vanilla

- Mix puddings with 3 cups milk; when it starts to thicken stir in whipped topping.

- Line a 9x12-inch pan with whole graham crackers and spread ½ of pudding mixture on top; repeat and top with graham crackers; you should have 3 layers of graham crackers.

- Prepare icing; melt chocolate and butter over low heat; remove and add syrup, milk, confectioners sugar and vanilla.

- Blend until smooth and ice tops of graham crackers.

Yield: 10 to 12 servings.

Frozen Raspberry Dessert

1 cup all-purpose flour
½ cup light brown sugar
½ cup chopped walnuts
½ cup butter, melted
2 egg whites, room temperature
½ cup white sugar
2 teaspoons lemon juice
1 (10-ounce) package frozen red raspberries, thawed and drained
1 (12-ounce) carton whipped topping, thawed

- Combine the first 4 ingredients, mixing well and spread on an ungreased cookie sheet ½-inch thick. Bake at 350° for 20 minutes, stirring with a fork every 3 minutes to crumble; set aside to cool.

- Sprinkle half the crumbs in a 13x9x2-inch pan; reserve remaining crumbs. Beat the egg whites until foamy; continue beating while adding the sugar 1 teaspoon at a time. Beat until stiff peaks form. Fold in lemon juice, drained raspberries and whipped topping; freeze.

- Remove from freezer a few minutes before serving.

- May keep frozen for several days.

Yield: 10 to 12 servings.

Macaroon Tortoni

1   package coconut macaroons,
    crushed
    Sherry to taste
½   gallon rich vanilla ice cream,
    softened
1   small jar maraschino cherries,
    drained and chopped
1   cup toasted slivered almonds

- Soak crushed macaroons in sherry for 15 minutes. Blend well with other ingredients.
- Spoon into individual serving containers such as Jefferson cups and freeze.

Yield: 8 to 10 servings.

Raspberry Trifle

2   (10-ounce) packages frozen red
    raspberries, thawed
4   teaspoons cornstarch
1   (14-ounce) can condensed milk
1   cup cold water
1   package instant vanilla pudding
2   cups cream, whipped
¼   cup orange juice
1   loaf frozen pound cake, cut in
    cubes
⅓   cup sliced almonds

- Drain raspberries, reserving 1 cup syrup. Cook syrup and cornstarch until clear and thick; chill. Mix milk and water; add pudding and beat well. Chill 5 minutes and fold in whipped cream.
- In a large glass bowl, place ½ of cake cubes; sprinkle with orange juice. Place ½ raspberries on top, then syrup, then ½ pudding; repeat layers.
- Top with almonds and chill.

Yield: 8 to 10 servings.

Mocha Ice Cream

4   eggs, beaten
1   cup sugar
1   (14-ounce) can condensed milk
1   tablespoon vanilla
1   carton half-and-half
1-2   teaspoons instant coffee, dissolved
      for color
¼   cup Kahlúa
      Milk

- Beat eggs very well; add sugar, condensed milk, vanilla and half-and-half; mix well. Add instant coffee and Kahlúa; pour into ice cream freezer container. Add milk to fill line; freeze according to your freezer directions.
- After cream is done, pack to ripen with additional ice and salt.

Yield: 16 to 20 servings.

Sherry Custard

1   quart milk
¾   cup sugar
3   tablespoons cornstarch
⅛   teaspoon salt
3   egg yolks
1   whole egg
1   teaspoon rum or rum flavoring
½   cup cream sherry

- Cook milk, sugar, cornstarch, and salt over medium heat, stirring constantly until slightly thickened. Beat egg yolks and 1 whole egg. Add 1 cup hot milk mixture to eggs, stir and return to hot milk. Continue cooking (do not boil) until custard consistency. Add sherry and rum. Cool and serve over cake.
- This is perfect to serve as a topping for Tipsy Cake.

Mountain Top Bread Pudding

¼ loaf plain white bread
4 ounces melted butter
6 whole eggs, beaten
1 quart milk
½ pound sugar
1 cup raisins
   Vanilla to taste
   Vanilla Sauce

- Cut bread slices into 1-inch squares and toast in a hot oven. Place in the bottom of a casserole and drizzle with melted butter.

- Combine remaining ingredients and pour over bread.

- Bake at 350° until custard is firm, approximately 45 minutes.

Vanilla Sauce: (may be served hot or cold)

2 cups heavy cream
½ cup sugar
4 egg yolks
1 tablespoon flour
1 tablespoon vanilla extract
¼ teaspoon salt
2 scoops vanilla ice cream

- Combine cream and sugar in a 2-quart saucepan and bring just to a boil. Remove from heat.

- Beat egg yolks, flour, vanilla and salt; stir in a little of the hot cream. Add this mixture to the rest of the hot cream. Cook, stirring constantly until just thickened; do not overcook.

- Remove from heat and add ice cream, stirring until melted.

- Strain.

- Serve over bread pudding.

Pavlova

4 egg whites
   Dash of salt
¾ cup sugar
½ teaspoon vanilla
1 teaspoon vinegar
1 tablespoon cornstarch
   Fresh fruit (not citrus)
½ pint whipping cream

- Trace a 10-inch circle onto waxed paper; butter the paper and place it on a cookie sheet; set aside.

- In the small bowl of an electric mixer, beat the egg whites and salt until foamy.

- Continue beating while adding the sugar gradually, 2 or 3 tablespoons at a time.

- When half the sugar has been incorporated, add the vanilla.

- Continue beating while adding the remaining sugar, vinegar and cornstarch. Beat until stiff but not dry.

- Spread in circle on waxed paper, piling the whites about 1½-inches thick.

- Bake 15 minutes at 275°, then 1½ hours at 250°.

- Cool on cookie sheet, pull off waxed paper and serve covered with fresh fruit and whipped cream.

Yield: 6 to 8 servings.

Pots de Crème Elegante

6   **eggs, separated**
½   **pint whipping cream**
1   **teaspoon instant coffee**
2   **teaspoons vanilla**
1   **(6-ounce) package semi-sweet chocolate, melted**
1   **(1-ounce) semi-sweet chocolate square**

- Whip whites of egg in a small bowl until stiff but not dry. In a separate bowl whip cream and add instant coffee; set aside.
- Whip egg yolks then gradually add melted chocolate pieces and vanilla. Fold stiff egg whites into chocolate mixture.
- Spoon this pots de crème mixture into 6 (6-ounce) wine glasses or other favorite serving glasses. Refrigerate at least 4 hours.
- Top each pot de crème with whipped cream mixture. Garnish with chocolate curls cut with paring knife from 1 ounce of chocolate.

Yield: 6 servings.

Raspberry Fantasia

1⅔ **cups all-purpose flour**
1¾ **cups dry oats**
¾   **cup brown sugar**
3   **tablespoons white sugar**
¾   **teaspoon baking powder**
1   **cup margarine or butter**
1   **(21-ounce) can raspberry pie filling**
    Lemon juice
1   **cup confectioners sugar**
½   **teaspoon vanilla**
1½ **tablespoons milk**

- Mix together thoroughly until crumbs: flour, oats, sugars, baking powder and butter.
- Pack ¾ of crumb mixture over bottom of greased 9x13x2-inch pan; carefully spread raspberries over crumbs, then sprinkle lightly with lemon juice. Top with remaining crumbs; try to cover all the raspberries.
- Bake in preheated oven at 350° for 25 to 30 minutes; bake until top is a soft, golden brown; remove and let cool.
- Mix confectioners sugar, vanilla and milk; drizzle over top in a zigzag pattern.
- Serve chilled with or without whipped topping.

Yield: 10 to 12 servings.

Toffee Dessert

2   **cups butter, softened**
4   **cups powdered brown sugar**
6   **eggs, separated**
6   **squares unsweetened baking chocolate, melted**
2   **tablespoons vanilla**
2   **cups chopped nuts (optional)**
2   **graham cracker pie crusts**

- Combine butter and sugar. Add beaten egg yolks to sugar mixture. Add melted chocolate and vanilla.
- Beat egg whites until stiff. Add to above mixture. Nuts may be added if desired.
- Pour into graham cracker crusts or into 9x13-inch buttered and crumbed (vanilla wafer or graham cracker) pan. Sprinkle a few crumbs on top.
- Refrigerate for at least 6 to 8 hours or overnight.
- Recipe can be halved for 8x8-inch pan.

Yield: 12 servings.

Peppermint Ice Cream

(Wonderful anytime but especially at Christmas)

4 eggs
5 cups milk
2 tablespoons vanilla
2½ cups sugar
4 cups whipping cream
¼ teaspoon salt
1½ cups crushed peppermint candy

- In a large mixing bowl beat eggs until foamy; gradually add sugar and beat until thickened. Add cream, vanilla and salt; mix thoroughly.
- Pour into ice cream freezer can; add milk to fill line on can and stir well.
- Add peppermint candy to ice cream after it has frozen until it is mushy, about 15 minutes of freezing.
- Continue freezing as directed.
- Can add a few drops of red food coloring to give it a brighter pink color.

Yield: 2 quarts.

Orange Ice

1 (12-ounce) container frozen concentrate orange juice, undiluted
1 pint of 7-up
1 pint of Sprite or Tom Collins mix
Pinch of grated nutmeg

- Blend all ingredients and pour into 9x10-inch oblong cake pan.
- Freeze until firm.
- Serve in chilled glass bowls with a sprig of mint.

Yield: 4 to 5 servings.

Milky Way Ice Cream

(Yummy)

4 eggs
2 cups sugar
1 (14-ounce) can sweetened condensed milk
2 teaspoons vanilla
1 (14½-ounce) can evaporated milk
6 Milky Way or Snickers bars
Milk

- Beat eggs; add sugar, condensed milk, vanilla and evaporated milk. Mix well; melt bars in a small amount of milk. Add to mixture and pour into ice cream freezer.
- Pour milk to fill line of ice cream freezer and freeze according to your directions.

Yield: 20 to 25 servings.

All American Pie

5 medium red apples, peeled and sliced
1 cup sugar
1 tablespoon all-purpose flour
1 tablespoon nutmeg
1 teaspoon cinnamon
1 tablespoon lemon juice
½ cup butter or margarine
2 deep dish pie shells

- Combine apples, sugar, flour, nutmeg and cinnamon in a bowl mixing well to coat apples. Pour into one pie shell; sprinkle lemon juice over apple mixture. Slice butter and place over apples.
- Top with other pie shell, pinching edges to seal; make 3 to 4 slits in top of shell.
- Bake for 1 hour at 350°.
- Can top a slice with vanilla ice cream.

Yield: 1 pie.

Chocolate Fudge Pie

(A must for chocolate lovers)

Meringue:

4   egg whites, room temperature
1   teaspoon vanilla
½   teaspoon cream of tartar
1   cup sifted granulated sugar

- Preheat oven to 225°.

- Beat egg whites until very foamy.

- Add vanilla and cream of tartar; add, while continuing to beat, the sugar, 1 tablespoon at a time.

- When mixture stands in stiff peaks, fill the 9-inch pie plate which has been lightly greased and shape into dish in form of crust.

- Bake for 1 hour and allow to cool gradually by turning off oven and leaving oven door open; after a few minutes allow to cool at room temperature.

- Fill with chocolate mixture, top with whipped cream and refrigerate.

Filling:

1   (14-ounce) can sweetened condensed milk
2   ounces unsweetened chocolate squares
¼   teaspoon salt
½   cup hot water
½   teaspoon vanilla extract
½   cup whipped cream

- In top of double boiler, combine condensed milk, chocolate and salt. Heat over boiling water, stirring constantly until mixture is very thick.

- Gradually stir in water, keeping mixture smooth and continue cooking, stirring often until mixture thickens.

- Remove from heat and stir in vanilla extract.

- Cool at room temperature, about ½ hour.

- Pour into meringue crust and refrigerate at least 3 hours.

- Top with whipped cream.

Yield: 6 servings.

Best Ever Fresh Peach Pie

½   cup sugar
3   tablespoons all-purpose flour
½   teaspoon ground cinnamon
¼   teaspoon salt
6   large ripe peaches, peeled and sliced
1   tablespoon lemon juice
¼   teaspoon almond extract
2   frozen pie crusts
Milk or water
Sugar

- Combine sugar, flour, cinnamon and salt in a small bowl.

- Put peaches in a large bowl; sprinkle with lemon juice and almond extract. Toss to coat; add sugar mixture; mix gently. Spoon peaches into thawed pie shell.

- Put other pie shell over the top of the pie and cut several vents in the pie shell for steam to escape. Brush pastry with milk or water; sprinkle with sugar.

- Bake in 425° oven for 15 minutes. Lower heat to 350°; bake 35 minutes longer or until golden and juices are bubbly.

- Cool.

Yield: 6 servings.

Caramel Pie

1 (8-ounce) package cream cheese, softened
1 can condensed milk
1 (12-ounce) container whipped topping, thawed
¼ cup butter
1 (7-ounce) can flaked coconut (optional)
1 cup chopped pecans
1 (21-ounce) jar caramel ice cream topping
2 graham cracker crusts

- Combine cream cheese and condensed milk, beating until smooth. Fold in whipped topping.
- Melt butter in frying pan. Add coconut and pecans and cook until golden.
- Into graham cracker crusts layer in the following order: Cream cheese mixture, caramel ice cream topping, cream cheese mixture, coconut and pecan mixture. Repeat layers.
- Cover and freeze until firm. Serve frozen.
  Yield: 12 servings.

Chocolate Nut Delight

1 cup sugar
1-2 tablespoons flour
2 eggs, slightly beaten
½ cup margarine, melted
1 cup walnuts or pecans, chopped
1 cup chocolate chips
1 teaspoon vanilla
2 unbaked pie shells

- Preheat oven to 325°.
- Mix sugar, flour, butter and eggs together.
- Add nuts, chocolate chips and vanilla.
- Place in unbaked 8-inch pie shells.

- Bake for 40 to 45 minutes.
  Yield: 2 pies.

Easy Peach Cobbler

(Delicious when made with fresh peaches)

¾ stick butter or margarine
¾ cup flour
1¾ cups sugar, divided
2 teaspoons baking powder
 Dash of salt
½ cup milk
2 cups sliced fresh or frozen peaches

- Melt butter or margarine in 2-quart deep casserole.
- Make batter by combining flour, sugar, baking powder, salt and milk. Pour batter on top of melted margarine; do not stir.
- Dump in 2 cups peaches mixed with ¾ cup sugar; do not stir.
- Bake uncovered for 1 hour at 350°.
  Note: Serve warm or cold with cream or ice cream.

Easy Lemon Tarts

(Quick and good, especially with seafood)

16 (3-inch) tart shells
4 eggs
1½ lemons, quartered and seeds removed (may use limes)
2½ cups sugar
½ cup butter, softened

- Mix all ingredients except shells in the blender; pour into tart shells.
- Bake 30 to 35 minutes at 350°.

Coconut Pie

(Sinfully good)

2 cups milk
½ cup all-purpose flour
1½ cups sugar
3 egg yolks
½ cup butter
2 cups coconut
1 teaspoon vanilla or lemon flavoring or one of each
Dash of salt
1 cooked pie shell

- Heat milk in double boiler.
- Mix flour and sugar well and pour hot milk over mixture, stirring constantly to avoid lumping. Place back in double boiler and cook until thickened.
- Beat yolks of eggs and add to mixture, stirring well.
- Add butter and coconut and cook until rather thick, stirring constantly. Remove from stove and cool; add salt and flavoring. Place in cooked pie shell.

Meringue:

3 egg whites
1 teaspoon lemon or vanilla flavoring
Dash of salt
6 tablespoons sugar

- Beat 3 egg whites until stiff; add flavoring, salt and sugar; beat to mix.
- Spread mixture on top of pie; cook 4 to 6 minutes at 400°.

Favorite Lemon Pie

1 cup sugar
1 tablespoon cornstarch
3 egg yolks
3 lemons, juiced and rind grated
1 cup boiling water
1 baked pie crust
3 egg whites
1 tablespoon ice water
½ cup sugar

- Mix first 5 ingredients together in saucepan and cook over low heat until thick. Pour into baked pie shell.
- Combine last 3 ingredients and beat until stiff. Spread on top of filling, sealing egg whites to crust. Leave sharp peaks in egg whites.
- Bake at 350° until lightly browned.

Yield: 1 pie.

Olde South Pecan Pie

(A Deep South tradition)

½ cup white corn syrup
¾ cup granulated sugar
½ cup brown sugar
4 tablespoons butter, melted
1 teaspoon vanilla
3 eggs
1 cup broken pecans
1 unbaked deep dish pie crust

- Combine syrup, sugars, butter and vanilla. Add eggs, one at a time, beating after each addition.
- Sprinkle broken nuts over bottom of pie crust. Pour in filling.
- Bake at 350° for 50 to 60 minutes.

Yield: 1 pie.

Fresh Peach Pie

½	**cup sugar**
2	**tablespoons cornstarch**
½	**teaspoon finely shredded orange peel**
¼	**teaspoon ground nutmeg**
1½	**cups peach nectar**
½	**teaspoon vanilla**
4	**cups sliced, peeled fresh peaches**
1	**(9-inch) pie shell, baked Whipped cream or vanilla ice cream**

- In a small saucepan, combine sugar, cornstarch, orange peel, nutmeg and peach nectar. Cook and stir over medium heat until bubbly and thick; continue cooking two additional minutes stirring constantly. Cool 5 to 10 minutes.
- Arrange fruit in pie shell and pour cooled mixture evenly over peaches.
- Chill for 2 hours.
- Serve cold topped with whipped cream or ice cream.

Yield: 1 pie.

Honeymoon Pie

1	**quart fresh raspberries, hulled, or 2 packages frozen raspberries, drained**
1¼	**cups sugar**
2	**teaspoons gelatin**
3	**tablespoons water**
3	**tablespoons boiling water**
1	**tablespoon lemon juice**
2	**cups heavy cream, whipped**
4	**egg whites**
¼	**teaspoon cream of tartar**
1	**cup sugar**

- Heat oven to 450°.
- Beat egg whites until stiff; add cream of tartar and 1 cup sugar, adding one tablespoon at a time and continuing to beat until well mixed.
- Grease two 9-inch pie plates; spread crust mixture in pie plates and make a nest. Put pie plates in oven; turn off oven and leave overnight.
- The next morning, combine the raspberries and remaining sugar. Soak gelatin in cold water; dissolve it with boiling water. Stir into berries with lemon juice.
- Cook the gelatin mixture. Cool and when it is about set, fold in lightly whipped cream. Pour into 2 pie shells and cool.
- Can add drops of red food coloring to raspberry mixture.

Raisin Pie

2	**cups seedless raisins**
2	**cups water**
½	**cup brown sugar**
2	**tablespoons cornstarch**
1	**teaspoon cinnamon**
⅛	**teaspoon salt**
1	**tablespoon vinegar**
1	**tablespoon butter**
1	**(9-inch) double crust pie crust**

- Boil raisins in 1¾ cups of water for 5 minutes.
- Combine brown sugar, cornstarch, cinnamon and salt; moisten with remaining ¼ cup cold water. Add to raisins, stirring until mixture boils. Remove from fire and add butter and vinegar. Pour into pastry-lined pie pan; cover with top pastry.
- Bake 25 minutes in 425° oven. Cool and enjoy.

Yield: 1 pie.

Peaches and Cream Pie

¾ cup all-purpose flour
1 teaspoon baking soda
1 small package instant vanilla pudding
1 egg
½ cup milk
½ teaspoon salt
3 tablespoons butter
6-8 medium peaches, peeled, sliced and drained
1 (8-ounce) package cream cheese, softened
3 tablespoons peach juice
½ cup plus 1½ teaspoons sugar
1½ teaspoons cinnamon

- Combine the first 7 ingredients to form crust; press into pie plate, covering the bottom and sides.
- Place peach slices over crust.
- Beat together the cream cheese, peach juice and ½ cup sugar. Beat for 2 minutes; spread over peaches.
- Combine 1½ teaspoons sugar and cinnamon; sprinkle over top.
- Bake at 350° for 30 to 40 minutes. Cool completely.

Yield: 1 pie.

Pumpkin-Pecan Pie

(A yummy end to a holiday dinner)

½ cup chopped pecans
1 cup brown sugar, divided
¼ cup butter, melted
2 eggs
1¾ cups cooked pumpkin
½ teaspoon salt
1 teaspoon cinnamon
½ teaspoon nutmeg
½ teaspoon ginger
1 (14-ounce) can evaporated milk
1 (9-inch) pastry shell, unbaked

- Combine pecans, ¼ cup brown sugar and melted butter in small bowl.
- Beat eggs slightly in a large bowl; add remaining brown sugar, pumpkin, salt and spices, mixing well. Stir in evaporated milk; pour into pastry shell.
- Bake at 425° for 15 minutes; reduce heat to 350° and bake for 20 minutes.
- Arrange pecan mixture around edge and in center of pie. Bake for an additional 10 minutes.

Yield: 8 servings.

Lemon or Lime Tart

(A delicious end to any meal, especially seafood)

Crust:
1¼ **cups unbleached all-purpose flour**
2 **tablespoons sugar**
¼ **teaspoon salt**
½ **cup unsalted butter, chilled and cut into pieces**
1 **egg yolk**
1 **tablespoon cold water**

• Mix first 3 ingredients in a food processor; add butter and pulse off/on until mixture resembles coarse meal. Add egg yolk and water and blend until dough begins to stick together. Roll dough into a ball and flatten; wrap in plastic and refrigerate for 30 minutes.

• Roll dough out on lightly floured surface to a 13-inch circle; transfer to a 9-inch diameter tart pan with a removable bottom. Press dough into the pan; trim edges and freeze for 1 hour.

• Preheat oven to 400°; line crust with foil. Fill with dried beans or pie weights; bake for 12 minutes or until crust is set.

• Remove foil and beans; continue to bake until crust is golden in center, about 15 minutes, then remove to rack and cool.

Filling:
½ **cup whipping cream**
2 **tablespoons cornstarch**
2 **large eggs**
6 **large egg yolks**
¾ **cup sugar**
¾ **cup fresh lime juice**
½ **cup orange juice**
¼ **cup unsalted butter**

Lime or lemon strips
Granulated sugar

• Blend cornstarch and whipping cream in a bowl; let stand for 1 minute then blend again. Whisk in eggs and yolks.

• Combine sugar, lime juice, orange juice and butter in heavy saucepan over medium heat, stirring until sugar dissolves and butter melts. Bring to boil and whisk juice mixture into egg mixture; return mixture to the saucepan and boil for 1 minute, stirring constantly.

• Spoon filling into tart shell; chill for several hours or overnight. Garnish each slice with lemon or lime strips curled and sprinkled with granulated sugar.

Note: The filling is tart if made as directed. If you prefer a sweeter flavor, add another ½ cup sugar.

Yield: 8 servings.

Strawberry No-Fool Pie

6 **tablespoons butter**
¾ **cup sugar**
1 **cup self-rising flour**
¾ **cup milk**
2 **cups strawberries, sliced**

• Melt the butter in a 9-inch pie plate, and set aside.

• Mix sugar and flour with half of the milk, combining well. Add the rest of the milk and stir until smooth.

• Pour into the pie plate containing the melted butter, but do not mix.

• Spread fruit carefully on top.

• Bake at 350° for 30 to 40 minutes.

• Cool before serving.

Yield: 6 to 8 servings.

Rum Pies

1   envelope gelatin
½   cup hot water
6   egg yolks
1   cup sugar
½   cup light rum
1   pint whipping cream
2   (8-inch) chocolate crumb crusts
    Shaved chocolate or chocolate
    sprinkles

- Dissolve gelatin in hot water; cool.
- Beat egg yolks until foamy. Continue beating while adding sugar slowly. Beat until sugar is dissolved.
- Whip the cream stiffly. Combine the cooled gelatin and the egg/sugar mixture. Fold in the whipped cream; fold, don't stir.
- Pour into crusts and chill until set. Garnish with chocolate.

Yield: 2 (8-inch) pies.

Riverside Pecan Pie

½   cup butter
3   tablespoons all-purpose flour
1   (1-pound) box light brown sugar
6   tablespoons milk
3   eggs
2   teaspoons vinegar
1½   teaspoons vanilla
1   cup broken pecans
2   pie shells, uncooked

- Melt butter; set aside to cool.
- Mix flour, sugar, milk and eggs, beating well. Stir in vinegar, vanilla, butter and nuts. Pour into crusts and place in a cold oven.
- Bake at 300° for 1 hour.

Yield: 2 pies.

Shredded Apple Pie

*(A different way for the
All-American pie)*

1   (9-inch) pie shell, frozen, unbaked
3   Granny Smith apples,
    approximately
    Lemon juice
¼   cup margarine
1   cup sugar
1   teaspoon vanilla
1   egg, beaten

- Grate enough peeled apples to fill pie crust; sprinkle lemon juice over apples.
- Melt margarine and combine with sugar, vanilla and egg. Mix well and pour over apples.
- Bake at 375° for 40 to 45 minutes or until pie is set.

Note: Top with vanilla ice cream and enjoy!

Unholy Pie

1   cup sugar
½   cup flour
    Pinch salt
1   pint heavy cream
1   unbaked pie shell

- Combine dry ingredients and sift twice.
- Place in unbaked pie shell. Pour cream slowly over top; stir in a figure 8 motion lightly.
- Bake 90 minutes at 350°. Cool before cutting.

Yield: 1 pie.

Swedish Toscas

Crust:

6   **tablespoons butter, softened**
¼   **cup sugar**
1   **cup all-purpose flour, sifted**

- Cream butter and sugar until fluffy, then blend in flour.
- Divide into 12 ungreased muffin tins and press into the bottom and part way up the sides.
- Bake at 350° for 10 minutes.

Filling:

2   **tablespoons butter**
¼   **cup sugar**
2   **teaspoons all-purpose flour**
1½   **tablespoons cream**
⅓   **cup slivered blanched almonds**

- Combine all ingredients in a saucepan and bring to a boil, stirring constantly.
- Remove from heat, divide among baked shells and bake at 350° for 10 to 15 minutes.
- Cool slightly and remove from pans to finish cooling. Store in tin can.

Yield: 12 toscas.

Kahlúa Hot Fudge Sauce

(The Kahlúa gives it a little added taste that is super)

1   **cup unsweetened cocoa**
⅔   **cup granulated sugar**
½   **cup light brown sugar, well packed**
1   **cup whipping cream**
¼   **cup Kahlúa**
½   **cup margarine**
1½   **teaspoons vanilla**

- Stir the cocoa and sugars in heavy saucepan; add cream, Kahlúa and margarine.
- Stir over medium heat until mixture boils; boil for one minute.
- Remove from heat and stir in vanilla.
- Serve over ice cream or hot fudge cake.

Chocolate Sauce

1   **cup sugar**
¼   **cup cocoa**
⅓   **cup evaporated milk**
1   **teaspoon vanilla**
6   **tablespoons butter**

- Mix sugar and cocoa in a saucepan. Add milk, vanilla, and butter, in that order.
- Bring to a boil and boil for 5 minutes. Beat for 2 minutes.

Yield: 1½ cups.

Table of Measures

Pinch ....less than ⅛ teaspoon
60 drops.. 1 teaspoon
3 teaspoons............................. 1 tablespoon
4 tablespoons....................................... ¼ cup
5⅓ tablespoons..................................... ⅓ cup
2 tablespoons .... 1 fluid ounce
1 cup ....8 fluid ounces
1 cup .... ½ pint
2 cups .... 1 pint
2 pints .... 1 quart
4 quarts.. 1 gallon
8 quarts .... 1 peck
4 pecks .... 1 bushel
16 ounces.. 1 pound

Can Sizes

No. 300........ 14 to 16 ounces .... 1¾ cups
No. 303........ 16 to 17 ounces ....2 cups
No. 2½........ 1 lb. 13 ounces ....3½ cups
6 ounce .... ¾ cup
8 ounce .... 1 cup
10½ ounce .... 1¼ cups
16 ounce .... 2 cups
20 ounce .... 2½ cups
29 ounce .... 3½ cups
46 ounce .... 5¾ cups

Converting To Metric

Length

When You Know:	Multiply by:	To Find:
millimeters	0.04	inches
centimeters	0.4	inches
meters	3.3	feet
kilometers	0.6	miles
inches	2.54	centimeters
feet	30	centimeters
yards	0.9	meters
miles	1.6	kilometers

Weight

When You Know:	Multiply by:	To Find:
grams	0.035	ounces
kilograms	2.2	pounds
ounces	28	grams
pounds	0.45	kilograms

Volume

When You Know:	Multiply by:	To Find:
milliliters	0.2	teaspoons
milliliters	0.07	tablespoons
milliliters	0.03	fluid ounces
liters	4.23	cups
liters	2.1	pints
liters	1.06	quarts
liters	0.26	gallons
teaspoons	5	milliliters
tablespoons	15	milliliters
fluid ounces	30	milliliters
cups	0.24	liters
pints	0.47	liters
quarts	0.95	liters
gallons	3.8	liters

Temperature:

When You Know:	Multiply by:	To Find:
degrees Celsius	⅗, and add 32	degrees Fahrenheit
degrees Fahrenheit	⅝ (after subtracting 32)	degrees Celsius

Quantities to Serve 100 People

Coffee	3 lbs.	Cauliflower	18 lbs.
Sugar	3 lbs.	Cabbage for slaw	20 lbs.
Whipping cream	3 quarts	Carrots	33 lbs.
Milk	6 gallons	Bread	10 loaves
Fruit cocktail	2½ gallons	Rolls	200
Tomato juice	4 no. 10 cans (26 lbs.)	Butter	3 lbs.
Soup	5 gallons	Potato salad	12 quarts
Oysters	18 quarts	Fruit salad	20 quarts
Hot dogs	25 lbs.	Vegetable salad	20 quarts
Meat loaf	24 lbs.	Lettuce	20 heads
Ham	40 lbs.	Salad dressing	3 quarts
Roast pork	40 lbs.	Pies	18
Hamburger	30-36 lbs.	Cakes	8
Chicken for chicken pie	40 lbs.	Ice cream	4 gallons
Potatoes	35 lbs.	Cheese	3 lbs.
Scalloped potatoes	5 gallons	Olives	1¾ lbs.
Vegetables	4 no. 10 cans (26 lbs.)	Pickles	2 quarts
Baked beans	5 gallons	Nuts	3 lbs.
Beets	30 lbs.		

To serve 200 people, double these quantities
To serve 50 people, divide by 2
To serve 25 people, divide by 4

Substitutions

Ingredient called for: *Substitute*

1 tablespoon cornstarch .... 2 tablespoons all-purpose flour

1 cup sifted cake flour .... 1 cup sifted all-purpose flour minus 2 tablespoons

1 cup sifted self-rising flour .... 1 cup sifted all-purpose flour plus 1½ teaspoons baking powder and
½ teaspoon salt

1 teaspoon baking powder .... ½ teaspoon cream of tartar and ¼ teaspoon baking soda

1 whole large egg .... 2 egg yolks and 1 tablespoon water

1 whole large egg .... ¼ cup frozen egg substitute, thawed

1 cup whole milk.. ½ cup evaporated milk and ½ cup water

1 cup buttermilk or sour milk .... 1 tablespoon white vinegar and whole milk to equal 1 cup
(let stand 5 minutes)

1 cup sour cream .... 1 tablespoon lemon juice and evaporated milk to equal 1 cup

1 cup half-and-half .... ¾ cup plus 2 tablespoons whole milk and ⅓ cup melted butter

1 cup whipping cream .... ¾ cup whole milk and ⅓ cup melted butter or margarine
(not appropriate to whip)

1 ounce unsweetened chocolate .... 3 tablespoons unsweetened cocoa and 1 tablespoon shortening

4-ounce bar sweet baking chocolate .... 4½ tablespoons sugar plus 3 tablespoons unsweetened
cocoa and 2⅔ tablespoons shortening

6 ounces semi-sweet chocolate .... 6 tablespoons unsweetened cocoa plus 4½ tablespoons sugar
and ¼ cup shortening

1 cup honey .... 1¼ cups sugar and ¼ cup water

1 teaspoon grated lemon or orange rind .... ½ teaspoon lemon or orange extract

Tomato juice .... equal parts tomato paste and water

Tomato sauce .... equal parts tomato paste and broth

1 cup chicken or beef broth .... 1 teaspoon chicken or beef-flavored bouillon granules
dissolved in 1 cup hot water

1 tablespoon minced fresh herbs .... 1 teaspoon dried herbs

1 clove fresh garlic .... ⅛ teaspoon garlic powder

1 teaspoon lemon juice .... ½ teaspoon white vinegar

1 cake compressed yeast .... 1 package dry yeast

1 cup ketchup or chili sauce ..... 1 cup tomato sauce plus ½ cup sugar and 2 tablespoons white vinegar

1 small onion, chopped .... 1 tablespoon instant minced onion

1 cup corn syrup .... 1 cup sugar dissolved in ¼ cup hot water

1 cup dark corn syrup .... ¾ cup light corn syrup plus ¼ cup molasses

Substitutions

Ingredient called for:	Substitute
1 cup sugar	1⅓ cups brown sugar, lightly packed
1 cup sugar	1 cup molasses or honey plus ¼ to ½ teaspoon soda *(reduce liquid in recipe by ¼ cup)*
1 cup molasses	1 cup honey
1 teaspoon dry mustard	1 tablespoon prepared mustard

Equivalents

Dairy

Food	Amount	Approximate Measure
Butter or margarine	1 pound	2 cups
Cheese, American	4 ounces	1 cup shredded
Cheese, Cheddar	4 ounces	1 cup shredded
Cheese, cottage	1 pound	1 cup
Cheese, cream	3-ounce package	½ cup plus 2 tablespoons
	8-ounce package	1 cup
Cheese, Parmesan	8 ounces	2½ cups grated
Eggs, large	4 eggs	1 cup
Eggs, large	1 egg	¼ cup frozen egg substitute, thawed
Egg whites	7 to 9 egg whites	1 cup
Sour cream	8 ounces	1 cup
Whipping cream	½ pint	1 cup unwhipped or 2 cups whipped

Fruits and Vegetables

Food	Amount	Approximate Measure
Apples	3 medium	2¾ cups sliced
Asparagus	1 pound	16 to 18 spears
Bananas	1 medium	½ cup mashed
Broccoli	1 pound	2 cups flowerets
Cabbage	1 pound	4 cups shredded
Carrots	2 medium	1 cup sliced

Equivalents

Celery	2 medium stalks	1 cup sliced
Corn	1 medium ear	½ cup kernels
Green beans	1 pound	3 cups cut
Green pepper	1 large	1 cup chopped
Iceberg lettuce	1 medium head	6½ cups torn
Lemon	1 medium	2 to 3 tablespoons juice or 1 tablespoon grated rind
Okra	1 pound	3 cups sliced
Onion	1 pound	1 cup chopped
Orange	1 medium	⅓ to ½ cup juice or 1½ tablespoons grated rind
Peaches	2 medium	1 cup sliced
Peas and beans, dried	1 pound	2 to 2½ cups
Pineapple	1 pound	3 cups diced
Strawberries	1 pint	2 cups whole
Sweet potatoes	1 pound	1½ cups cooked, mashed
Tomatoes	1 pound	2 cups diced

Pasta and Rice

Food	Amount	Approximate Measure
Pasta, egg noodles	6 cups	4 cups cooked
Pasta, elbow macaroni	2 cups	4½ cups cooked
Pasta, spaghetti	8 ounces	4 to 5 cups cooked
Rice, brown	1 cup	4 cups cooked
Rice, converted	1 cup	4 cups cooked
Rice, instant	1 cup	2 cups cooked
Rice, long-grain	1 cup	3 cups cooked
Rice, wild	1 cup	3 cups cooked

Equivalents

Staples

Food	Amount	Approximate Measure
Chocolate, unsweetened	8 ounces	8 (1-ounce) squares
Chocolate, morsels	6 ounces	1 cup
Coconut, flaked	4-ounce can	1⅓ cups
Cornmeal	1 pound	3 cups
Cracker crumbs	23 soda crackers	1 cup
	15 graham crackers	1 cup
Flour, all-purpose	1 pound	3½ cups unsifted
Flour, cake	1 pound	4½ to 5 cups sifted
Flour, self-rising	1 pound	3½ cups unsifted
Flour, whole wheat	1 pound	3½ cups unsifted
Gelatin, unflavored	1 envelope	2½ teaspoons
Nuts, almonds	1 pound shelled	3½ cups
Nuts, peanuts	1 pound shelled	3½ cups
	1 pound	2½ cups nutmeats
Nuts, pecans	1 pound shelled	3 cups
	1 pound	2¼ cups nutmeats
Nuts, walnuts	1 pound shelled	4 cups
	1 pound	1⅔ cups nutmeats
Oats, regular	1 pound	6¼ cups
Oats, quick-cooking	1 pound	5⅔ cups
Shortening	1 pound	2 cups
Sugar, brown	1 pound	2¼ cups packed
Sugar, granulated	1 pound	2 cups
Sugar, powdered	1 pound	4 cups
Yeast, dry	1 package	2 teaspoons

Contributors

Our sincere appreciation to the ladies of **Christ Episcopal Church** and their friends and relatives throughout the community who contributed recipes to our cookbook. We regret similarity of context and limitations prevented us from including all the recipes which were submitted.

Libby Allen
Susan Alverson
Audrey Turner Austin
Darrah Bagley
Pam Barber
Anne Barker
Carolyn Kramer Belvin
Lou Blades
Anna Biggs
Patricia Britt
Jean Brooks
Gin Brown
Sarah Bunn
Virginia Bunn
Clint Cameron
Richard Carpenter
Valerie Carpenter
Jeri Carson
Sybil Carson
Gerry Chory
Lily Chou
Jane Clark
Janice Cook
Bessie Culpepper
Jane Culpepper
Brenda S. Daniels
Wanda Daniels
Carolyn Davis
Judy Debnam
Phyllis M. Dixon
Cecelia G. Dudley
Patty Duff
Shirley Dunbar
Nancy Eadie
Dee Hull Everist
Janet Farmer
Cora G. Fearing
Nancy Ferebee

Brent Flickinger
Deede Foreman
Edla Foreman
Jo Ann P. Foreman
Mary Foytik
Frances Gaither
Jessie Gaither
Diana Gallop
Alma Gregory
Angie Halen
Mary H. Harrell
Jane Harris
Jane Haynes
Betsy Wright Hinton
Eleanor Hinton
Harriet Hornthal
Ann Hughes
Camilla Hull
Kay Hull
Bobbie Hunsberger
Blair Jackson
Kathrine P. Jackson
Janie Jacobson
Lois Jennette
Lynn Bright Jennings
Holly Johnson
Joy Johnson
Van Jones
Clarine Jordan
Ada Kee
Frances King
Claudia Lee
Nora Lee
Sarah Ann Light
Gray Little
Love Little
June Liverman
Jeanne K. McCain

Claudia McDaniel
Peggy McPherson
Betty MacKenzie
Beverly Madrin
Vera Mawson
Sherry Meads
Mildred Mercer
Mary K. Merritt
Susan H. Milbrath
Fred Moncla
Kay Moncla
Kay Morrisette
Nell Morrison
Ginny Nash
Bonnie O'Neal
Eunice Overman
Dorothy Owens
Katie Owens
Anne Parrish
Louise Peters
Joyce Porter
Jean Poston
Myrtle Pritchard
Thomas Pritchard
Penny Raby
Jane Reisenger
Jerry Rhees
Shirley Rhees
Todd Rich
Jan Riley
River City Seafood Co.
Flora Robinson
Jane Robinson
Peggy Robinson
Tapp Robinson
Dian Ross
Anne Sanders
Barbara C. Sanders

Isabelle Sawyer
Phil Sawyer
Linda B. Sawyer
Helen Scott
Betsy B. Selig
David Seymour
Emily Sheely
Beverly M. Small
Adrienne Southworth
Bea Southworth
Carolyn Spence
Charles Squires
Margaret Stallings
Paula Lassiter Stevenson
Patricia Sweeney
Carrie Symons
Jean Tarkington
Dru Thompson
Judy Thorne
Sally Toxey
Jane Umphlett
Marie Value
Melba Van Dalsum
Barbara Waldo
Alice Weatherly
Beans Weatherly
Faye Ellen Weatherly
Eunice Weeks
Dianne Wells
Lillian White
Patricia White
Anne B. Williams
Trudy Wilson-Williams
Jean Winslow
Virginia H. Wood
Winnie Wood
Holly Wright
Nancy Wright

INDEX

ORDER FORM

Christ Episcopal Church ECW

200 McMorrine Street
Elizabeth City, North Carolina 27909

Please send _____ copies of **Pasquotank Plate**	@ $17.95 each	$ _____
Postage and handling	@ $ 2.75 each	$ _____
Gift Wrap	@ $ 1.00 each	$ _____
North Carolina residents add sales tax	@ $ 1.08 each	$ _____
	TOTAL	$ _____

Name _____

Address _____

City _____ State _____ Zip _____

Make checks payable to **The Pasquotank Plate.**

ORDER FORM

Christ Episcopal Church ECW

200 McMorrine Street
Elizabeth City, North Carolina 27909

Please send _____ copies of **Pasquotank Plate**	@ $17.95 each	$ _____
Postage and handling	@ $ 2.75 each	$ _____
Gift Wrap	@ $ 1.00 each	$ _____
North Carolina residents add sales tax	@ $ 1.08 each	$ _____
	TOTAL	$ _____

Name _____

Address _____

City _____ State _____ Zip _____

Make checks payable to **The Pasquotank Plate.**

Notes